ORDER IN THE CHURCH
[Proper Church Etiquette and Protocol]

Bishop Alton A. Smith

AuthorHouse™
1663 Liberty Drive
Bloomington, IN 47403
www.authorhouse.com
Phone: 1-800-839-8640

© 2011 Bishop Alton A. Smith. All rights reserved

No part of this book may be reproduced, stored in
a retrieval system, or transmitted by any means
without the written permission of the author.

First published by AuthorHouse 10/28/2011

ISBN: 978-1-4567-6936-9 (sc)
ISBN: 978-1-4567-6937-6 (e)

Library of Congress Control Number: 2011908053

Printed in the United States of America

Any people depicted in stock imagery provided by Thinkstock are models,
and such images are being used for illustrative purposes only.
Certain stock imagery © Thinkstock.

This book is printed on acid-free paper.

Because of the dynamic nature of the Internet, any web addresses or
links contained in this book may have changed since publication and
may no longer be valid. The views expressed in this work are solely those
of the author and do not necessarily reflect the views of the publisher,
and the publisher hereby disclaims any responsibility for them.

CONTENTS

Dedication vii
Acknowledgements ix
Foreword x
Introduction xiii
Definitions xv
Chapter 1   The Worship Service 1
Chapter 2   Church Organization and Structure 8
Chapter 3   Care and Respect for the Church Facility and Property 14
Chapter 4   Church Etiquette 17
Chapter 5   Pulpit Etiquette 21
Chapter 6   Clergy Attire and Ministerial Vestment 24
Chapter 7   The Bishopric 29
Chapter 8   Funeral Etiquette for the Bishop and the Elder 37
Chapter 9   Guide to Leadership in the Church 40
Chapter 10 Five Steps to Heaven 46
Bibliography 51

DEDICATION

This book is dedicated to my parents
Deacon and Mrs. John Frank (Louise Barnes) Smith
who instilled within me from a child the importance
of loving and obeying God. They taught me the
significance of love and family. Without their
nurturing and tender care from the beginning, I
would not be who and where I am this moment.

To my late Father & Mother-in-Law
Deacon and Mother Lenlie (Lela Russell) Benton
who were an inspiration to me and who endeavored to
teach me about the early members
and the beginnings of the
Church of Christ, Disciples of Christ.

It is also dedicated to my loving wife, ***Doris*** – my typist,
my sounding board and my partner in life. She has been
there for me since we met over forty years ago. I never
knew when we met at Carver Heights Junior High School
that we would share a lifetime of joy and happiness. I am
blessed and thankful that we are one in Christ Jesus.

To my daughter, **Damesha**, I dedicate
this book to you because you
are so special. I am so happy that God gave
you to us as our wonderful daughter. You have
proven to be the young lady that we are so
proud of and pray that God will continue
to do His Mighty Work
with you and through you…

In memory of our first born –
Marissa Davon Smith ~ August 17, 1977

To my **Late Grandparents** for their wisdom
and guidance and my extended family, **Dan,
Contina, Erika** and **Devon**. I love you all.

To the **Church of Christ, Disciples of Christ**
and to all **Disciples** everywhere…
*"Go ye therefore, and teach all nations, baptizing them in
the name of the Father, and of the Son, and of the Holy
Ghost: Teaching them to observe all things whatsoever I
have commanded you: and, lo, I am with you always, even
unto the end of the world. Amen." Matthew 28:19-20*

ACKNOWLEDGEMENTS

It is my pleasure to thank the following friends for their sacrifice and assistance in the completion of this book:

My Wife
Doris Benton Smith
Typing, editing, proofreading

~

Friend and Confidant
Rev. J. O. Williams
Foreword

~

Retired Educator and
faithful member of St. Mark Church
of Christ, Disciples of Christ
Mrs. Martha Smith
Editing and Proofreading

FOREWORD

Rev. J. O. Williams, Sr., BTH, DD
Retired Pastor and Associate Regional Minister
for the Christian Church (Disciples of Christ) in
North Carolina Former Secretary of the Goldsboro-
Raleigh District Assembly 1965 – 1977

Bishop Alton A. Smith was elected to the office of the General Bishop of the General Assembly of the Church of Christ (Disciples of Christ), International in the spring of 2009. The General Assembly is composed of nine subordinate assemblies of the Church of Christ (Disciples of Christ) along the Eastern Seaboard of the United States and congregations in West Africa, Panama and Jamaica.

I knew Bishop Smith as a lay person in the St. Mark Church of Christ (Disciples of Christ) in Goldsboro, North Carolina before he responded to the call to ministry. He is deeply religious and a lover of law, order and decency and proper protocol, believing that the same should be done in the House of the Lord. He is married to Mrs. Doris Smith and is a family man. His determination as a minister and most certainly as the General Bishop, is to restore order to the churches affiliated with all of the assemblies within his jurisdiction and fully aware that "we are not the only Christians, but Christians only".

As further proof of his orderliness and timely conviction, he has sought to bring order in the church by the writing of this book: <u>ORDER IN THE CHURCH: Proper Church Etiquette and Protocol</u>. He has been inspired by the Apostle Paul who had himself, preferred, and advised the Corinthians to be orderly and practice Christian charity (protocol) to all. Here he taught them among spiritual gifts, which they should prefer, and by what rules they should make comparative instructions, practice proper behavior or protocol being defined as the rules of correct or appropriate behavior of a group, organization, or profession. By all means, Let all things be done decently and in order.

Bishop Alton Smith has been deeply influenced by the writings of the Apostle Paul especially in setting some order in the Assemblies just as Paul had done in Corinth. That congregation who called themselves followers of Christ, yet plagued with many different problems that needed to be set in order. *36 Or did the word of God come originally from you? Or was it you only that it reached? 37 If anyone thinks himself to be a prophet or spiritual, let him acknowledge that the things which I write to you are the commandments of the Lord. 38 But if anyone is ignorant, let him be ignorant. 39 Therefore, brethren, desire earnestly to prophesy, and do not forbid to speak with tongues. 40 Let all things be done decently and in order. I Corinthians 14:36-40 KJV.* **Bishop Alton A. Smith has sought to do likewise in his writing of the book, "Order in the Church."**

In these verses the apostle closes his argument, with a just rebuke of the Corinthians for their extravagant pride and self-conceit; they so managed with their spiritual gifts as no church did like them; they behaved in a manner by themselves, and would not easily endure control or regulation.

Now, says the apostle, to beat down this arrogant humor, "Came the gospel out from you? Or, came it to you only? Did Christianity come out of Corinth? Was its original among you? Or, if not, is it now limited and confined to you? Are you the only church favored with divine revelations that you will depart from the decent usages of all other churches, and, to make ostentation of your spiritual gifts, bring confusion into Christian assemblies? How intolerably assuming is this behavior!" *COMMENTARY OF THE WHOLE BIBLE VOL. 4.*

This book, ORDER IN THE CHURCH: Proper Church Etiquette and Protocol, will be a great value in setting forth the rules for correct or appropriate behavior of constituencies of the Assemblies, Churches and the Clergy composing the General Assembly of the Church of Christ (Disciples of Christ). It is a tool in helping the church to have order and spiritual class in its attempt to be the Body of Christ in a fragmented society.

INTRODUCTION

For as long as I can remember anything, the church has stood out in my life. Not only was I carried, but when old enough I was required to actively participate. As I became older, it became a part of me. I have always watched, observed and wondered why things were done the way they were. As I grew older and accepted Jesus as my personal Savior I began to study and read His Holy Word. Some things began to become clearer as to why we do some of the thing that we do in our worship.

As I studied the history of our church, some things were not as clear to me as I desired. I began to dig deeper and to pray for understanding. As I looked for and at the order and the workings of the church and the requirements for leaders to be guided by, I discovered that there is a high standard required of each of us. It soon became obvious that we should be good stewards of the work assigned our hands.

We live in a day and time when it seems that any old way is all right. For many, a sense of right and wrong is unclear. One might ask what determines right from wrong when it comes to order in the church. I based all of these writings on the truth of God in His Word and the wisdom of the ages that lines up with that truth.

I am grateful for the guidance of the Holy Spirit for

enabling me to properly and positively present this book. God the Father gets all the glory and I remain just one of His humble servants. I am truly blessed that He has chosen me for this assignment.

As you read this writing, please know that I write not as an authority, but as a practitioner of what I have learned.

This book concludes with a Guide to Leadership in the Church to use to implement insight and strength for the assignments that we have been charged to carry out.

Blessings,
Alton A. Smith
2011

DEFINITIONS

Protocol
A set of guidelines for use in various circumstances.

Etiquette
The forms required by good breeding or prescribed by authority, to be observed in social, official, professional or church life. Conformity to accepted standards or conduct. Ceremonial code of polite society.

CHAPTER 1
THE WORSHIP SERVICE

This information that follows is the basic order of worship. It is not meant to be exclusive nor inclusive. The author realizes that each church has its own order of worship with both additions and/or deletions of this basic order. The basic order of Worship is a guide…

The Basic Order of Worship

Musical Prelude
Call to Worship
Processional
Doxology
Invocation
Response
Aim and Plea of the Church/Church Affirmation
Morning Hymn
Scripture
Prayer
Chant
Hymn of Praise/Mission

Bishop Alton A. Smith

Announcements
Offering
Offertory Prayer
Inspirational Selection
Sermon
Invitation to Discipleship
Invitational Hymn
Benediction

The Worship Service

WHAT IS WORSHIP?

Worship is an expression of reverence, praise and thanksgiving for God.

THE WORSHIP SERVICE INCLUDES FOUR ASPECTS OF WORSHIP:

The Act of Reverence (Psalms 100:3)
Musical Prelude
Call to Worship
Processional
Doxology
Invocation
Response
Aim and Plea of the Church/Affirmation of Faith

The Act of Fellowship (Hebrews 10:25)
The Morning Hymn
Scripture
Prayer
Chant
Announcements

The Act of Dedication/Reconciliation (Malachi 3:10, Matthew 7:11)
Offering

Offertory Prayer

The Act of Renewal (Psalms 119:11, 33-45, 105)
Inspirational Selection
Sermon
Invitation to Discipleship
Altar Prayer
Benediction

Components of the Worship Service

Musical Prelude – *(The congregation should enter silently and be seated in meditation.)* The prelude sets the tone for Worship. Its function is to call the congregation together in a spirit of devout meditation and prayer. The people are to turn their thoughts from the things and concerns of the world towards reflection on God. It is not a time for talking and moving around.

Bishop Alton A. Smith

Call to Worship – *(Scriptural)*

A call to attention to the purpose of the gathering – The Worship of God.

Processional – *(The congregation should be standing and joining in the singing.)* The processional represents the approach of the people of God into God's presence. The processional represents our journey to God, an onward march toward a definite goal – *the Altar.)*

Doxology – *(Congregation remains standing.)*

The Doxology is an expression of praise to God, a *short* hymn.

Invocation – *(Congregation standing.)*

The invocation is a *short* prayer that invites God to become involved in the Worship Service.

Response – *(Congregation standing.)*

Short choral response.

Aim and Plea of the Church/Church Covenant –

The congregation responsively repeat in unison the beliefs and teachings of the church.

Order in the Church

Morning Hymn

The first hymn of worship. It is a hymn expressing praise and thanksgiving to give glory and honor to the name of God. Preferably a chosen hymn familiar to the congregation that they may join in.

Scripture

The reading serves as a religious meditation guiding toward a diving revelation. The scripture should be complimentary of the occasion or the service or program. Sitting or standing is optional and at the discretion of your Shepherd. The congregation should conform to the request of the pulpit.

Prayer

The universal prayer to voice the needs of persons and the desire for God to meet those needs.

Chant

A short, soft song at the end of the prayer.

Hymn of Praise/Hymn of Mission

The Ministry of Kindness.

Bishop Alton A. Smith

Announcements

A *brief* reading of concerns and invites related to the congregation.

Offering

The congregation's gifts to God through tithes and offerings.

Offertory Prayer

The offertory prayer or selection should be short and confined to words concerning giving of offerings to God.

Inspirational Selection

Selection intended to prepare the congregation to receive the Word of God.

Sermon – (THE WORD OF GOD)

The central focus of the service, bringing a united search of deeper meaning and concern for a Holy and righteous living.

Invitation to Discipleship

An invitation to offer our lives to God or to renew our commitment to the Kingdom of God.

Order in the Church

Invitational Hymn

An appropriate hymn that encourages the unsaved to consider their relationship with Jesus Christ and to focus on making a commitment to Him. *The hymn should not interfere with or overshadow the Invitation being extended, but should complement the Invitation and the appeal for salvation.*

Altar Prayer

A universal prayer for people coming to the altar with prayer requests.

Benediction – *(Congregation standing with bowed heads.)*

A prayer in which the blessings of God are asked upon the congregation.

> **To leave the service before the benediction is to leave without your blessing.**

CHAPTER 2
CHURCH ORGANIZATION AND STRUCTURE

CHURCH ORGANIZATIONAL STRUCTURE

The HEAD of the Church
Jesus Christ – Son of God

↓

PASTOR

↓

DEACONS

↓

MOTHERS

↓

TRUSTEES

↓

DEPARTMENT OR MINISTRY LEADERS

↓

MEMBERS

Order in the Church

Organization and Structure of the Church

1. JESUS CHRIST - THE HEAD OF THE CHURCH

- Alpha & Omega *(the First & the Last)* Revelations 1:8
- Atoning Sacrifice for our Sins — I John 2:2
- Bishop of our souls — 1 Peter. 2:25
- Chief Shepherd — 1 Peter 5:4
- Deliverer — Rom. 11:26
- Eternal Life — 1 John 1:2; 5:20
- Hope of Glory — Colossians 1:27
- King of Kings — Revelations 19:16
- Lamb of God — John 1:29
- Lord of Lords — Revelations 19:16
- Our Great God and Savior — Titus 2:13
- Son of the Most High God — Luke 1:32
- The Only-begotten Son of God — John 3:6
- The Resurrection and the Life — John 11: 25
- The Way — John 14:6

2. PASTOR - THE UNDER SHEPHERD

- An ordained member of the clergy.
- Ordained leader of the church
- Congregational Leader
- Duties of the Pastor include:
  - ✓ *Live Holy and Above Reproach* – I Timothy 3:2 - A bishop *(elder)* then must be blameless, the husband of one wife, vigilant, sober, of good behavior, given to hospitality…"
  - ✓ *Preach the Word of God* – II Timothy 4:2 - Preach the word; be instant in season, out of

season; reprove, rebuke, exhort with all long suffering and doctrine.
- ✓ *Teach the Word of God* – I Timothy 3:2 - A bishop then must be blameless, the husband of one wife, vigilant, sober, of good behavior, given to hospitality, apt to teach
- ✓ *Oversight of the church* – Acts 20:28 - Take heed therefore unto yourselves, and to all the flock, over the which the Holy Ghost hath made you overseers, to feed the church of God, which he hath purchased with his own blood.
- ✓ *Shepherd the Congregation* – I Peter 5:7 - Feed the flock of God which is among you, taking the oversight thereof, not by constraint, but willingly; not for filthy lucre, but of a ready mind.
- ✓ *Pray For and Minister to God's People* – Acts 6:4 - But we will give ourselves continually to prayer, and to the ministry of the word.
- ✓ *Minister to the Sick, Widows and Elderly* – James 5:14 - Is any sick among you? Let him call for the elders of the church; and let them pray over him, anointing him with oil in the name of the Lord.
- ✓ *Provide Spiritual Care and Discipline for the People of God* – I Peter 5:2 - Feed the flock of God which is among you, taking the oversight thereof, not by constraint, but willingly; not for filthy lucre, but of a ready mind;

3. DEACONS – I Timothy 3:8-13

"Likewise must the deacons be grave, not double-tongued, not given to much wine, not greedy of filthy lucre; Holding the mystery of the faith in a pure conscience. And let these also first be proved; then let them use the office of a deacon, being found blameless. Even so must their wives be grave, not slanderers, sober, faithful in all things. Let the deacons be the husbands of one wife, ruling their children and their own houses well. For they that have used the office of a deacon well purchase to themselves a good degree, and great boldness in the faith which is in Christ Jesus."

- *Duties of the Deacon include:*
  - ✓ To assist the Pastor in Spiritual Leadership of the church
  - ✓ To support the Ministry of the Word of God
  - ✓ To assist in carrying out the Ordinances of the Church
  - ✓ To care for the physical and spiritual well-being of the congregants.
  - ✓

4. **MOTHERS – Titus 2:3-5**

"The older women likewise, that they be reverent in behavior, not slanderers, not given to much wine, teachers of good things, that they admonish the young women to love their husbands, to love their children, *to be* discreet, chaste, homemakers, good, obedient to their own husbands, that the word of God may not be blasphemed".

- *Duties of the Mother of the Church:*
  - ✓ Mothers must be Godly women
  - ✓ Must be willing to serve and to support the Ministry of the Church.

- ✓ Must be a role model for the younger women of the church and community.
- ✓ Must be responsible for preparing and maintaining the Communion elements.

5. **TRUSTEES** – *(No Biblical Reference for church trustees)*

   Church Trustees should possess the following qualities:
   - They should be born again.
   - They should be in obedience of God's plan for supporting His church – Tithes and Freewill Offerings.
   - They should be trustworthy.
   - They should have a servant's heart.
   - They should be diligent and faithful to the Kingdom of God.
   - They should possess the qualities of patience, understanding, and self-control.
   - *Duties of the Church Trustee:*
     - ✓ The trustees are the legal agents of the church.
     - ✓ Trustees are responsible for maintenance and supervision of the physical facility of the church.
     - ✓ Trustees should support the ministry of the total church.

6. **DEPARTMENT OR MINISTRY LEADERS**

   Members of the church who have been elected or appointed to serve as officers of a church auxiliary or ministry. These officers include:
   - ✓ President or Chair

- ✓ Vice President
- ✓ Secretary
- ✓ Treasurer

7. **MEMBERS – People that assemble themselves together for worship and for service in the house of God. Church membership may be attained by the following circumstances:**

    - ✓ Attendance for church worship and activities of the church
    - ✓ Be baptized through immersion
    - ✓ Support the church with tithes and offerings.
    - ✓ Agree to abide by the teachings of the Holy Scriptures and commit to the Ordinances of the church.
    - ✓ Grow in grace and knowledge of our Lord and Savior, Jesus Christ
    - ✓ Invite and bring others to Christ and His Church

CHAPTER 3
CARE AND RESPECT FOR THE CHURCH FACILITY AND PROPERTY

The church is the temple of God and should be treated as such. Care and concern must be exhibited for honoring the house of God. We must be careful to treat the symbols of the church with respect, care and honor. This includes:

- *The Bible* – God's Holy Word. We must not write in the church Bibles, nor allow our children to use them as a toy or playful distraction. Pew Bibles are the property of the church and should not be taken home by parishioners.

- *The Altar* – The Altar is the most important Church furnishing. It is the focal point of Divine worship. The altar is a symbol of God's presence and the sacrifice of Christ. The altar reminds us of God's omnipotent presence. Personal items should never be placed on the altar.

- *Hymnals* – Hymnals are provided so that the congregation might join in with songs of the church. We must be careful to protect bindings and the spines of hymnals so that they might last and be of service

Order in the Church

during the worship services of the church. Hymnals are the property of the church and should not be taken home.

- *Church Furniture* – Care and respect of church furnishings is the same as the care and respect of the furnishings in our homes. Abstaining from eating and drinking in the church sanctuary will help to avoid staining the furniture.

- *Baptismal Pool* – Baptism is an ordinance of the church. The act of baptism is symbolic. It symbolizes an outward sign of an inward change. No one should enter the baptismal pool unless instructed by a church official (pastor, deacon or trustee).

- *Communion Table and Elements* – The communion table and the communion elements are used only for the communion service. This table and these elements should be set aside solely for use during this sacred ordinance of the church. Only those who have been ordained or consecrated by the church should perform the duties using these sacred items. Personal items should never be placed on the communion table.

- *Pulpit* – The pulpit is an elevated place or enclosed stage, in a church, in which the preacher or another member of the clergy stands while preaching. This pulpit area is reserved for clergy. Any other member of the congregation should use the lectern (speaker stand) designated to the left or the right of the pulpit.

It is our responsibility as children of God to honor Him in all that we do and to honor His House. It is our responsibility to keep the temple clean. Whether we are members of the church custodial staff, the administrative board, or a member of the laity, it is our responsibility to maintain the house of God in a clean and respectable condition.

The exterior of the church should be neat and orderly. A well maintained exterior is inviting to visitors and members as well and helps to determine whether someone will choose your church as their place of worship.

CHAPTER 4
CHURCH ETIQUETTE

"But if I tarry long, that thou mayest know how thou oughtest to behave thyself in the house of God, which is the church of the living God, the pillar and ground of the truth." I Timothy 3:15

1. **Entering the Church Sanctuary**

   ☦ Worshippers should arrive early in order to select a comfortable seat in the sanctuary.
   ☦ Worshippers should enter the church sanctuary quietly.
   ☦ Worshippers should not stop to speak or to greet another worshipper upon entering the sanctuary during service.
   ☦ Food, candy, gum or drinks should not be brought into the sanctuary at any time.

2. **The Church Service**

   ☦ All church services should begin at the appointed time. Late arrivers should be allowed to enter the service only during times that will not interfere with the Worship Service and should sit or be seated in the rear of the Sanctuary.
   ☦ The Order of Service is not rigid, but is provided to serve as a guide. All service participants should be

present and in their proper places when the service begins and should follow the guide of the shepherd of the congregation. No program or worship service participant should take their place after the worship service has begun. If late, they should take a seat in the audience.

☦ Selecting a seat near the front of the sanctuary is a common courtesy. Rear seats should be left for those who arrive late, so not to disturb the worship service.

☦ Always remember that strangers are often guest of church members. Treat them with the courtesy that you desire when you are a visitor.

☦ Only a minister of the Gospel should enter the pulpit. Children should be taught that the pulpit is sacred and not an area for play, walking or entertainment.

☦ A lectern or speakers stand should be provided to the left or right of the pulpit. All worshippers, speakers, soloists or anyone who is not an ordained elder should use this stand.

☦ If worshippers must leave the sanctuary during the Worship Service, do not pass in front of the pulpit. Use side aisles so that you do not disturb the concentration of other worshippers.

ADDITIONAL ETIQUETTE REMINDERS

☦ **Inviting Speakers or Preachers** – No speaker should be invited or confirmed without prior approval of the pastor.

☦ **Music** – Music should be selected that is appropriate to the occasion. Instrumental music should not be so loud as to overpower the vocalists.

Order in the Church

- ✟ **Introduction of Speakers** – Introduction of any guest speaker should be kept brief. Introductions and resumes should be acquired from guest speakers or guests in advance so as to familiarize yourself with the content.

- ✟ **Recognitions** – When giving recognitions, the speaker should be careful not to omit anyone. In recognizing officers, the highest ranking officer(s) should be recognized first, then proceed down the list in order of office held.

- ✟ **Illness** – In the event that someone should become ill during a service, a trained first aid representative, a nurse or an usher should be notified. All other persons should remain seated and quiet.

- ✟ **Funerals** – Funerals should be carefully planned centered around the deceased, if possible. The funeral program should be done by the family, the pastor and/or his/her appointee.

- ✟ **Walking During the Worship Service** – Walking during the service should be kept to a minimum. There are times during the service that *no one* should be walking, except for an emergency.

These times include during the:

- ✟ *Scripture* – Reading of God's Word
- ✟ *Prayer* – Giving thanks and making petitions before God
- ✟ *Sermon* – The Word of God demands our undivided attention.
- ✟ *Invitation to Discipleship* – Walking may prove a

distraction to someone who is making the critical choice between heaven or hell.

✟ ***Benediction*** – Bestowing the blessings of God upon the people of God.

CHAPTER 5
PULPIT ETIQUETTE

PULPIT ETIQUETTE ~
"The Work of the Ministry"

1. Be on time to enter the pulpit. If late, take a seat in the congregation. Always wait to be invited to the pulpit.

2. Wear conservative attire that does not call attention to you and distract attention from the Worship Service. (Dark suits, white shirts, dark shoes, etc.)

3. Ladies should always wear long skirts/dresses or robes in the pulpit.

4. Be observant and attentive while in the pulpit. Take brief notes. Save extra reading for your study time. Always support the preacher.

5. No excessive talking in the pulpit.

Bishop Alton A. Smith

6. Sit erect in the pulpit. Look the part.

7. When asked to make remarks, be brief. Remarks should be appropriate for the service or program occasion.

    ☦ Allow the sermon to stand for itself. Do not try to re-preach another minister's sermon.
    ☦ When asked to read the scripture, just read. Do not comment or try to preach it.
    ☦ When presiding, lead the congregation into worship – not drive them.

8. Always remember the season of the year and the occasion for the service that you are in.

9. Remember the purpose, the length and the differences between the Invocation, Morning Prayer, Offertory Prayer and the Altar Prayer.

    ☦ *Invocation – short prayer* that invites God's presence into the service.
    ☦ *Morning Prayer – universal prayer* to voice the needs of persons and the desire for God to meet those needs.
    ☦ *Offertory Prayer – short prayer* to bless the tithes and offerings and those who participated in giving.
    ☦ *Altar Prayer* – prayer for those gathered around the altar.
    ☦ *Benediction* – Blessings and a prayer for Divine protection.

10. Learn and use several benedictions.

Order in the Church

11. Learn how to extend the Invitation to Discipleship.

    ✞ Remember and be aware that every person that comes forth isdifferent.

12. When presiding over a Worship Service, remember that you are in charge. You must lead by the Holy Spirit and be in control at all times during the service.

<u>*Remember at all times*</u>
"Let all things be done decently and in order."
1 Corinthians 14:40

VISITING (Guest) MINISTERS

1. Be sure to understand that you are a guest in another's home. You must present yourself with an attitude of submission, as a servant.

2. Make sure that you ask in advance if there is anything that you need or of which you are not sure.

3. Be proficient in performing the task that you are assigned or asked to complete. If you are asked to preach or pray, don't sing. If you are asked to read the scripture, don't try to preach or expound, etc.

4. Do not try to correct or change any part of the service. It is your obligation to comply with the standard that the pastor has set. Remember, you are a guest and you are there to serve.

CHAPTER 6
CLERGY ATTIRE AND MINISTERIAL VESTMENT

Personal Grooming – This is a very important factor.
- ✟ Be cognizant of your breath, especially after eating. (pocket mints…)
- ✟ Hair, beard, mustache should always be neatly trimmed.
- ✟ Fingernails should be clean and trimmed.
- ✟ Shoes should be shined and well maintained.

Note to Remember: As members of the Clergy, you represent God, our Father here on earth. Your attitude and your appearance help to set or destroy the demeanor for worship and how our congregations and our communities perceive who we are.

Clerical Vestments

The history of ministerial vestments goes back to old Roman everyday clothing and it has determined contemporary formal dress of Christian Clergy of all persuasions. Basic black is considered the traditional color throughout the Universal Church.

The attire worn by Clergy should at best enhance the Worship Service. Color, material and design should not draw attention to us, but the focus should at all times be on the Glory of God.

Before you open your mouth, your clothes speak. As ambassadors for God, we cannot wear anything that might distract the focus from God and the service that we are doing to Him.

Ministers must always be aware of their appearance, whether in ministerial settings, public settings, visitations, formal or casual settings. They must always check, especially in clerical settings, what is the acceptable or expected attire for that setting.

Significance of wearing the robe in the pulpit

> *Robe - A long loose flowing outer garment, especially an official garment worn by high church official.*

- ✟ The pulpit robe emphasizes the office of the preacher.
- ✟ The pulpit robe de-emphasizes the personality of the man or woman in the pulpit.
- ✟ The pulpit robe gives testament to the office of the preacher as a representative of Christ.
- ✟ The robe serves to hide the personality of the man (or woman) and highlights his/her special calling.
- ✟ The pastor represents Christ (the husband), to the church, (His bride).
- ✟ The pastor does not act for himself, but for Christ.

> "...*that they may make* Aaron's garments *to consecrate him, that he may* minister *unto me in the* priest's office. *And these [are] the* garments *which they shall make; a* breastplate, *and an ephod, and a* robe, *and a broidered*

Bishop Alton A. Smith

> *coat, a mitre, and a* girdle: *and they shall make holy* garments *for* Aaron *thy* brother, *and his sons, that he may* minister *unto me in the* priest's office. ` *Exodus 28:2-4*

Various members of society, such as a policeman, the ball player, a doctor or a nurse wear the uniform of their profession because they do not act for themselves. They are under orders. In the same way, a minister or an Elder is also under orders and must be appropriate robed.

The robe of the preacher signifies his calling to his office. The clothing and vestment of the clergy signifies the office that he/she holds and the responsibility to the congregation which he/she serves.

Ministers –
- ✞ Ministers are un-ordained members of the clergy (preachers).
- ✞ Ministers may wear a plain dark (black or navy) suit or plain black robe when preaching or presiding over a Worship Service.
- ✞ No other clerical attire may be worn by ministers until after their ordination to the Gospel Ministry.

Elders (Ordained Preachers) –
- ✞ Elders are preachers who have been ordained to the Gospel Ministry.
- ✞ Clerical collar shirts may be worn by persons who have been ordained to preach the Gospel.
- ✞ *EVERY* member of the clergy should have at least one of each of the following:

    1) Standard black suit

    2) Plain black pulpit robe

    3) Plain white pulpit robe
- ✞ Civic Dress for Elders – Dark suits, white shirt or

clergy shirt with two inch white tab, black shoes and socks.
✞ Some Elders choose to wear the tab or full collar.
  1) Tabbed collar – Elders may wear the two inch tabbed collar with their tab collar clergy shirt, or
  2) Full collar – Elders may wear the two inch full color with the full collar clergy shirt.
✞ Elders may wear the silver cross with a silver chain or scarlet cord exposed over the breast.
✞ Female Elders
  1) Each of the statements concerning Elders will also apply to female elders.
  2) Pulpit attire should be long enough without the assistance of scarves or lap kerchiefs.
  3) Earrings, if worn, should be studs or small hoops - one in each ear.
✞ *Reminders*
  1) The color purple, the gold chain, the gold cross and the three inch collar are reserved for Bishops only.
  2) The color red is reserved for the *Presiding* Bishop at the time that he is presiding.

WHAT TO WEAR, WHEN:
✞ When invited to a meeting that you will represent clergy or the church congregation, always wear civic or business attire.

Bishop Alton A. Smith

☦ It is appropriate to wear a robe during the following services:
1) Worship Services *(when preaching or presiding)*
2) Funerals
3) Weddings
4) Baptisms

CHAPTER 7
THE BISHOPRIC

Biblical Qualifications of the Bishop

1 Timothy 3:2-7 – *"A bishop then must be blameless, the husband of one wife, vigilant, sober, of good behavior, given to hospitality, apt to teach, Not given to wine, no striker, not greedy of filthy lucre; but patient, not a brawler, not covetous; One that ruleth well his own house, having his children in subjection with all gravity; For if a man know not how to rule his own house, how shall he take care of the church of God? Not a novice, lest being lifted up with pride he fall into the condemnation of the devil. Moreover he must have a good report of them which are without; lest he fall into reproach and the snare of the devil."*

Titus 1:5-9 – *"If any be blameless, the husband of one wife, having faithful children not accused of riot or unruly. For a bishop must be blameless, as the steward of God; not self-willed, not soon angry,*

> *not given to wine, no striker, not given to filthy lucre; But a lover of hospitality, a lover of good men, sober, just, holy, temperate; Holding fast the faithful word as he hath been taught, that he may be able by sound doctrine both to exhort and to convince the gainsayers."*

The word Bishop is derived from the greek word, "*episcopos*", which means a spiritual overseer, superintendent or director. The apostle Paul, in addressing the elders of the Church at Ephesus stated, *"Take heed therefore unto yourselves, and to all the flock, over the which the Holy Ghost hath made you overseers, to feed the church of God, which he hath purchased with his own blood."* (Acts 20:28)

Leadership Model of the Bishop:
- ✞ The bishop is the Pastor to Pastors.
- ✞ The bishop must be an example in leadership.
- ✞ The bishop must know the structure and organization of the church.
- ✞ The bishop must have knowledge of the doctrine of the church and ascertain that it is being taught.
- ✞ The bishop must teach Pastors, Elders, Ministers and congregations the ordinances and mandates of the church.
- ✞ The bishop must have clear knowledge of the constitution and the laws that govern the church.
- ✞ The bishop must know the difference between the organization and the organism.
- ✞ *The organization is the direction that we follow the carry out the program of the church.*
- ✞ *The organism is the living spirit of Jesus Christ that*

Order in the Church

guides the church. In order to hear from Him there must be "Order in the Church".

✟ The bishop must always demonstrate and display leadership within the church.
✟ The bishop should train Elders and Ministers in pulpit etiquette, ministerial dress, how to conduct the Worship Service and how to carry out the ordinances of the Church.
✟ The bishop must be punctual for meetings, services and appointments.
✟ The bishop must teach those whom he leads to be astute in matters of business. Leaders must begin meetings and services on time, have a working agenda and end on time.
✟ The bishop must require Elders, Pastors and Ministers who serve under you to constantly seek training in their field of ministry.
✟ The bishop must require that all under his charge maintain the proper credentials at all times.
✟ The bishop must be loyal to the pastors and congregations under his charge.
✟ The bishop must ascertain that the churches in his charge have the proper insurances (fire, flood, counseling, etc.)
✟ The bishop must ascertain that the churches in his charge have the proper deeds for church properties.
✟ The bishop must encourage church leaders to tithe. The New Testament church is built on evangelism and tithes.
✟ The bishop at all times must exercise fairness and impartiality.
✟ The bishop must encourage community outreach.
✟ The bishop must have a sound mind, but never forget that good common sense will go a long way.

Bishop Alton A. Smith

- ✞ The bishop must lead by Godly example.
- ✞ The bishop must use Godly judgment in decision-making.
- ✞ The bishop must be a Kingdom Administrator (overseer).
- ✞ The bishop must be sensitive and careful in handling pastors, ministers and members of the church because each need is different. This is where the bishop must exercise prayerfulness and Godly wisdom.
- ✞ The bishop must at all times be cognizant of the strengths and weaknesses of those whom he leads.

The Bishop's Attire (Vestments)

The Latin word *vestment* refers to "clothing". In language translations now used, it refers to the garments worn by ministers in the performance of their sacred duties. In the Church, vestments are to be set apart and blessed by the Church to increase devotion in those who see and wear them. Vestments serve as the uniform of those who wear them.

These garments are used to identify the Bishop as a "follower of Christ", a scholar or one who imitates Christ. The Bishop is one who oversees other members of the clergy or pastors.

The following garments identify the Bishop as a follower of Christ or "imitator of Christ". He is the shepherd of the House. These regal garments are sometimes referred to as *"Ceremonial Attire"*. The Ceremonial Attire is worn for ceremonial activities of the church, including Consecrations, Ordinations, Baptisms, Dedications, Holy Communions and Weddings.

The Cassock – The cassock comes from the word "casaque" which means cloak. The cassock is not reserved for the Bishop only, but may be worn by any member of the Cleric. The cassock is a black, ankle-length, long sleeved, close fitting garment and is the first layer of clothing that the Bishop wears. The cassock worn by the Bishop is of the color Roman Purple (Fushia), a mixture of Red and White, symbolic of blood. It is a princely color. The members of the cleric may wear black cassocks. A modest garment, it covers the body from neck to feet and typically closes in front with a series of small buttons. Some cassocks have thirty-three buttons down the front to represent the years of Christ on the earth.

The Cinture – The Cinture is girded about the waist and serves as a symbol of humility. Taking its symmetry from the towel with which our Lord girded himself, it speaks of the Bishop's willingness to "wash his brethren's feet" pursuant to the example of our Lord.

The Rochet – The Rochet is a symbol of the priesthood. It is symbolic of Aaron's white linen ephod and is a reminder to the Bishop that his role as Celebrant and Worship Leader is prominent in the total mandate of the office.

The Chimere – The Chimere is a loose, sleeveless robe worn by the Bishop. It is worn over the Rochet. It serves as a symbol of the Mantle of the Prophet. This garment is worn by the bishop because it signifies him as a Chief Proclaimer and Defender of the Faith in the apostolic tradition.

The Tippet – The Tippet is sometimes called a "Preaching Scarf" and represents the Bishop as the bond slave; yoked to Christ by the bond of love. The Tippet is

Bishop Alton A. Smith

either seven or nine inch width denoting Perfection *(seven)* or Judgment *(nine)*. The Pastor's Tippet is five inches wide symbolizing grace. The Tippet is also symbolic of the priest carrying the burdens of the people.

Gold Chain – This precious metallic element is made of very heavy, malleable and refined gold. The gold chain is a symbol of endurance which emphasizes that the wearer is not a novice. The gold represents deity and wealth. As a gift to the Christ child, it symbolizes His kingship. Bishops only, shall wear the gold chain with Pectoral cross.

The Pectoral Cross – The Pectoral Cross represents the instrument of suffering on which Christ died and redeemed the world. It also stands for whatever pain or endurance that a Christian undergoes, and voluntarily accepts, in order to be joined with Christ and cooperate in the salvation of souls. It also represents the victorious Risen Savior. The cross is attached to the gold chain, which he wears around his neck. It hangs on his breast and is usually three feet in length. The cross can be worn outside suspended by the chain while in choir dress or other high ceremonial vestments. When wearing civic attire, the Bishop will wear a black suit and will tuck the cross inside the left pocket of his clerical shirt. This symbolizes that the Lord is close to his heart.

The Episcopal Ring – The ring is a sign of Son-ship. It is a signet of authority and indicates that one is a Prince in the family of God. The stone of the bishop's ring is amethyst and is worn on the third finger of the bishop's hand. It is symbolic of his marriage to the church.

Mitre – The mitre is the hat of the bishop, a protection for the head; the seat of wisdom, knowledge and understanding.

Order in the Church

It symbolizes a crown of glory and honor, of spiritual leadership, having gifts of the Spirit and the ability to use them to the glory of God.

Crozier – The bishop's staff is called the crozier. The crozier is in the shape of a shepherd's hook. The bishop carries the staff as a reminder that he is the "shepherd" of the flock of God. The bishop holds the crozier with his left hand, using his right hand to bestow blessings upon the people.

Bishop's Seal – There is not a specified design for the bishop's seal. Each seal is custom designed according to the character, beliefs and obligations of the bishop. The seal of the bishop is his/her emblem used to identify their church and their commitment and homage to the church.

Additional Notes regarding the Bishop's Dress:
* The bishop must adorn the attire and vestments prescribed by your church. The proper colors for the bishop include:
  Purple Red, Purple Blue, Purple
* Bishops must teach Elders that they must refrain from wearing the Bishop's colors.
* The bishop should teach Ministers and Elders to wear appropriate colors in the pulpit. (*Loud colors should never be worn. Remember, we are Christ's representatives.*)
* The bishop's dress should always include the pectoral cross and the Episcopal ring even when wearing civic attire.

- * When wearing a robe, the pectoral cross should hang free.
- * When not wearing a robe, the pectoral cross should be placed in the left breast pocket of the shirt.

CHAPTER 8
FUNERAL ETIQUETTE FOR THE BISHOP AND THE ELDER

The office of Elder or Bishop is the highest office held in the church. It is only right and considerate that the Elder or the Bishop be given proper courtesy at the time of their demise. The following is proper protocol for these officers.

The Deceased Elder (and Minister)
In the event of death of an Elder, the family should notify the office of the District Bishop, who will in turn notify the General Bishop. The District Bishop (or his designee) will meet with the surviving spouse (or responsible immediate family member) to assist with planning and preparation of the funeral service.

Upon receiving the information of a death in the Ministerial Community, the bishop should proceed to inform the members of his diocese. Information should include funeral arrangements, instructions for participation, contact information for the family and funeral home assignment.

The Bishop (or designee) should meet with the responsible members of the family to discuss the proper funeral service for an Elder of the church.

Please be cognizant of the following:
- ☦ Elders should be buried in their black robe.

Bishop Alton A. Smith

- ✞ If the deceased Elder is a Pastor, the Officiating Minister and/or the Eulogist should be the District Bishop and/or the Elder's Pastor.
- ✞ If the deceased Elder is not a pastor, or is a Minister of that congregation, the Officiating Minister may be an Associate of the church and the pastor should serve as the Eulogist. The District Bishop should be notified.
- ✞ Attire for Elders during the funeral is the black robe. Attire for ministers is black suits. Robed Elders should line up first. Ministers wearing suits may follow Elders. Elders not wearing robes should line up with Ministers.
- ✞ The family should request *reserved* seating for Elders and Ministers.
- ✞ If the deceased is an Elder, *robed* Elders may serve as casket attendants to stand watch at the head and the foot of the casket during the funeral service.

The Deceased Bishop

In the event of the death of a Bishop, the family should notify the General Bishop. The General Bishop (or his designee) will in turn notify all other District Bishops. The General Bishop (or his designee) will meet with the surviving spouse (or immediate family member) to assist with the planning and preparation of the funeral service. This information will in turn be passed on to all District Bishops.

- ✞ The Bishop should be buried in his Ceremonial Attire. This is the highest honor for a Bishop.
- ✞ The office of Bishop is the highest in the church. For this reason, the General Bishop should deliver the eulogy for a Bishop.

Order in the Church

- ☦ Presider for the funeral service should be the Vice General, District or a Senior Bishop.
- ☦ Casket attendants should be the Elders of the Church (dressed in black robes).
- ☦ The Board of Bishops should be dressed in their Ceremonial Attire.
- ☦ All other Elders should be seated in reserved seats wearing their black robes, black clergy shirt and white two inch collar.
- ☦ Ministers may participate by following the robed Elders in line and wearing a black suit, white shirt and black necktie.

The funeral service for the Elder and the Bishop should be dignified, orderly and reverent. It should be the goal of each participant to make the service smooth, impressive and respectful and to provide comfort and care for the family during their time of bereavement. Our services should be memorable and give homage to the memory of one who has given his/her life to the church.

CHAPTER 9
GUIDE TO LEADERSHIP IN THE CHURCH

The driving force for church leadership and growth is:

The Great Commission

"Go ye therefore, and teach all nations, baptizing them in the name of the Father, and of the Son, and of the Holy Ghost: Teaching them to observe all things whatsoever I have commanded you: and, lo, I am with you always, even unto the end of the world. Amen." Matthew 28:19-20

A leader in the church must have a relationship with the Shepherd. A leader in the church must have accepted Jesus Christ as his Lord and Savior and must be one of His disciples.

What is a disciple? What does a disciple do?

A disciple is one who loves God and His Son, our Lord and Savior Jesus Christ, with all his heart, soul, and mind. A disciple tries to become more and more like Jesus through a life of faith and obedience. Jesus came into the world and

Order in the Church

lived a few brief years to set an example for us. He sacrificed His life for us so that we would have a chance for eternal life with Him and His Father. Eternal life is a choice for us to make. If we choose Him, we must live for Him. We must live as He taught us to live. We must live a life that others will see Him in us. Therefore, we are His Disciples.

In order to be a leader in the church one must follow the discipleship model. We must be servants *(But he that is greatest among you shall be your servant. Matthew 23:11)* As servants we must be willing to work, to be involved, to serve the body of Christ.

A servant leader is concerned about the needs of others first. He/she takes into account, how can I help others become a vital part of this ministry? What can we, as a ministry do to further the cause of Jesus Christ?

The servant leader is not a dictator, but is an activist. The servant leader does not constantly and only give orders, but takes into consideration how we together can accomplish our mission.

The leader must be a practitioner and the first partaker of all the ministry's undertakings. *("The husbandman that laboureth must be first partaker of the fruits." 2 Timothy 2:6)*. The leader must not only give direction, but must become involved in the undertakings of the ministry.

The involved, working leader is an example and an inspiration to those who follow.

How do we serve? First of all we serve with our presence. We are present and on time for activities and events of the church and our place in ministry. The leader must be in place to give direction. Never let members of your ministry go where you are not willing to go or do what you are not willing to do for your ministry.

The servant leader is an encourager. He/she allows

others to take part in the ministry and lets them know how necessary their role is in the ministry.

The servant leader must have a vision. This leader must lead in the direction of the ministry, have a goal in mind and know how the organization must proceed to reach the goal.

As Christians, we must be aware that each of us has a ministry and must be in submission and obedience of *The Great Commission*. We are to go into the world on the mission of our Lord and Savior.

Each of us has been bestowed with spiritual gifts and we will be held responsible for faithfully working within our gifts. No one is excluded from using these spiritual gifts to serve the body of Christ.

What is our purpose in the ministry of leadership in the church? Our purpose is to bring souls to Jesus Christ.

Attributes of a Spiritual Leader
- *Prayerful* – James 5:16 – "the effectual fervent prayer of a righteous man availeth much.
- *Faithful* – I Corinthians 4:2 – "Moreover it is required in stewards, that a man be found faithful.
- *Lover of God's People* – I Corinthians 13:13 - And now abideth faith, hope, charity, these three; but the greatest of these is charity.
- *Listens to and follows the voice of God* – John 14:23-24 - Jesus answered and said unto him, If a man love me, he will keep my words: and my Father will love him, and we will come unto him, and make our abode with him.
- *Sanctified* - Romans 15:16 - That I should be the minister of Jesus Christ to the Gentiles, ministering the gospel of God that the offering up of the Gentiles might be acceptable, being sanctified by the Holy Ghost.

Order in the Church

- ✞ *Spiritually Mature* – I Peter 5:2-4 - Feed the flock of God which is among you, taking the oversight thereof, not by constraint, but willingly; not for filthy lucre, but of a ready mind; Neither as being lords over God's heritage, but being examples to the flock. And when the chief Shepherd shall appear, ye shall receive a crown of glory that fadeth not away."
- ✞ *Able to Teach* – II Timothy 2:24 – "And the servant of the Lord must not strive; but be gentle unto all men, apt to teach, patient…"
- ✞ *Compassionate* – Colossians 3:12 – "Therefore, as God's chosen people, holy and dearly loved, clothe yourselves with compassion, kindness, humility, gentleness and patience."
- ✞ *Family Life in Order* – I Timothy 3:17 – "One that ruleth well his own house, having his children in subjection with all gravity; For if a man know not how to rule his own house, how shall he take care of the church of God?"
- ✞ *True Servant of God* – Matthew 6:24 – "No man can serve two masters: for either he will hate the one, and love the other; or else he will hold to the one, and despise the other. Ye cannot serve God and mammon."
- ✞ *Diverse* – II Peter 4:8 – "And above all things have fervent charity among yourselves: for charity shall cover the multitude of sins."
- ✞ *Knows what to do and how to do it* – Psalm 37:23 – "The steps of a good man are ordered by the LORD: and he delighteth in his way."
- ✞ *Patient* – Galatians 6:9 – "And let us not be weary in well doing: for in due season we shall reap, if we faint not."
- ✞ *Must have a working knowledge of the Bible and the*

doctrine of the church – John 3:11 – "Verily, verily, I say unto thee, We speak that we do know, and testify that we have seen"

✞ *Enthusiastic* – Colossians 3:23 – "And whatsoever ye do, do it heartily, as to the Lord, and not unto men"

✞ *A Positive Influence* – Matthew 5:16 – "Let your light so shine before men, that they may see your good works, and glorify your Father which is in heaven."

Who are we leading?

We are leading God's people, the sheep of His fold. Sheep must be led and not driven. The leader must be in front and not behind them. From the study of the shepherd, we know that the shepherd keeps a watchful eye. In order to maintain a watchful eye, one must be able to observe when the sheep are in line or one goes astray.

Good shepherds (pastors, evangelists, teachers, spiritual leaders) spot danger and lead the sheep away from it. He leads them to greener pastures where they can be fed with knowledge and understanding. That greener pasture in found in Jesus Christ. He is the Good Shepherd . . .

Psalms 23 ~ *A Psalm of David*

1. *The LORD is my shepherd; I shall not want.*

2. *He maketh me to lie down in green pastures: he leadeth*

   me beside the still waters.

3. *He restoreth my soul: he leadeth me in the paths of*

   righteousness for his name's sake.

4. *Yea, though I walk through the valley of the shadow of death, I will fear no evil: for thou art with me; thy rod and thy staff they comfort me.*

5. *Thou preparest a table before me in the presence of mine enemies: thou anointest my head with oil; my cup runneth over.*

6. *Surely goodness and mercy shall follow me all the days of my life and I will dwell in the house of the Lord forever.*

life: and I will dwell in the house of the LORD forever.

As leaders of God's people, let us keep before us that our ultimate goal is to bring lost souls to Jesus Christ, to teach them that in Him they can find peace, comfort and salvation; in Him they can find everything that they need.

In finality, let us be reminded that in service, our ultimate goal is to obey the Great Commission – **Matthew 28:19-20 -*"Go ye therefore, and teach all nations, baptizing them in the name of the Father, and of the Son, and of the Holy Ghost: Teaching them to observe all things whatsoever I have commanded you: and, lo, I am with you always, even unto the end of the world. Amen.***

CHAPTER 10
FIVE STEPS TO HEAVEN

(How to be Saved and Know It)

Step One: ***Acknowledge that you have sinned.***
Each of us that has been born into this world was born in sin.

> *"For all have sinned, and come short of the glory of God."*
>
> *Romans 3:23*

> *"As it is written, There is none righteous, no, not one."*
>
> *Romans 3:10*

Step Two: ***Realize that there is a penalty for sin.***

> *"For the wages of sin is death…"*
>
> *Romans 6:23a*

The word "death" means separation. The death referred to in this verse means eternal separation from God into the lake of fire as stated in Revelation 21:8.

Order in the Church

> *"But the fearful, and unbelieving, and the abominable, and murderers, and whoremongers, and sorcerers, and idolaters, and all liars, shall have their part in the lake which burneth with fire and brimstone: which is the second death."*
>
> *Revelation 21:8*

Step Three: Acknowledge that Christ paid the penalty of sin for you.

> *"For God so loved the world, that he gave his only begotten Son, that whosoever believeth in him should not perish, but have everlasting life."*
>
> *John 3:16*

> *"But God commendeth his love toward us, in that, while we were yet sinners, Christ died for us."*
>
> *Romans 5:8*

Step Four: Acknowledge that Christ wants to give you the free gift of eternal life in heaven.

> *"But the gift of God is eternal life through Jesus Christ our Lord."*
>
> *Romans 6:23b*

Step Five: You must believe in Christ and ask Him to be your Savior.

> *"That if thou shalt confess with thy mouth the Lord Jesus, and shalt believe in thine heart that God*

> *hath raised him from the dead, thou SHALT BE SAVED."*
>
> *Romans 10:9*
>
> *"For with the heart man believeth unto righteousness; and with the mouth confession is made unto salvation."*
>
> *Romans 10:10*
>
> *"For whosoever shall call upon the name of the Lord shall be saved."*
>
> *Romans 10:13*
>
> Think about these truths, and just confess your sins to Jesus Christ and He will come into your heart and life. For the scripture saith, *"Whoever believes on Him will not be put to shame."*
>
> *Romans 10:11*

Good works will not bring salvation to our souls. Being a good person is not salvation.

The Bible declares that we are saved through faith and not by works.

> *"For by grace are ye saved through faith; and that not of yourselves: it is the gift of God: not of works, lest any man should boast."*
>
> *Ephesians 2:8,9.*

Order in the Church

Because of the love of a caring and compassionate Savior who loved us so much that He provided a way for man to be delivered from all of our sins. He saved each of us through the free gift of salvation that we could ***be saved and know it*** according to the Word of God.

Salvation is the work of a loving Savior that saves men from the eternal doom of sin. In salvation, He gives to each of us the riches of His Grace, which means eternal life now and forever. Salvation is the work of Christ Jesus and not the work of man.

The meaning of salvation is "*deliverance from sin*" and as written in the Old and New Testament implies that we are delivered and safely preserved until His coming when we will reign with Him in heaven.

BIBLIOGRAPHY

Dictionary and Thesaurus - Merriam-Webster Online. Web. 2011. http://www.merriam-webster.com.

Bass, Rev. Shelley & Josephine. "Bishops Vestments" www.nationalrobe.com.   2010

St. Mark Church of Christ Book Ministry. *Pressing Toward the Mark*. Authorhouse, Bloomington, IN   2008.

The Holy Bible. Nashville: Thomas Nelson, 1993. Print.

CPSIA information can be obtained
at www.ICGtesting.com
Printed in the USA
BVHW03s1406080218
507481BV00001B/15/P

9 781456 769369

THE TRIALS OF APHRODITE

MISALIGNED MYTHS 1

VICTORIA MOXLEY

Copyright © 2024 by Victoria Moxley

Cover Design © 2024 by Victoria Moxley in collaboration with Tea With Coffee Media via Adobe Photoshop and Dreamstime

Internal Images © Kelsey Anne Lovelady via Canva and Atticus

Published by Tea With Coffee Media

Tea With Coffee Media and the colophon are trademarks of Tea With Coffee Media

All rights reserved.

No portion of this book may be reproduced in any form without written permission from the publisher or author, except as permitted by U.S. copyright law.

DEDICATION

For all the smut lovers who just want a scarred and muscled god with rough hands to break them and leave them begging for more.

ACKNOWLEDGEMENTS

JESSIE SADLER. YOU NOT only helped me with your flawless Alpha reading skills, but you also helped me 'Wet Daddy' Hephaestus when I was completely lost and getting a feel for him early on. Thank you.

To the incredible Kelsey Anne Lovelady for helping me figure out these trials and for reading things over. You are an absolute treasure.

To Vervain Moxley, my best friend and unofficial twin, for helping me to build this world with our other idiots that will one day see the light of day. And for being the best editor ever!

Look, grandma! Look, mom! I finished a book. I wish you both could've been here to see it. And then never read it.

~ Victoria Moxley

TRIGGER WARNINGS

YOUR MENTAL HEALTH MATTERS

Graphic violence
dismemberment
blood
gore
injury
mentions of past cheating
pregnancy
forced marriage
forced proximity
BDSM
rough sex
face fucking
rough anal sex
attempted assault

APHRODITE'S PLAYLIST

"Wide Awake" – Katy Perry
"Only Love Can Hurt Like This" – Paloma Faith
"Tie Me Down" – Gryffin
"Never Let Me go" – Florence + The Machine
"Who You Are" – Jessie J
"React" – The Pussycat Dolls
"Want U Back" – Cher Lloyd
"Touch" – Little Mix
"Leave While I'm Not Looking" – Paloma Faith
"Treat You Better" – Shawn Mendes
"Like I'm Gonna Lose You" – Meghan Trainor
"I'm a Mess" – Bebe Rexha
"Bound to You" – Christina Aguilera
"Soap" – Melanie Martinez
"She Keeps Me Warm" – Mary Lambert
"Fidelity" – Regina Spektor
"Almost Lover" – A Fine Frenzy
"She's So Gone" – Naomi Scott
"Love Me Like You Do" – Ellie Goulding

"Unholy" – Sam Smith ft. Kim Petras
"Bad Guy" – Billie Eilish
"Clarity" – Zedd ft. Foxes
"Tears of Gold" – Faouzia
"War of Hearts" – Ruelle
"Tattoo" – Loreen
"Tip of My Tongue" – The Civil Wars

HEPHAESTUS' PLAYLIST

"Another Life" – Motionless In White
"Remember Everything" – Five Finger Death Punch
"Lifelines" – I Prevail
"Just Pretend" – Bad Omens
"Masterpiece" – Motionless In White
"Help" – Papa Roach
"Face Down" – The Red Jumpsuit Apparatus
"Hunting Season" – Ice Nine Kills
"Tears Don't Fall" – Bullet For My Valentine
"I Don't Belong Here" – I Prevail
"Grow Up, Peter Pan" – Adept
"Eternally Yours" – Motionless In White
"Your Betrayal" – Bullet For My Valentine
"This Is The Time" – Nothing More
"I Will Not Bow" – Breaking Benjamin
"Suffocating Under Words of Sorrow" – Bullet For My Valentine
"Dear God" – Avenged Sevenfold
"Crawled From The Shadows" – Deicide

Contents

		XIV
1.	Prologue	1
		6
2.	Chapter 1	7
		14
3.	Chapter 2	15
		28
4.	Chapter 3	29
		38
5.	Chapter 4	39
		48
6.	Chapter 5	49
		58
7.	Chapter 6	59
		68
8.	Chapter 7	69

		80
9.	Chapter 8	81
		98
10.	Chapter 9	99
		108
11.	Chapter 10	109
		126
12.	Chapter 11	127
		138
13.	Chapter 12	139
		152
14.	Chapter 13	153
		166
15.	Chapter 14	167
		180
16.	Chapter 15	181
		194
17.	Chapter 16	195
		222
18.	Chapter 17	223
		236
19.	Chapter 18	237
		246

20.	Chapter 19	247
		258
21.	Chapter 20	259
		266
22.	Chapter 21	267
		282
23.	Chapter 22	283
		288
24.	Chapter 23	289
		298
25.	Chapter 24	299
		310
26.	Chapter 25	311
		328
27.	Chapter 26	329
		338
28.	Epilogue	339
29.	Hephaestus' Anime List	343
30.	About the Author	347

PROLOGUE

My gaze was fixed on the worn blue and green rug between us, as I did my best not to squirm. The woman sat across from me was the single mortal who could cause me discomfort. Meeting her gaze was the last thing I wanted to do at that moment. Through all the years we'd known each other, she'd learned my tells, my signs of discomfort or dishonesty. I never thought I would meet anyone that could reduce me to such, much less a human. "Dita," she called my mortal name. "If you're not ready to talk about it, then we can try another day." We'd been doing this dance for enough years that I didn't want to take the out she was offering me. She'd helped me more than I ever thought a mortal could, paved the way for me to take my redemption. It was time that I finally stopped running from the things that scared me most.

"You know who I truly am. Why continue with the pretense of my mortal identity?" Was I stalling? Yes. But it was something that I wondered since I had shared the truth of who I was with her. I wasn't Dita, the blessed mortal with an estranged husband that was figuring out her relationships while helping others with theirs. The truth was far more interesting. I revealed to her that I was the goddess Aphrodite, that I was confused about the things I had done and how I had recently started to feel. Why did my past actions haunt me so?

"Because it's still strange to think that you're a living breathing goddess. And Dita was what I called you until you chose to share that information with me last month." Dr. Frost sighed as she set her pen down on the notepad in her lap. "I mean it. If you're still not ready, we can wait."

"No, I am." It was my turn to sigh as I sat back on the soft couch, my fingers playing with a loose thread on the azure cushion beside me. "You want to know about our wedding, how I felt that day." That was a confusing memory. I know how I had felt at that moment, but my feelings had changed at some point and my thoughts and emotions about that day were different, drastically so. Where to begin. "You know the myth?"

"I know there are two versions. One didn't paint him in a good light, the other didn't paint you in a good light either."

"He never attacked Athena. Hera did not throw him from Olympus. Zeus did, when he attempted to spare Hera from Zeus' attentions. And he held resentment towards both for the fate he had after. Even Hera since she did nothing to help him after his banishment. He

CHAPTER 1

THE SLAP ROCKED ME back on my heels. I could taste metal pooling at the corner of my mouth. It was more surprising because I hadn't seen Hera show that level of anger towards any god other than Zeus. Licking the ichor that blossomed, the gold color stark against the crimson I'd donned for the meeting, I looked up into those glowing hazel eyes. "I understand why you would never trust me. My intentions are pure. For once, I see the truth of the situation, about myself, and what I need to do. All I want is the chance to make amends." My gaze shifted to the large, dark wooden desk in front of the window of her office. Anything to keep the fury in my gaze from being seen by her. She'd take it as an insult, and I had only a little more contrition in me. Especially when the sting of her slap was still burning my face. I took a few deep breaths, trying to calm myself. I would never achieve my goal if I didn't try to appease her first. While I understood why she was prideful, the insults she'd taken over the ages, her pride was standing in my way.

Her bark of laughter made me flinch. We'd never been truly at odds before, but there was no one else I could turn to. Of everyone in the pantheon, she was the only one that I knew would have the information I needed. That was the only reason I was willing to crawl on my belly before her. "Pure? Truth? All you know is cruelty and lust. I would never help you hurt him again."

I knew that she'd made amends with him long ago, that she regretted her actions, or lack thereof, and had fixed their relationship. But all I wanted was the chance to do the same. While I knew I was most likely too late, I wanted to try. "Please. I mean every word. I just need to know where he is. Would you not prefer to hear tales of how I crawled on my belly for forgiveness? With how things ended the last time I saw him, you will most likely hear about him spurning me." I was really voicing my fears, but if she wouldn't trust me, maybe I could appeal to her desire to see me humbled. As though begging her for information wasn't humbler than I had been in centuries. My heart raced as I wiped the throbbing wound on my lip. Her expression proved she was thinking it over. The malicious glint in her eyes made me wonder if she'd do something to ensure that I was humiliated. It was a risk that I had to take though.

"I will not tell you where he is. He deserves his freedom." My face fell at her words. "However, I might pass a message to him from you." Perhaps it was the relief on my face, the hope that I felt bubbling up, that made her say what she did next. "Prove yourself worthy of him."

My face fell. If I had to prove myself to her, there was no way she'd ever pass on a message to him. "How?" I could point out that I would never get to see him if she had her way, but angering her further, insulting her honor, wouldn't help me.

Maybe she could hear my thoughts, not that it was one of her abilities, but she seemed to have figured out what I was thinking. "I will pass your message to him. If he accepts, you will prove yourself to him. And I believe you know how."

Unfortunately, I did. I wasn't a demigod, but she'd put me through the same sort of trials one of them would have to face to prove themselves worthy. I knew the tasks that they underwent. What could she possibly choose for me? I had no illusions that anyone but Hera would set the tasks for me. And I shuddered to think what she might come up with to humble me completely.

"Well? Will you prove yourself if he accepts your apologies? While I don't agree with my son's choice of wife, I won't take the decision away from him." I could hear in her voice that she wanted to do exactly that. She wanted to make sure that I was never near him again. Taking a moment to breathe through the nerves, I looked her over. There was no questioning why Zeus had chosen her. She was the epitome of what a goddess should be. Those sharp cheekbones, those defined features, her curvy figure. Her chest was more generous than mine, and I was by no means lacking for my own endowments. She'd drawn her mahogany-colored hair back into a no-nonsense bun, making her features even more striking. My own had been a turquoise for some time, but I knew she would be snide over such a thing and had quickly changed it back to a true black before the meeting. An impatient click of her heel drew me back from thoughts. It was a weakness for me, reveling in the beauty of others. Even when that beauty held nothing but resentment for me.

"I accept. Will you have a set limit for these trials?" It would be better to know how many trials I had ahead of me. Not that I could prepare myself for them, she would never be so kind as to tell me anything she had planned.

I wondered if that would earn me another strike, but she just looked at me curiously. It was like I could taste her doubt on my tongue, but she nodded her head. "Seven. You will undertake seven trials of my choosing. If he wishes to give you the chance to redeem yourself," she added. Of course, she'd remind me that even if I was willing to do whatever it took, Hephaestus could still refuse to let me prove myself.

"I will gladly undertake them." Did I expect to come out the other side? Not really. But if I did, I could only hope that he would be waiting for me there. And that I wasn't too late.

"And what message would you have me pass on to him?"

"You really cannot even give me his phone number?"

"No. I won't have you harass him and manipulate him into forgiving you. If that was what you wanted, perhaps you should have gone to your beloved Ares."

That made me pause. "Has he forgiven Ares? Are they in contact with one another?" All that she gave in answer was a slight nod as she moved to sit at her desk once more. "Then there is hope."

"Forgiving his mother and brother does not mean he will accept the cruel goddess that crushed his heart. Be quick with your message. I have important matters to attend to." And I wasn't one of them. Her concise and true statements stung, but I wouldn't be deterred. Sighing, I pulled a paper from my bag, a pre-written message asking him to hear me out and a place to meet on it. Her words smothered that small spark of hope that I had been clinging to, but it wasn't fully out yet as I placed the note on the edge of her desk. "One last thing before you go." Her words stopped me as I turned to leave, my heart dropping into my stomach. "I wouldn't want you to think you could weasel your way out of the trials should you grow tired of them and try to run away with my son." I knew where this was going, and I knew that there was no way around it.

"You want me to swear by the ichor." I glanced over my shoulder to watch her nod. To my surprise, she didn't look haughty or smug in any way. Her face was careful, neutral. Or perhaps just guarded so I couldn't use it as an excuse later. Either way, I knew what I had to do. There was still ichor that had pooled at the corner of my mouth. It would be enough. I swiped my thumb over it and held it up for her to see. "I swear it by the ichor. May I face a true death should I break this oath. I will undertake the trials should Heph forgive me. I will prove myself worthy of him." There wasn't a show of lights, a visual sign that it was done. But we could feel the magic in the air, the bond that was formed between us. I could only hope as I left her office that I didn't hang myself on it.

CHAPTER II

MY HEART RACED AS I cradled a clear glass with some iced coffee concoction in it. I really didn't even taste it, nor the pastries on the table. All I could taste was my trepidation. It was a vile thing on my tongue and I was drowning in how my heart thrummed in my ears. The din of other patrons in the cafe didn't even register. My eyes were fixed on the door as my maroon fingernails tapped a staccato rhythm on the glass in my hands.

Each time the door opened my heart leaped into my throat. And each time it wasn't him, my heart sank heavily into my gut. It was a roller coaster of emotions, and I was even more exhausted given how I had been unable to sleep the night before. *Would he come?* There was a chance I could just sit in the cafe, alone, and he would never show. All I could envision was Heph receiving my note from Hera and ripping it to shreds. He hadn't passed word back whether he would meet with me. Or maybe he had, and she refused to pass it along. That was a better outcome. That was the one that I hoped for.

Because if that was the case then maybe he would still show up.

I glanced at my phone where it lay untouched on the table. Each notification indicating that my mortals were checking in on me lit up the screen and I saw the time. The minutes felt like years with how slowly it was moving. Perhaps showing up half an hour early was a way to torment myself even more than I already had been. But as the time approached, my heart sank even lower. All the hope I had clung to was being crushed under the memory of our past interactions.

With lessening hope, I looked up as the door opened, and my heart nearly stopped. There he was. His fiery hair combed back, his beard that was meant to look unkempt, but I could tell was regularly trimmed. He wore a faded brown leather jacket over his grey Henley, dark jeans, and well-worn boots. My eyes were transfixed on his face, taking in the small burns decorating his cheek above his beard on the right side, and the long line that went from the side of his face, stopping at the line of his strong nose. I saved those eyes for last as he approached me. They were gray-blue, swirling, and deep, intense. And as he looked me over, I could feel that intensity grow. How could I ever think there was nothing between us? But I knew the answer as soon as the question passed through my mind. For so many centuries, I had fooled myself into thinking I knew what love was when it came to my own relationships. I'd spent so long mistaking fighting and hate fucking as passion and a healthy relationship. I was an expert at everyone's relationships but my own. It was my weakness.

My gaze fell on his scarred, calloused hands, one grasping the top of his cane, the other laid over it, gripping tightly until his knuckles turned white. I looked back up at his face and offered a smile. "Sit, please. Thank you for joining me." He wasn't late, not really. It had perhaps been a minute or two I had sat there waiting since the actual meeting time passed. But it had felt like an eternity. "I was unsure if you would be able to make it."

"I was unsure if I wanted to," he replied, the grit in his voice sending a shiver through me. "I didn't know if it was a ploy for public humiliation."

"Not unless it is mine." That made his frown lessen as he looked at me in surprise, his brows rising and allowing me to see more of those incredible eyes. I offered a soft smile. "It is good to see you again. I really am unsure where to even start." Heph looked more confused by the moment. Was I really that untrustworthy? That wasn't really a question that I wanted an answer to.

"Why am I here? You made it clear last time we met that you had no desire to see me again." He sighed and took the chair across from me. That was fair. I had been hateful towards him for so long, I didn't blame him for thinking the worst of me.

"I wanted to admit that I was wrong. I know it is likely too late to do so, but I want to earn your forgiveness." I wasn't sure his eyes could get any wider, but they did at that moment. It was short-lived, anger filling his eyes, and a suspicious look replacing it quickly.

"I'm tired, Dite. What's the game this time? Just tell me the rules so I can lose, and you can go off with Ares again." I could sense the years of pain and exhaustion, his exasperation just flowing from him in those words.

I winced at his words, but especially at that name. "I have not seen him in decades. Far too late, I realized that what we had was not true love, it was . . .something else. And I chose to spend the time since figuring out what I truly wanted, what I needed." It wasn't as though I loved Heph, I knew that wasn't it. But for the first time, I could feel the potential there. *If* he wanted to give it a chance.

"Say I believe you." he started, tapping his fingers on the table. "What is it exactly you want and need?" He was wary, and I didn't blame him in the least.

"To see if you have enough love left for me in your heart to try this for real. To salvage our marriage, to give it a real try, or to allow me to let you go if you crave freedom from me." That was not the answer he was expecting. His face was a storm of emotions, flitting across so quickly I couldn't keep up. Finally, he pushed himself up, setting his cane against the table and moving to my side with his hand steadying himself on the polished surface. It drew a few looks our way but they quickly glanced away once I stared back at them. Meeting in public was meant to feel safe for him, but I wouldn't let them make a side show of our reunion.

"This is the cruelest trick you have tried so far. If this is how far you will go to hurt me, I will take my freedom from you," he growled as he leaned down, his face inches from mine. "Or perhaps we should see how true your words are. Could you bear the touch of someone as ugly as me?" he hissed in my ear, his breath hot against my skin.

"You are not ugly," I whispered, the words shifting to a soft moan as he wrapped his hand in my hair. My face was utterly at peace as he leaned closer. He'd left enough slack that I could turn my head as I had done every other time he tried to kiss me before. The anger in his face flickered to surprise at the moan, and his eyes widened as one of my hands rose to brush my fingers over the deep scar on his left cheek before cradling his face. Determination settled on his face as he leaned in, expecting me to stop him at the last moment. But as his lips brushed mine, tentative and soft, I couldn't hold back, pressing into the kiss and devouring him as though he'd disappear if I didn't take all of him into me.

He pulled back with a small gasp, lowering himself to one knee beside me. His hand released my hair as he gripped my chair to hold himself up. I wasn't sure if it was the kiss that had brought him to his knees or if it was the realization that I had finally given him the smallest bit of something he'd craved for so long. I turned in my seat, my hands gripping his shoulders, unsure of how to help him at that moment.

Clearing his throat, he slowly stood and moved around the table, sitting back in his original chair. He grabbed the cane, fidgeted with it, and avoided my gaze. "You don't find me hideous anymore?" His voice was cautious, asking tentatively for something he hoped to be true. If I was truly still as cruel as everyone believed me to be, I would've been able to break him completely at that moment. But that was the farthest thing from what I wanted.

"I never did." I answered honestly. It was my turn to fidget, my heel clicking as I tapped it against the floor, my fingers rubbing the rim of the abandoned glass on the table. It wasn't the interaction I'd been expecting. He'd leaned in, towards me, wanting to expose my lies, but I bared myself and my truth to him. I wanted him. Even that kiss had been him moving out of anger, wanting to break whatever façade I had put on. There was nothing there. I had never been as open with him as I was being, sitting across the table from him.

"Then why?" It was full of meaning, not just the now, but the centuries of animosity and pain. The question was far heavier than what seemed to be a simple interaction to those around us.

"I was a foolish child. I never took the time to get to know you. I was angry that I was some prize to be given away when–" I stopped, my gaze going to the scars on his cheeks. It wasn't just that Heph had been thrown from Olympus. Zeus had scarred him first, taking out his anger on the young god when he refused to bow to Zeus' demands. "Heph, I was afraid. I was caught up in something that I thought was love, I was angry, and I had just been gifted to someone that everyone feared and reviled. It should never have taken as long as it did for me to see the truth, but I was too stubborn to look at my own faults. There are plenty of things I regret."

"Like Medea?" Once again, his words cut me to the core, making me wince. All I could do was nod. "So, what you're saying is that after all the years of refusing me, you want to do this? For real?" I could tell that he was skeptical of me, that he was unsure how honest my intentions were. His face was easy for me to read in that moment, his brows furrowed as he tried to gauge what I truly meant.

Nodding again, I felt my heart leap into my throat once more. Would he deny me? It would serve me right. I had made him miserable and lonely for so long. And while I was ignorant about my own relationships, I could tell that he had never strayed. He'd remained loyal to me while I was far from willing to do the same. After I realized what was really going on with Ares and myself, I went on a bender. Orgies, drunken nights, flashing myself across the planet before my powers finally failed me and I ended up at the door of Dr. Frost's office. There I collected mortals that were lost, giving them a home and a way of making a living. They were my little family, but I wanted something more with the man sitting across from me, *if* we could find a way to work through our past. "I do. Am I too late?" I asked, looking up through my lashes at him, that spark of hope flaring in me.

Heph leaned back in his seat, looking thoughtful. Tenting his fingers, he thought for a moment, before settling his eyes on mine "I don't know. But why should I believe you now?" he asked. I could sense in his voice that he had that same hope I did, but I knew why he couldn't trust it; why he couldn't trust me.

"Your mother had an idea about that."

"She did?" he replied, skepticism apparent in his voice as he leaned forward. His brows rose as he combed his fingers through his beard, drawing my attention to the coarse hairs. I couldn't stop myself from taking a moment to admire his hands.

"Trials." One word but I knew the weight it held. He looked pained and then furious. Those intense eyes darkened with it, and I worried he might do something foolish.

His teeth clenched, his jaw tense beneath that fiery beard. "How many?" he growled.

"Seven." My gaze lowered to the table, to the untouched treats and I felt my stomach twist in on itself. Food was the last thing I wanted.

"Seven?!" He nearly roared but somehow managed to hold back his voice in the crowded cafe. Still, it drew some glances our way before they nervously looked back to their tables. There was no doubt that he could bring the building down around us if he didn't rein in his ferocity.

His fury surprised me, but I gave a slight shrug. "I honestly anticipated more. I told her I would do whatever it took to prove myself and my intentions. This was her price for passing my message to you and allowing me to do so."

"And you accepted?" he demanded as a storm brewed in his eyes. "Why? Why now? Why this time?" His gaze searched mine, looking for whatever he missed, whatever I was hiding, whatever game I was playing. When he found nothing hidden, a small hint of a smile crested on his lips.

"Of course, I accepted, Heph." I did my best not to shrink under the ire I could feel coming off him. "Because I finally sought help. I was at my lowest and I found someone to help me figure out what was happening and what I had been running from for so long."

"And this help, it led you back to me?"

"Yes, it did. Therapy is a beautiful thing," I answered with a small smile. He reacted in kind, a small smile forming on his lips, his stormy eyes flashed with hope. There was still a small spark there. My heart leapt, maybe there was still a chance. "If you accept, then let your mother know so she can give me the first of the trials. She awaits your decision."

"You mean to do this?" he asked, incredulous. "You would do the trials, no matter what they are, just to prove yourself, for whom? Me, Hera, or yourself?"

"They were her price, but I want to be sure there is never any doubt in you as to my intentions. I suppose the answer is for all of us." The cafe continued moving around us, as I held his gaze, trying to make him see, to understand.

"You don't have to," he said quietly, looking at me with the full intensity of his gaze. "You could just take the time with me, be with me."

"If I could, I would want nothing more. But Hera would never allow that. I have tasted enough of her ire that I would rather not test her again by backing out." I couldn't even if I wanted to. But I knew that he was holding on by a fraying thread. If I told him that his mother had me swear by the ichor, it wasn't just the café that he likely would've brought down around us. It would be better for everyone if I kept that information to myself for a little while. Lying by omission right then was the better option in my eyes.

"That I understand. Her wrath is not something I wish to see you incur." he sighed and leaned back again. I wouldn't tell him how I had already incurred some, the strike she delivered when I asked after him. The last thing I wanted was to get between him and his mother. "Aphrodite," he rumbled, and my name in his mouth caused my body to react. A pool of warmth settled in my chest. I loved how my name sounded in his gravelly voice. It was surprising how easily I reacted to him once I stopped trying to fight something I'd been running from for so long.

"Yes, Heph?" I answered, doing my best to mask what his voice did to me.

"Be sure you come back to me. Don't you dare fall to her trials and let her best you." I would. And I promised as much. There wasn't really anything left to talk about after that exchange. But we did chat for a few more minutes before he stood to go do as I wanted, to tell his mother that I would do her trials.

Standing with him, I moved in front of Heph and smiled up at his curious face. One of his strong hands held onto the cane, the other loose at his side. My arm wrapped around his neck, my fingers buried in his hair as I gave him another kiss. It shocked him, his free arm sliding around my waist as though it were an automatic response. I had never initiated contact before, but I loved how it felt to do so. Tears filled his eyes as I pulled away, my own filled as well as I tried to smile. My heart ached and I wondered if I would succeed in the trials and if I would get the chance at a life with him. Only time would tell. As well as my ability to take whatever Hera threw at me. For the man with his arm around me, looking at me as though I was the most precious treasure he had ever seen, it would be worth it.

CHAPTER III

"Boss, where are you?" Micah always kept an even tone, but I could hear the panic edging in through the phone.

"I told you, I needed to work on fixing things. I will be back when I can. Right now, I must go meet Hera." My hands were sweaty as I stood outside the door of her office. I didn't know what she'd choose for my first trial, and I worried about what would happen to my mortals if I failed.

"You're doing something dangerous. That's why you left us here?" He was far too intelligent for comfort. I'd found him in the lowest part of his life while wading through mine. Micah was great at being my faux muscle and helping me to adapt to the modern mortal world.

"Yes. I feared what might happen if I brought you with me. Take care of them. If anything happens, I will be sure that you all want for nothing." Before he could reply, I hung up the phone and turned it off. He'd keep the two women that worked alongside him for me safe. I didn't have to worry about that. Tori and Callie were in good hands with him. That was what I reminded myself of over and over as I opened the door to Hera's office.

She was sitting behind her desk, a deep blue dress that flattered her perfectly hugging what I could see of her body. Beside her stood Hephaestus, just as handsome as when I'd seen him the day before. His presence made my lips curl into a smile. His face shifted from frustration to something more mirthful when he noticed me. The Henley was an olive color but everything else was the same as the last time I saw him. "I was wondering how long you'd stand talking in the hall," Hera said as she pushed herself up from her seat and waved Heph off.

"Apologies, I had some matters to deal with before undertaking your trials." I licked my lips, my hands wiping at the white jeans I'd donned. While I wasn't sure what I would have to face, I knew that it wouldn't be something I needed to dress up for. My faded red t-shirt was cut to a mid-drift and my white sneakers had seen plenty of use. I was dressed for comfort, and hopefully whatever fate awaited me.

"Were those matters more important than this?" Her derision was clear in her words, but I brushed it off.

"No. Just settling affairs. Surely you can understand that. What if I never make it back from the trials? There are those that depend on me still."

"I wasn't aware you were close with your children again," Hera replied.

"While I sent word to Eros and Adrestia, that was not who I was worried about." At the way both the gods before me raised their brows, I sighed. "I have mortals that depend on me. They help me and I take care of them. It is a simple arrangement."

"And where are they now?" Hera asked. That was why I hadn't wanted to bring them, talk about them. I didn't want to risk her using them against me.

What would be the best way to answer her? Fidgeting with my pockets, I looked at the carpet and tried to decide. "At my home. The one I have been in for the last several years. They will remain there until things are done and decided." Hopefully that would put an end to things and leave them out of the line of fire.

Hera started to say something, but Heph placed his free hand on her shoulder and shook his head. "Very well. I look forward to meeting them when you feel it's time to bring them here," he said with a smile I couldn't decipher. All I could do was offer a smile in return, and a nod.

"Let's begin with your first trial." That drew my attention back to Hera. "You will take up your sword once more."

My stomach churned at the thought. I had given up being a warrior long ago. It was another point of contention with Ares, my desire to step away from violence. I'd laid my sword down long ago and had no intention of ever raising it again. Of course, that would be her first choice in choosing my trials. "Fine." I wanted to ask who or what I'd be fighting, or if she'd just make me fall on it. I was smart enough not to at least.

"I have arranged for a very special prey. You will bring proof of its death to me, and I will consider the first trial complete." I had to kill. Of course, I had to kill. I had more than enough blood on my hands, it was the last thing I wanted to do. My gaze shifted to Heph and I knew it was worth it. When all the trials were done, he would never ask me to pick up a sword again. He would help me to wash the blood from my hands. I wrapped that thought around me, to ease the pain spreading through my chest.

"Whatever you say. You are the boss here," I replied, doing my best to keep my voice bland.

Her top lip curled in distaste, but she continued. "You will face a gorgon." That wasn't so bad or special. They weren't particularly difficult for a female to go up against. Perhaps she sensed the relief that went through me, because she drove it away with her wicked grin. "I have arranged for a male gorgon to be made especially for you." That would prove more challenging.

"Mother!" Hephaestus roared, his face unbelieving as he turned to look at her. I was terrified but my chest warmed at the knowledge that he truly had no part in what was happening. And he was furious with his mother for me. I could do it for him.

"Something special indeed. I will bring you his head." I interrupted before Hera could answer Hephaestus' outrage.

Hera huffed but nodded. "Then summon your sword and I will tell you where to go."

That made me cringe. "One small issue. My abilities have been less than reliable." Hera chewed the inside of her cheek, frustration leaking into her expression. I had expected her to laugh, but I saw the tiniest bit of hesitation in her. Had she realized that I was more likely to fall without my abilities? Perhaps she also realized that if I did, Heph would suffer. As a mother, I knew that the last thing she'd want was to cause him more pain. The pain he suffered physically each day was because he'd protected her from Zeus. I watched her look to him, her face flashing with guilt before looking at me again.

"Very well. I will send you there." Her gaze traveled down my body, and I sighed, knowing I'd need a lot more than jeans and a supportive bra to help me. "Hephaestus." He knew what she wanted.

I watched him walk closer, my heart racing as I took all of him in. I reveled in how he made me feel small, how I knew he could hurt or protect me with that strength. Licking my lips, I looked up into his face, one hand rising to brush through his beard. The shiver that went through him made me smile. "Worry not, my sparrow, I will return," I murmured. Did I believe that

I would? Not entirely. But if I turned to stone, he could always put me in his forge so I could watch him work for the rest of eternity.

The sadness that filled his gaze made me want to take his hand and run away from everything. But I wouldn't break my word. I would pay the price. Not that I could if I really wanted to. I leaned up to give him a tender kiss. That drew a gasp from Hera, but I ignored her. I knew she was at our wedding and saw other occasions as well that I had refused his kiss. Never again. His kiss felt like sparks igniting with each touch and I craved more. That would help me get through the trials, his fiery kisses that I needed to return to.

"I trust you, little dove. For the first time, I trust you to keep your word." He still held resentment, and I deserved it, but I could feel him warming up to me again. He let go of his cane, but his power spread through the room, and the cane remained standing at his side as he moved his hands to my shoulders. A gasp escaped my lips at the touch and then his power caressing my skin. As he moved his hands over my body with feather light touches, my clothes disappeared, replaced by white ornate armor. It was perfectly formed to my body and decorated with roses, daggers, and small birds that looked like doves and sparrows. I raised the vambrace on my left arm and smiled at the anatomical heart he'd placed there.

"It is beautiful," I murmured, smiling up at him as tears filled my eyes. I could feel and see every bit of love and worry he'd put into the armor he'd summoned for me. "As are you. Never doubt how much I want to worship your beauty. No amount of scars will change that." The surprise on his face amused me, but I watched his eyes fill with tears. "No. Only weep if I break my promise and am unable to return," I murmured, my thumb catching the first tear that fell onto his scarred right cheek.

"You will return." His left hand wrapped around my right, and I felt my sword he'd forged for me so long ago materialize in my grasp. I glanced down at the white and silver blade, my chest tight. It was just as beautiful as the armor, but I hated that I needed it. "And I will erase the guilt you feel," he promised. Pressing a kiss to my head, he released me, grabbing his cane once more before returning to Hera's side.

I finally looked at her and found her conflicted as she looked between us. As much as I wanted to ask her about it, I needed to go before I lost my nerve. I parted my lips to ask her to go before she lifted her hand. It should've angered me that she wanted to silence me, but instead she moved forward, a turquoise piece of cloth in her hands as she approached me. Instinctively, I took a step back. "Fear not. You will need this," she explained. Hera touched my hair, and it was suddenly pulled up into a high ponytail, making it far easier for her to tie the cloth over my eyes. "You are a war goddess. Use those long slumbering skills to come back to him. Make him happy and I will forgive you. Prove you can protect him," she whispered, making sure the cloth was secure before walking away. I was glad she could no longer see my eyes. There was no way to hide the shock. Before I could say anything else, I felt her power hook into my abdomen and yank me from the room.

As I fell to one knee, my gloved hand brushing the rough stone of the ground, I knew there was no time to hesitate or dwell on what had just happened. The trial had begun, and I had prey to destroy.

CHAPTER IV

I DIDN'T HAVE TIME to dwell on my surroundings. Before I heard the slithering of scales over the ground, I could smell his approach. It was the musty smell of snakes mixed with the inherently masculine smell of a man. "You've come," he hissed, growing closer.

"You are brave to face me," I replied, my hands gripping the sword and sheath, pulling it free. I'd mourn the loss of the sheath later. Right then, I could only worry about the enemy that Hera had created for me. How kind of her to make an opponent that should be just as wary of me. There was one thing, one ability, I didn't seem able to lose, and that was the aura that surrounded me and made non-divine beings fall hopelessly in love with me at first sight. It was the first thing I'd learned to control, reining it in to keep every mortal that crossed my path from becoming my willing slave. But faced with my new opponent, I released the hold I had on it.

"The queen mother of all gods warned me of your abilities. We are matched in that I cannot look upon you as you cannot look upon me. Perhaps she wanted to be fair." *Dammit.* I cursed internally as I realized he must have been as blind as I was then. So much for that advantage that I hoped to have over him.

Hera does not play fair, I thought with another silent curse. Why would she want me to face a male gorgon who wouldn't fall in love with me because she warned him to close his eyes? Unless she was testing to see whether I would give into temptation and fall prey to his advances should he look at me. And whether I could defeat him before he did. Devious didn't even begin to describe Hera.

It made the urge to let loose the bloodlust I kept stifled grow. That desire to slaughter my enemies, to bathe in their blood as I stood over their corpses, was always looming beneath the surface. It was like a dark voice whispering sweet nothings to me, a primal urge I had been battling for eons. But I couldn't just unleash it because Hera put a sword in my hand. I wouldn't give in. I wouldn't be the one thing I hated more than anything. It was always something that made Ares resentful. I stopped riding into battle with him. I refused to pick up a sword even to spar. It made me think he fell in love with my thirst for blood, not me. Perhaps that was closer to the truth than I might like to admit.

Hearing the scales slithering closer, I moved as quietly as I could in the opposite direction. My arm smacked into a pillar, giving me just enough time to stop my head from doing the same. But it alerted him to my location. Quickly, I skittered as silently as possible to the left, trying to stay out of his range as my heart pounded in my ears. Without being able to see where he was, I knew it'd be difficult. I had to depend on my hearing and sense of smell to fight. Fighting down my pulse would be the lesser battle. Fighting with those senses was something I'd never tried to do before, even when I was still a goddess that thrived in battle. Twirling the sword in my hand, it felt familiar still, like I had never put it down. All I had to do was get over my squeamishness about fighting again and I would be fine. Easier said than done, but I would try. Well, that, and keep myself from reveling in the bloodshed.

I felt the air shift before the sound of scales had me throwing myself backwards, the rush of wind as his hand struck out at the spot I'd been a moment before. *Fuck.* My senses were fine, but his were better. He didn't need his eyes to find me when he had other heightened senses. "Come on, can we not talk this out in a civil manner?" I asked before throwing myself back again, praying there wasn't a pillar in my way. I landed on the ground, and he skidded into either a pillar or wall as he missed me. He'd thrown all his weight into it, as I hoped he would. Was that how I would win? Skittering around on the ground like an insect? I hated it. That was not the fight I wanted to have to endure. It was humiliating, and the stakes were far higher than just facing another beast or god with a sword. Hera had truly made it as difficult as possible.

"There is no civility. Cruel goddesses don't deserve any. All you have to look forward to is death. Perhaps you will look first, and I will add you to my collection." There was no chance of that. If he did manage to turn me to stone, I knew that Heph would never leave me on the battleground his mother had gifted us. But I couldn't cling to that hope. I would thrive on the knowledge that I wouldn't break first. I wouldn't look first. Let him break, let him fall hopelessly in love with me so I could take his head back to the queen of all gods. The image of his blood staining the carpet in her office made my lips curl up into a devious smile. I wondered how furious that would make her. The pettiness of it warmed me as I moved quickly and silently as far from him as I could.

I could hear him getting closer and I knew he could hear my racing heart. The worries I was carrying were making it thrum in my chest like a homing beacon for him. Taking a deep breath, I turned to face him, searching for that warrior calm I knew lived inside me. As he struck, I felt where the air shifted with his strike and dodged, my sword swinging out and finding home in a fleshy part of him. The hissed curse he gave made me grin. But it was short-lived. I felt sharp fangs sink into my left upper arm as I fell with the momentum of my strike. The pain of my fall and the bite to my arm drew a gasp from me. I was barely able to bite back my cry of pain before it escaped. They were small fangs; it was from the snakes on his head. *Fuck!*

Were they venomous? How would it affect me with my depleted powers? I didn't know, and it took all my self-control not to panic as I scurried away, putting my back to a pillar. The more I gave into the panic, the worse it would be. For the moment, it just stung and burned. I had to hope that I was immune to his venom. If not, I needed to finish the fight quickly. Licking my lips, I turned my head, listening to him curse and grumble as he slid around the area. "Are you ready to speak civilly now?" It was taking all my control to keep the desire to swim in his blood and dismember him piece by piece at bay. That wasn't my goal. I just needed his head as proof that I had defeated him. Or I hoped that was what Hera had meant by proof.

"Why? I know you've been bitten. Your temptress abilities and adulterous ways will do little to shield you from its effects. They can't save you. Soon, you will be mine to add to my garden." Dammit. That was not what I wanted to hear.

"And how do you know it will even work on me?"

"Because the queen of gods assured me it would. When I was changed, she wanted to make me a formidable opponent for you." That sounded about right. I was fucked.

Though I didn't know what his venom would do to me, I knew I couldn't just hide and wait for him to come to me. He could draw out the fight until I was completely useless. That just wouldn't do. "What else did she tell you? Did she tell you what I looked like? Have you seen me before?"

"I have never seen you." Maybe that was something I could use.

"And you have never found yourself curious what the goddess of love and beauty looks like? Have you never wondered why so many mortals have fallen over themselves to offer up their lives and bodies to me?" Not that I enjoyed it, but I could play the role he was setting up for me. For just a short time, I needed to embrace everything I once was and that I hated so much. I slid my hand over the ground, searching for something to use, anything. A small rock shifted under my hand and I quickly grabbed it, throwing it around the pillar. It hit the ground a good distance away, and the sound drew him towards it. That was a start. I needed to control where he went, where he was. Not that talking was helping, but at least facing the wall as I was, my voice was echoing through the area. We had to be in an enclosed space of some kind for that to be the case.

"Of course. Who wouldn't want to lay eyes on one such as you? But I'm not foolish enough to do so until it is time to turn you into my very special ornament." That didn't sound like a fun time for me. I shuddered to think what he meant by that. Rather than find out, I would remove his head. Obviously, talking was going to get me nowhere. And I realized that the pain had started to subside, numbness spreading through my upper left arm. *Shit!* So that was how he'd win. He'd paralyze me and then force me to look into his eyes. No amount of love aura was going to stop him from wanting to possess me. Especially if I was unable to fight back. I felt my stomach clench because I knew what could likely happen before he turned me into his personal statue, and I would be helpless to stop it. For a moment, I considered trying to pull that aura back in, but decided against it. Perhaps I could use it to my advantage before he got the upper hand for real. I could only hope that Heph or Hera would have an antidote for whatever venom he had that was coursing through my veins.

Steeling myself with thoughts of returning to Heph, I leaped from my hiding place, purposely slamming the heel of my white boot down on the ground. His hiss grew closer, and drew the corners of my lips up into a smile. Those coils and scales were large enough that he couldn't silence them. Perhaps if he could move quickly enough, but I was trusting in the fact that he was still new enough not to be able to. Later, I would question who was in his collection or how he already had one, given how recently he'd been made. But it wasn't relevant right then. All that mattered was making sure that no one else was added. Especially not me.

Rolling my head side to side, I did my best to loosen the tension in my body. I was determined and letting him get the better of me because I was out of practice would be humiliating. The pounding of my heart against my ribcage was harder to move past. The panic of losing the ability to move before I had beaten him was rising. I did my best to dampen both those things down for the moment. Later, I could let all those locked up emotions out. There would be a later. I was going to make sure of it.

There was one last thing I could do, and I would use it to draw him to me. Enough running, chasing, and chatting. It was time to end it. Only one of us would survive and I would use every last drop of godly power I had left to make sure it was me.

CHAPTER V

Lashing out that part of my power, or aura, or whatever one might like to call it, that made those lesser beings fall hopelessly in love with me, I moved out from behind the pillar. I found him to my right, the slithering of his belly shifting the rocks, the scent of snake and blood drawing me towards him. Without waiting for him to react to my revealing myself again, I lashed that power at him. I knew what it would do. He'd crave to come nearer, drawn to me as though I were playing a siren's song. He wouldn't be under my control yet, but it was a start. It wasn't as strong as him seeing me, but it would spark the beginnings of obsession in him. Weak, but hopefully still effective. Biting my lip, I felt my left hand drop heavily to my side. It was useless and I couldn't feel anything from it. I needed to be quicker. The moment it spread to my legs or sword arm I would be useless. At least I hadn't tried to dual wield.

"What have you done?" he growled; his voice so close I knew he was within reach. I struck my right arm out, the tip of my sword digging through scales. If the sound was any indication, I knew I had managed to knock at least one or two loose. The sound of them hitting the ground was satisfying, as were his shouts. But before I could shift to strike again, he backhanded me. It wasn't a gentle strike. My body was airborne, and I did my best to put my right arm back so that I could soften the blow of whatever I landed against. The wall suddenly stopped my momentum, and I was barely able to keep hold of my sword, the blade nicking my leg where the armor was spaced to allow movement. Biting down on my lip, I stifled my cry of pain. It wasn't as though he couldn't tell where I landed from the thud of my body hitting the wall. I just refused to show that weakness. I would not cry out in pain for him.

"What I needed to do," I answered, voice straining to hide the pain he had blossomed in me. He inhaled deeply, and I knew he craved a look then far more than he did before. That was what I had ignited in him with that brief flash of power. He wanted to look, he wanted to come nearer and give himself over to his baser desires. It was a risk, but I hoped I could distract him long enough to gain the upper hand back. Every time I wounded him, I ended up with a wound of my own. It was time to tilt the scales in my favor.

I could feel his desire as he neared me again. Breathing hard, I pushed myself up from the floor, using the wall that had just been used against me to steady myself. A headache was forming, and I didn't even want to know if I had made my head bleed as I had done my leg. Tightening my grip on my sword, I let him come to me. There was just enough energy left in me to lash out again, willing him to open his eyes. Exhaustion was settling in, and I had lost feeling in my left side, but I would use everything I had to come out of the trial the victor. No matter what state I was left in after.

The moment he opened his eyes, I knew it. A rush of energy went through me. The adoration he had for me was palpable and gave me a small boost. I didn't know if it'd be enough, but I had to use it to my advantage. "You are lovelier than I had imagined, cruel goddess. I think I will keep you as you are once my venom runs its course," he whispered, his breath hot on my skin as he neared. A shudder went through me as I felt just how much he enjoyed my appearance.

"Touch me with that again, and I shall remove both your heads." All my threat managed to do was draw a laugh from him.

"I plan to do far more than just touch you with it. I will know the bliss that others say is found when buried inside your delectable body." With him looking at me, I was at a greater disadvantage, and I knew it. But since his goal was no longer to kill me, I could work with it.

I did my best not to tense or give any sign of what I intended, quickly turning and using the momentum to drive my sword into him. His scream of pain was a victorious sound for me. My sword had gone halfway into a part of his human half. Yanking it free, I fell backwards as his tail knocked my feet out from under me. *Dammit.* His snake half had surrounded me, and I didn't realize it. *Stupid, stupid, stupid,* I cursed myself. How could I be so careless as to forget that he had a far greater reach because of that stupid tail?

Before I could react or move, he was on top of me, his blood soaking my armor as he pressed his body against mine. His new curse would be that he wouldn't care how much he bled as long as he was able to touch me. For a moment I laid there, relearning how to breathe after he knocked the air from my lungs, letting him rub his body against mine. With the amount of armor Heph had put on me, I had a feeling he knew what could happen if the gorgon got the better of me. Or maybe he was just worried about my safety. It was great armor. I just happened to have less luck than the next goddess at the moment and it wasn't able to protect me as much as he obviously wanted it to. A more skilled goddess would've been able to walk away without a scratch with such skillfully crafted armor. Perhaps I owed him another apology once I returned to him.

The one good thing about releasing such a potent aura towards him was that he was utterly infatuated, and in his lust, he didn't stop to disarm me. His hands were busy running over the armor that hugged every curve from my breasts down to my hips. At least I couldn't feel more than the weight of the armor being pressed against my skin more. His actual touch was distant enough that I didn't retch. But a shiver of disgust still went through me. I knew that there was only one set of hands I wanted on my body and that they were scarred and calloused from centuries of hard work.

Heph's face flashed in my mind, and I screamed as I swung my sword to where I guessed his head was. I was rewarded with a gurgle, but my blade had stopped. Damn. I hadn't had the leverage that I needed to fully behead him in one swing. Not that a short sword was a great weapon for doing so. His hands that had been trying to find a way into the lower half of my armor stilled as his head reared back, a garbled shout sounding.

One of his clawed hands ripped at the blindfold Hera had given me and I cursed as the side of it snapped, allowing him to remove it. The action left a scratch that narrowly missed my eye, saved only by how tightly I squeezed them shut. I pulled my sword back and struck again, his arm knocking mine so that I merely slashed across his chest. While he roared in agony, I scooted back with my legs, trying to get distance from him as he thrashed around. The numbness was spreading through my left leg. I was running out of time.

As quickly as I could, I pushed myself to my feet, my left leg nearly giving out. A cry of my own sounded as I launched myself at the gorgon, my blade digging into his throat. Instead of pulling it out, I pushed the blade into the still connected tissue, trying to sever the remaining portion of his injured throat. I put my entire body into the movement, trying to get his head free of his body. When his head didn't fall to the ground, I knew that there was something still holding it on. I reached blindly into the warm, wet mess with my sword hand, slashing and trying to free it from his body. There were no more roars or shouts, or gasps from him as I did. He was silenced. All that he could do was claw at the back of my armor and neck, creating gashes in it as his panicked snakes tried to bite my face. One landed a strike on my cheek before I finally felt the gorgon's head come fully off. I landed hard on my back as his body fell to the side, thudding against the ground, my sword falling from my hand. His head rolled against my leg, and I prayed that there was no more life in the snakes. But no more bites came. I tampered down that blood lust that told me to finish ripping his body to pieces, to cover myself in even more of him. It was a mark of victory. No, I wouldn't be the barbarian. I wouldn't give into those urges. Reaching blindly, I found the torn blindfold. I turned my back to his head, just to be safe, and I opened my eyes.

It took a few moments to adjust to the low light in the ruins; the sun peeking through the small opening in the ceiling. There were crumbling pillars and a smashed altar. I wasn't sure whose temple it once was, and I really didn't care. I fumbled with the blindfold, trying to tie it into something I could use on his head. It took all the coordination I had in my right hand and my teeth to manage. Closing my eyes once more, I felt for his head and shut his eyelids before opening mine once more. It would be foolish to win and still be turned to stone just because I was reckless. It took a few tries, but I slid the blindfold over his face, covering his closed eyes before pulling the bag I had tucked into the back of my belt free. I rolled his head into the sack and paused, glancing at my sword. A wicked smile played over my lips.

I should've been concerned about how I was supposed to make it back to Hera's office, but there was something I was more interested in at that moment. Grabbing my sword, I moved to his body, striking at it and laughing as what I wanted to add to my gift to Hera fell free. I set my sword aside and shoved it into the bag before grabbing both the bag and my blade once more. "I told you I would." Even being on my knees became impossible, and I fell forward.

As I did so, I felt the pull of Hera's power in my belly before I was yanked from the ruins and deposited on her rug. My blood-soaked sword fell from my hand as I thudded against her floor. The bag dripped more of the dark liquid as I lost the strength to hold onto it any longer. For a moment, I just laid there, letting the mix of gorgon blood and my ichor soak into the pale ornate rug beneath me. I couldn't move my left side, and I could feel my cheek numbing from the last bite.

"Dite!" Hephaestus cried as I struggled to roll myself over. Her carpet smelled like whatever was last used to clean it and it was making my nose itch. I just wanted to breathe. My breath caught as his cane fell beside me, Heph dropping to his knees and pulling my wounded body into his lap. His fingers hesitated over the bite on my cheek before looking at the bite on my arm and the cut on my leg. "Heal her! She did what you wanted!" he cried.

I heard Hera moving closer and smiled up at him. My right hand rose to brush his cheek as I took in the panicked look in his eyes. "I came back," I breathed, letting the numbness and exhaustion pull me into a sweet, restful nothingness.

CHAPTER VI

"-DITE," I HEARD SOMEONE distantly calling me. "Aphrodite! Come on, little dove," came Heph's voice. That was enough to pull me from whatever slumber I had been wrapped up in. Blinking my eyes open, I saw we were still in the same position, but I was no longer numb. There was an ache that seared through my body, but it was nothing. I was back and Heph was cradling me in his arms.

"Heph," I murmured. My head rolled to the side, and I saw Hera giving a wide berth to the bag I had brought her, trying to wipe the gorgon blood and my ichor from her hand with a baby wipe. For once I wasn't the one that was worried about being covered in blood. I knew I was coated, and I didn't care. My gaze returned to Heph as he looked down at me. "I think I need a bigger sword next time." Was I completely lucid? Likely not, but I got a choked laugh from him.

"There won't be a next time. You're done after this. No more swords. I know how much you hate this." It had been a struggle to hold on to other feelings during the fight and not let myself fall into bloodlust, but I managed. I had found a balance and came out just as disgusted with the violence as I had been before.

"Unless another trial demands she take up her sword again," Hera pointed out.

"Mother," he growled, his grip tightening around my shoulders and across my chest where he was hugging me.

I patted his hand and pushed myself up onto my knees. "How many monsters do you want me to slay? And will they all be during death season?" I asked, testing my balance before pushing myself to my feet. Bending down, I grabbed his cane, offering it to him as well as my free hand. It surprised me that Hephaestus took my hand, letting me help him up. As he took the cane, he pressed a gentle kiss to where the bite on my cheek had been.

"You still have six trials ahead of you. Don't dare think you are safe from anything until they are done." Hera crossed her arms under her breasts as she leaned back against the edge of her desk. That was a good point. I didn't know what else she had in store for me.

"Well, I'm saying it then. She's done slaying monsters. Period." We both looked at Heph, surprised, our brows rising. He wanted to keep me away from danger. I didn't have the heart to tell him that there were other forms of danger that she could use against me.

THE TRIALS OF APHRODITE

Hera watched as Heph drew closer to her, away from me, and nodded. "Very well, no more monsters. I had no more planned for her to face, but I don't want her to think that she has anything figured out."

After everything I had just gone through, I could feel my anger bubbling up. Reaching for the dripping bag, I opened it, face scrunching as the scent of snake and blood hit my nostrils. The acrid scent was just as disgusting as before. I grabbed the gorgon's head and pulled it out, tossing it at Hera's feet. She scowled as blood splattered her nude-colored heels. "As requested, my queen. One gorgon head."

"You did exactly as I instructed. I'm surprised." I had to roll my eyes at that. My body was aching, I felt nauseated, I was exhausted. All I wanted was a hot bath, junk food, and a soft bed. Yet, I was standing in her office while she continued to look down on me.

That was the only reason I had to explain what I did next. "Oh, I have another gift for you." They both looked at me in surprise and I could feel the devious grin spread over my face as I pulled the other body part I had taken from the bag. I tossed it beside the head at her feet and watched them both process the fact that I had just tossed an erect, scaled, gorgon penis on the floor.

"A gift? You call this a gift?" Hera hissed as she looked up at me.

Laughing, I did a mocking bow as I answered her. "That is so you can go fuck yourself, my dear queen. It is still hard and ready for you." Hephaestus choked on his air as Hera's face reddened. I could see the fury rising in her. "He wanted to use it on me, gave it a valiant effort, but I thought you would enjoy it far more than I ever would. I did not want it. I am curious about something though. How long has it been since you had a dick that did not come attached to our king?" That did it. I knew it was foolish, but I was just done with the day. Hadn't I done enough? Didn't I deserve a rest? Apparently not.

Before I could blink, Hera was in front of me, my head snapping back as she forcefully grabbed a handful of my hair, and I felt the sting of her slap across my once snake bitten cheek. "I was going to give you a reprieve before your next trial, but you seem eager to continue." All I did was laugh and let the ichor that had pooled in my mouth dribble out, some spattering her chest by 'accident'.

"I am looking forward to it." I could hear the hiss of the breath Hephaestus took. Did he know what was coming, or did he just know that his mother was a force to be reckoned with when pissed? Maybe I could ask him later. I didn't have the chance as Hera kept her grip on me, and I felt the pulling sensation from her power as she flashed us to what I recognized as Heph's forge. "Why?"

"You will see," was all she told me as she walked to a set of iron stairs, her grip on my hair made me follow along or allow her to tear it completely out. I stumbled down the stairs, doing my best to stay upright as she dragged me beneath his forge. Before I could ask anything else, she shoved me to the ground and looked at Heph as he appeared behind her. "Do it. Summon them."

"She should rest first," he pleaded.

"No! She made her choice. Do it. Or I will consider the trials forfeit and banish her somewhere she can never return from, and you won't ever see her again." The pain that threat caused Heph made her pause, her expression softening for a moment before steeling once more. "She chose this. This was her decision. Ask her if she would rather forfeit."

"No," I quickly answered. "I will not forfeit. Heph, please do whatever it is she is asking of you."

Hephaestus' face showed his confliction, the pain buried behind that internal battle, as he stepped closer to me. "You wouldn't ask if you knew what it was."

That made me sigh. "I have an idea. Please, my sparrow. Do as she commands. The sooner this is over, the sooner we can try for that life we both want," I promised. Not that I knew if we wanted the same things, but it did the trick. *Fuck it.* I wouldn't have a bath and bed. But at least I could have the second trial done. Or so I hoped.

A tear slid down his cheek as he cradled my face between his hands. As he leaned down to press his lips to mine, I saw Hera turn away out of the corner of my eye. I knew she was just angry and protective, that she wasn't just being cruel to be cruel. I'd pissed on her shoes, metaphorically, and she just wanted to keep her son safe from my brand of cruelty. My anger had abated as I saw the agony that Heph was going through because I chose to lash out. It was a reminder to bite my tongue the next time I faced Hera, whenever that might be.

I melted into the kiss, wrapping my arms around his neck and tangling my fingers in his hair as his beard tickled and scratched my face. His arms wrapped around my waist as he tried to drink me down through the contact of our lips. I didn't know how long the trial would be, but I knew it was enough to make him desperate to make the moment last.

Heph broke the kiss first, pulling back and smiling sadly. "This was not how I wanted to do this for the first time," he muttered. That made me chuckle, his hand running over my shoulders and causing the armor to dissipate. My clothes from before were gone. They wouldn't be allowed for the punishment I knew was coming. Oh, sorry, *trial*. Stepping back, he averted his gaze from my bared body and waved his hands. His power filled the halls of his own forge, a warmth that permeated the very air that surrounded us, a glowing fire and nearly suffocating pressure. Chains of iron grew from the walls and wrapped around my wrists; the warmth surprising as the cool metal settled against

THE TRIALS OF APHRODITE

my bare skin. The chains tightened, pulling my arms up and out, before turning into golden manacles. They were tight enough I couldn't slip free, but not so much that I would hurt myself unless I struggled. It was a kindness that I was surprised Hera allowed him to give me.

He was silent as he turned on his heel, hiding his face from me and hurrying up the stairs the best he could with his limp. I hadn't seen his cane and had completely forgotten that he needed it. How selfish of me. Just something else for me to think about as I sat under his forge. I missed his warmth, but the intense heat of the forge was already getting to me. I would manage. Somehow.

Hera sighed and approached me, looking up at the ceiling, seemingly thinking something over. "You will stay here for ten years. If in ten years, he is satisfied that you have proven yourself, you will be released. If not, you will remain for another ten." She paused, a smirk on her lips, "And it will continue until he is satisfied." Her gaze lowered to me, her hand rising to press to my chest. A pained gasp sounded as I felt her sealing my powers away. Even the aura was gone, pushed inside me, and locked up tight. I couldn't fight back the tears that fell as the heat and pain intensified with my abilities gone. The small bit of protection my godhood and aura granted me had been taken. All that was left was the immortality granted to us all. "You will suffer and never die here. You will have nothing but the heat and agony to keep you company, as was his curse for so long."

She turned to leave but stopped, stomping her heel against the stone ground. Above me, the ceiling cracked, and I couldn't bite back the scream that came as a drop of magma from the forge above fell onto my upper chest and trailed down, slowly hardening to rock before falling away. "For you to go fuck yourself with," she hissed over her shoulder before flashing away.

CHAPTER VII

I sagged in the chains, trying to breathe through the agony after more of the heat had seared my skin. *How long has it been?* I couldn't keep track of time. My body was exhausted, I was in constant agony, and more was added every time the magma dripped from the ceiling. It would've been nice if I could anticipate the next time it would fall, but I quickly learned that it never fell at the same rate. There was no way to know when the next round of agony would pile on top of what I was already wanting to die from. The other issue was that I was healing nearly human slow, which meant that I wasn't healing at all. I knew there was bone exposed on my shoulder and upper chest. It was a horrifying sight that made me even more happy to close my eyes and wait for my time to be over.

The question I had that really pissed me off was how I hadn't passed out from the pain of it yet. It was a sweet relief I had yet to be granted. If I managed to drift off to sleep for even a few moments, I was brought back to reality with a fresh round of heat burning my flesh away. The scent still clung to the air, and I had no idea if I would ever stop smelling it. I'd run out of tears long ago, my eyes throbbing with how dry they were. Was there any part of my body that didn't hurt? There was nothing I could focus on to ease the pain, no reprieve to be had.

As I took a deep breath, I felt the searing pain of the lava hitting my skin once more. I couldn't hold back my screams, the chains shaking as my body convulsed. Somehow, my body found fresh tears, the traitorous bastards streaming down my face. It would have been kinder to Heph to put me in Tartarus. There was enough of me left to feel guilty over the torment that he must have been going through, having to listen to me scream.

I was still trembling and whimpering from the misery that I would likely endure for eternity when I felt hands cradling my face and rough thumbs brushing my tears away. My eyes fluttered open as I bit my lip to keep any other sounds from escaping. Heph's face looked like he was feeling even more pain than I was. The guilt in his eyes was like a stab to my heart. Licking my lips, it took me several tries before I could speak. My throat was dry from lack of water and all the screaming I'd been doing. "H-how long?" I rasped out.

"Five years," he ground out. Halfway there. It had felt like a century had passed, but I was only halfway through the required amount of torment Hera had set forth. That was, if Heph didn't deem me unworthy and I remained beneath his forge for even longer. The thought made me shudder and my chest tighten. Looking into his eyes, I couldn't see him doing that, but I couldn't be sure. I doubted everything at that moment. The only thing I didn't doubt was that I would stay there for as many decades as it took.

"Gag me," I whispered. It wasn't fair that he'd had to listen to me for so long. I flinched as I saw another drop falling from the corner of my eye. But I watched as he lifted a hand and flung it upwards against the leaking forge. I didn't have the strength to see when it would fall again, but a feeling of relief went through me all the same. It was a moment of reprieve, but I would take it happily. "Please. Hate hurting you."

The turmoil on his face, the tears that decorated his cheeks before disappearing into his beard broke my heart. All I wanted was to keep from hurting him, and I couldn't even manage that. I was a failure. "No. You're not hurting me. You're doing everything you can to show me you don't want to, not anymore," he murmured, pressing his forehead to mine as he cradled the back of my head. It was such a tender and affectionate moment that it surprised me. I realized he had never reached for me, really, not outside of the trials. While he'd tried to kiss me before, he'd kept his hands to himself. All I could do was savor the bit of affection and remember it when the next round of torture began. "I'll be back," he promised with a kiss to my head.

I looked up for the torturous magma to spill onto me again. A small smile crossed my dry lips upon seeing that black obsidian hardened over the ever-falling heat. There was no new round of torment, the obsidian remaining dark and shining. No more heat found its way onto my aching body. I was lost in the shining facets of the dark gem, and finally gave into that long-neglected need to sleep.

"Come on, boss lady. You promised. Sit still and watch a movie with us." Callie's voice made me stop and sigh. How could I refuse her after everything she'd been through? I'd saved her from a true sadist that had lured her into a room at what was supposed to be a safe BDSM club. The only time I had turned to violence in the last few centuries was for her. I didn't regret it. I should've, I should've felt some sort of remorse. But the sight of her near death, broken and bleeding, it had pained me. That was the sight that haunted me.

Nodding, I sat between her and Tori as Micah handed me the remote before sitting at Tori's feet. Whenever he sat near her like that, she played her hands in his long blonde hair.

It was a comforting thing, and I understood their need for affection. That was why I didn't move away when Callie rested her head on my shoulder. I merely moved the remote to my other hand and lifted my free hand to pet her tight curls.

"Why would you think it wise to hand the remote to me? None of you enjoy it when I pick what we watch," I reminded them. A startled laugh escaped when Tori reached over and grabbed the remote from my hand before I could process her movements.

Holding the remote in front of Micah's face, she leaned down and wagged a finger at him. "Never give Dite the remote. Boss lady will torture us. How could you?"

His only answer was a shrug, but I knew that he just wanted to make sure I would stay with them. They depended on me for more than a home and money. I was their shield, their rock, and they were what kept me grounded. What would have become of me if I hadn't found them? Would I have kept up with therapy and still stayed in town? Or would I have abandoned my goals and run off to continue destroying myself? It wasn't anything I wanted to explore. Life was better working through things and valuing the people that had become my family. Of course, after the first couple of years together, I told them the truth. I had been amused that they had suspected something was amiss with me. They had even just simply asked which goddess I was. Somehow, given how horrible I had been before in my relationships, personal and romantic, I had finally found healthy friendships when I began to work on fixing myself. That was when I knew I needed to fix my marriage or end it once and for all. I wouldn't continue to be the toxic anchor that was weighing him down.

Ares was a good man, but we didn't belong together. Together, we were toxic. The only place we worked well was in battle and in the bedroom. There was nothing else for us. It took me a long time to realize that. The same went for my friendship with Amphitrite. I realized we were using one another and neither of us offered anything healthy to the relationship. Perhaps we'd both changed and could try again. But I had found a goddess that I had a healthy relationship with. She kept me in check and never judged me for what I had done. When I asked why, Itzpapalotl, or Lola as I called her, merely said that I judged myself enough for the both of us.

My gaze flitted between my three mortals as they argued over the 'chick-flick' they wanted to watch. I didn't care, really, I just wanted to enjoy my time with them. Movie nights like those, where we binged so many movies they blurred together, ate everything in sight, and fell asleep in a puppy pile; those were the nights that made it so I could finally feel happy again.

A scream escaped my dry throat as I was pulled from my blissful slumber. My aching arms were being moved, and a violent shudder coursed through my entire body.

The burnt flesh and exposed muscle, tissue, and bone reacted, sending wave after wave of agonizing pain. A faint voice barely registered over my own echoing screams as Heph whispered, "I'm sorry," over and over. He released the manacles holding me taut and caught my sagging body as it fell from its suspended state. He quickly wrapped me in a blanket, his hand trembling as it lingered just above the wounds I had from his forge. "A deal's a deal, Hera. Heal her."

"No, the deal was to release her. I will release her powers. She will have to heal on her own." My eyes were shut, but I could imagine the look on Hera's face. "I will not release her early and heal her wounds. One, but not both." Another cry escaped when I felt Hera's fingers hit the wound on my chest, but she did as she promised, and I felt the rush of energy go through me. My body began to slowly heal, but it still wasn't as fast as it would have been had my powers not gone haywire. "When she is healed, send her to me for the next trial."

I opened my eyes enough to see Heph start to argue but I lifted one hand to squeeze his arm weakly. There was no point in angering Hera further. "Please," I whimpered, pressing my head to Heph's chest. Was it still the same day? Had it really only been five years? Nothing made sense in my head, but maybe after some sleep and recuperation, I could figure out what had been happening.

"We will discuss this later," Heph hissed at Hera as he wrapped me in the blanket and lifted me into his arms. I worried that he'd hurt himself even as I cried out in pain at how I was jostled. How would his leg fare with me in his arms like that? But I didn't have the energy to ask. That darkness was threatening to drag me back under, even with the pain that was bringing tears to my eyes once more.

"There is nothing to discuss. But you are always welcome to visit, my son." If Heph answered Hera, I didn't hear it. Blissful unconsciousness took me away from the torment of the state of my body and their bickering.

When I woke again, I was sore, but nowhere near in as much pain as when I last remembered. The bed I was in wasn't mine. Over a decade and a half earlier, that would've been normal for me. But at that moment, panic took over me. Had I relapsed? I wasn't sore in a way that would indicate so. The memory of Heph releasing me early from my trial came rushing back, and I lifted the black sheet to my nose. All the tension in me eased as I smelled his scent clinging to it. It was the smoky scent that came first, followed by the heady musk of his skin, and something sweeter yet spicy, like cinnamon. The combination made me smile as I carefully laid back on the bed, burying my face in the pillow and pulling the sheet over me.

I wished he was there with me, but I understood why he would rather not share his bed with me. Or perhaps he was being respectful since I still had no clothing on. I knew it was because he worried about irritating the wounds that started to gradually close. They were still tender and healing slowly, but my bone was no longer exposed. Yes, I foolishly decided to try to touch them and ended up biting his pillow to keep my sounds of pain quiet. If he was there, I didn't want to disturb him with them. He'd heard enough of my pleading and agony for a lifetime. Sighing, I reached for the lamp on the bedside table.

As much as I would've loved to go back to sleep, I refused to waste what time I'd been given with him. Hera was probably livid that the time was being spent with him, but it was a risk I was willing to take. I glanced around the room in the low light. The walls of his room were a soft grey. There were dark, heavy curtains over each of the windows, shelves lining every wall but the one that the head of his enormous bed was pressed against. There were various books and collectables decorating them. The display around the large TV across from the bed intrigued me the most. There were weapons framing the TV mounted on the wall.

Some I recognized from a few of the anime shows that Callie enjoyed. The others weren't familiar, but they were all beautiful. I knew they were his work. Was he an anime nerd? The thought amused me, given my secret nerdy passion. It wasn't something that I flaunted, only sharing it with my mortal companions.

Carefully, I pulled the covers back and got up out of his bed, gradually settling my weight on my legs. I felt weak, which wasn't surprising in the least, given how little I'd used my body in the last five years. There was one of his large Henley shirts on the bed and I picked it up, smiling at the dark blue material that was nearly black. It wasn't comfortable at first as I put it on. At least it was large enough that I could drape it off my injured shoulder. Unbuttoning the top button made it close to indecent, but the wounds on my chest were able to breathe and I was still technically covered. I would just need to be careful not to flash him by accident. The bottom of the shirt was long enough that my lower body was shielded from view, the shirt brushing just below the tops of my thighs. It would do.

Playing with the material, I went for the cracked bedroom door, curious about what the rest of his home would look like and what I'd find when I saw him again.

CHAPTER VIII

WHAT I SAW WAS not what I was expecting. I followed the smell of smoke, and wondered what he could have possibly set on fire in his home. Did he have a forge in his house? That was an interesting thought. But it wasn't the reality.

He stood shirtless in his kitchen, cursing as he pulled a pan off the burner, the flames erupting from it quickly dying as he waved his hand over it. And what a back he had. The defined muscles shifted as he moved, drawing my eyes along his skin. "Why is this so godsdamn difficult?"

"You should never feel bad about that. As much as I enjoy the foods that mortals have to offer, I can cook very little. I have a private chef for that," I replied as I watched him drop the pan back to the stove. It was my turn to be surprised. Sure, the sight of his muscled back was incredible, even with the scattering of small scars across it. But the sight of him shirtless from the front floored me. He was muscled, as one would expect from his work in the forge, but it was bulky muscle.

There was nothing lean about him. It was a body that was carved from hard work and not lifting weights. It wasn't for show. His stomach was thick and solid, the barest hint of the abs that he could have if he tried to define them peeking through. I didn't even take in the scars decorating his skin. The physique alone made me clench my thighs together.

"Dite," he called, as though it might not have been the first time he tried to get my attention.

Shaking my head, I felt my cheeks burn as I lowered my head. He'd caught me staring at him like some virginal schoolgirl. What was wrong with me? "Sorry. Could you repeat whatever you asked me?"

The surprise on his face was worth risking looking at him. As was the absolute joy that took over his features at my question, realizing that I had been too preoccupied staring at him. "I thought I was the one that was supposed to marvel at your body?"

"You are more than welcome to enjoy it when I am finished enjoying yours," I teased back, feeling that heat creeping up my cheeks once more. What was wrong with me?

"Are you sure I'm not still dreaming?" he asked as he abandoned whatever he'd been attempting to make and moved closer to me.

"You dream of me?" That was surprising. He nodded in answer, and I couldn't help grinning up at him. "So, what were you asking me?"

It took him shaking his head for me to realize that he'd gotten distracted as well, his eyes shifting back up from where he'd been looking at the expanse of bare chest I was showing. "I was asking where home was so I could get your cook here before we starve."

"New Mexico." That earned me another raise of his brows. Apparently, I was just full of surprises. "Buckle up for this one. I went on a bender and woke up in a town called Truth and Consequences nearly a decade ago. Or a decade before the trials started. That is where I have been working on myself and collecting mortals." That sounded horrible, but it was the running joke they had with me.

Heph chuckled and reached out like he'd take my hand but then dropped his. "You're not the same Dite you were the last time I saw you. Are you?" It was my turn to just shake my head, my lower lip drawn between my teeth as I worried he'd find that unsatisfactory. "Guess I'll just have to take the time to get used to the new you."

"As will I. I never realized you were a lover of anime." I watched his pale skin flush and laughed, reaching out to cup his reddened cheek. "Callie, my chef, she enjoys it as well. I recognized some of the weapons and figures from her favorites. I think the two of you will get along well. If you still want to meet them some day." Even with my hand on his face, he still hesitated to touch me. I dropped my hand and smiled as I moved towards the stove. Apparently, without the threat of my demise, he was hesitant to lay his hands on me. It was a fear I'd driven into him after all. I couldn't really blame him for being afraid. "Would you like to know a secret that only my three mortals and my therapist know about me? Oh, and Lola. But she is quite cruel with her teasing." My question made me hesitate as I reached for the burned pan. It'd been five years. I knew my mortals would be fine because they had access to my accounts, but I was still worried that they'd think I abandoned them. Or worse. And Lola and I never went more than a week without speaking.

Heph didn't sense the turmoil in me. At least he didn't appear to as he approached, limping closer to me. "What's the secret?"

His question pulled me from my momentary panic. "I love sci-fi. Specifically, Battlestar Galactica, but I am weak for anything of that nature. And I enjoy fantasy things as well, but that is my first love." The surprised laugh he answered with made me grin up at him. "Heph, my sparrow, I truly would love to catch up, and we will. But, for the moment, I really need to find my phone."

He nodded and pointed at one of the corner tables in his living room. There was my phone in its iridescent case. I hadn't even taken the time to look around and enjoy his home. I was so transfixed by him. But I still wasn't ready to enjoy the masculine space. I needed to know how everyone I cared for was doing.

There were countless calls and texts from all three mortals, my therapist, and Lola. It was to the point that my phone could no longer count how many there were. I shot a quick text to the group chat for my mortals, another for my therapist, and one to Lola. It was a quick explanation that Hera had imprisoned me for five years and I was fine, just healing. I quickly received answers from all five. Lola's in the form of a call. "Hello, butterfly. What can I do for you?"

"Bitch, do you think you can just act like nothing happened after disappearing for five years? Do you have any idea how worried I've been about you?" Her anger was laced with panic, and I knew how badly I had scared her. "I told you Hera was setting trials for me. If Heph had not gone to her and asked for me to be released, it would have been ten years."

"TEN?" she screamed, making me pull the phone from my ear.

"I promise to explain everything fully soon. Please tell me you have refrained from torturing anyone from my pantheon." I knew her. She was a warrior and fiercely protective.

"Unless you count beating your ex in sparring, no. I've managed to keep my hands to myself. But I hope you know I expect a full rundown of everything. You're done now, right?" *I wish.*

Sighing, I wondered how to explain. I glanced at Heph who was watching me curiously. "No. That was only the second." That got another round of screaming that made me pull my phone from my ear, and I saw the smile on Heph's face. I held up a finger. "Lola, I only have a little time with Heph before I must start the next trial. Can you please update Micah and the others? I promise to explain everything soon." That made her hesitate before agreeing, promising that she'd been taking care of them all, which made me feel infinitely better. They were safe. With more promises of explaining later, I was able to hang up, answering my therapist quickly before turning my phone back off.

Lola's words finally registered, and I gasped as I looked down at my phone. My ex? Ares? Did I want to know badly enough to turn it back on or could it wait? As I saw Heph moving to finish putting the pan in the sink, I decided it could wait. Whatever they had going on wasn't my concern right then. Heph was. He was why I was going through everything.

As he started trying to wash the burned food off the pan, I couldn't resist moving behind him. I wrapped my arms around his waist, pressing my body to his back. There was obvious discomfort from my healing wounds, and I couldn't stifle the whimper of pain, but it was worth it. His body was stiff against mine before relaxing into the contact. I'd surprised him, I could tell. I smiled against his back, pressing my lips to his scars, one at a time. At least the ones I could reach without moving away from him. I was an affectionate person, though I hadn't been for most of my existence. All the nights of cuddling platonically made me a creature that needed touch to thrive. And five years without my platonic puppy piles with my mortals made me feel incredibly bereft. Though as I held Hephaestus, it wasn't platonic thoughts swirling around in my brain.

My grin widened until my teeth were pressed to his skin as my hands rubbed his stomach and shifted to his hips, my fingertips brushing the top of the dark jeans he still had on. What was it about a man topless, wearing nothing but a pair of jeans? As I dipped my fingers beneath the waist of his jeans to see if he had anything else on, he dropped the pan into the sink with a loud clang and grabbed my wrists. Well, at least I had gotten him to touch me. The action left me laughing as I pressed my head to his back.

"What are you doing?" he growled, glancing over his shoulder at me.

"I was curious if you had anything under your jeans." Why lie? That must not have been the answer he was expecting because he released one of my wrists and turned to face me, the other still in his grasp as he looked down at me.

"Why?"

I shrugged. "Why not? If you prefer that I keep my hands to myself, I can."

He hesitated and shifted his grip on my wrist, pressing my hand to the center of his chest as he leaned back against the sink. "No, that wasn't what I meant. I just...I don't know how this goes. Not in real life. I've never..." he trailed off and my heart broke.

"I know. And I am so very sorry for that. I promise to try not to surprise you anymore. But if you have questions, I am always available for answers."

"How do you know?" His brows furrowed, and I rolled my lips under as I debated how to answer.

Again, what was the point of not just telling him the truth? "My abilities. I could sense that you were still untouched. And I feel horribly selfish for admitting that I was glad. I am glad." He didn't ask why. Either he knew or he was afraid to, and I wasn't going to pry. Without saying anything else, he dropped my hand and I let my arm hang by my side as he turned back to the sink. "Let it soak."

I expected him to be stubborn and refuse but he just accepted my suggestion and turned away from the sink after filling the pan with water. He started to reach for my hand but decided against it, just limping towards the couch instead. I followed him, looking around his home. Everything was done in shades of dark brown and black. The furniture was black, as were the obsidian counters of his kitchen, and the dining table off to one side. It was an open concept, and I loved the way the spaces all flowed together. It was minimally decorated, just a few paintings of fire and volcanoes decorating the walls. They were beautiful, but I hoped to have another chance to examine them later.

He huffed as he sat, lifting his leg that I knew caused him problems onto an ottoman that made me believe it was his usual seat. I glanced at his foot, though I knew the myths of it being clubbed were just that. There were faint scars that started on the top of his foot, growing thicker and more pronounced as they traveled up his ankle and under his pants. Long ago, I'd seen his leg when it was healing and then again once it'd scarred over. Then, it disgusted me. Now, I was disgusted with the judgmental bitch I'd once been. I was blinded by youth and anger at the time.

Unsure if I should sit with him or on the couch perpendicular to the one he was on, I hesitated. After a moment, trying to keep it from being even more awkward, I sat one cushion away from him, giving him space but staying nearby. I wanted nothing more than to curl up against him and enjoy the feel of his body against mine. But I still didn't know if that was something that he'd enjoy. "So, the anime swords. Is that what you do?" I asked. "For work?" I needed to talk about something. The awkward silence was grating on my nerves, as was the lack of contact, the fear of failure. That fear of failure was my worry that we wouldn't be able to fix our marriage, that we would just crumble, and he'd walk away when everything was said and done. I needed distraction.

Heph met my gaze, and a slight tremble coursed through me as I wrapped my arms over myself. "I'll answer in a minute, promise," he said as he pushed himself up. I hated that he was already standing again, limping through his home. But I didn't move. If he wanted me to follow, he would've told me so. Instead, I just looked over at the fireplace that was across from the couch I was on. There was a large television hanging over it, books and tiny figures lining the mantle. I smiled, glancing to the left and seeing the wall of windows. They extended from the floor to the ceiling and with how dark it was outside, I couldn't make out much more than my reflection and the room around me for the moment. It occurred to me I had no idea where we were. I hadn't even thought to ask, just excited to be in his space with him.

The sound of him moving around his home drew me from my thoughts. Heph appeared again with several items in his hands. I laughed as he set the water bottle down on the coffee table in front of me before draping a fuzzy grey blanket across my lap and offering me a plush toy that was obviously from some anime I didn't know. Was he caring for me? It felt like aftercare, but I couldn't say anything like that yet. I just shifted the blanket on my lap and took the toy, cradling it in my arm as I reached for the water with my other hand. "I'll order some food," he promised. "Anything you're in the mood for?"

"Whatever you would like. I enjoy all sorts of food." It was the truth, and I was curious what he might pick. I was always interested in the dining habits of the people around me. Strange to say, but it was how I expanded my knowledge of food and it allowed me to try new things.

Heph nodded and returned to his previous seat with a grunt, lifting his leg before grabbing his phone and putting in an order for something through a delivery app. I didn't peek, preferring it to be a surprise. When he was done, he set his phone aside and looked at me. "I make weapons." It took me a minute to realize that he was answering my question about his work. "Anime lovers, LARPers, collectors. Sometimes cosplay people will ask for a blunt weapon. It's interesting work. My other work is something I don't really know how to talk about."

"Heph, I am a sex therapist that specializes in helping individuals in the BDSM community. Either those looking to try it to see if it helps them heal, or people who have been traumatized by the posers in the community and are looking to form a healthy dynamic." It was a strange niche, but I had a surprising amount of clientele. Especially since I did in-person sessions as well as virtual sessions for clients around the world.

The look of utter shock on his face made me laugh, hugging the plush toy to my stomach. Did I have a corner of stuffed animals around a bean bag chair I laid in to read from time to time? Yes. But I loved that he had his own plush toys and was willing to share them.

I watched his mouth open and close for a few moments, his blue-grey eyes widening as his brows rose higher and higher. It was an amusing sight. He took a few moments to figure out what to say, and I just grinned at him as I waited patiently. "So that other work I do I was talking about? It's for the BDSM community. Custom furniture, collars, other stuff. I just never imagined the overlap between our work." It was a strange coincidence, but I liked that if I wanted upgrades to anything I had, I could turn to him. Not that I had used anything of the sort for many years. It'd been too long to even remember the last time I had taken part in a scene.

"Neither did I. But that means I could speak to you about my work, and you might be able to understand things." He just nodded, and I settled against the arm of the couch, curling my legs under me. The blanket helped my modesty. Or, rather, helped me from causing him to blush even further. I never minded exposing my body, I had always been free, even outside of a sexual setting. But he seemed far shier than I remembered.

An awkward silence settled between us, and he turned his head to look at me. "Is there anything else you need?"

"I really appreciate the aftercare, but I promise there is nothing else I need. I usually would like a cuddle pile, but I am content with what you have given me." It was true. Would I have preferred to be cuddled right then, after everything I had been through? Yes. But I would respect his space.

"There's not really a cuddle pile that can happen right now. Would I suffice?" That was an incredibly adorable answer and the last thing I expected to come out of his mouth. Nodding, I watched his arm stretch over the back of the couch and took the invitation. It was an awkward shuffle over to him, soft whimpers escaping from the edge of the shirt rubbing at my healing skin, but I managed. Heph reached for me and wrapped his arm around me as gently as he could, helping to pull me against his side. It wasn't the most comfortable thing, and I couldn't stop all the pained noises from sounding as I settled against him, but it would have to do. Or so I thought.

A little yelp escaped my throat as he pulled me onto his lap. It was far more comfortable than pressing my wounds against his side, but I worried that I was hurting his leg. I shifted over to his good leg as much as I could, pressing the uninjured side of my body against him. His arm wrapped around my back as I rested my head on his chest, smiling at the fact that I was finally getting the chance to have that sort of contact with him.

His beard tickled my scalp as he settled his chin on the top of my head. But I loved it. The scratchy hairs were wonderful. I didn't care if I got a beard burn, I wanted to kiss him until our lips were swollen and we were gasping for air. I wanted to care for all of him, run my fingers through his beard as much as I wanted and to caress every scar he had, every inch of skin I could. But I settled for just enjoying the warmth and solid feeling of his body beneath mine, the strength of his arms around me. It was far more than I thought I would get.

That was how we sat, in silence, as he just rubbed his hand over my arm and I played my fingers over his chest, enjoying the way it felt to be so close to him. It was better than the dreams that had filled my head, and I wondered how much better reality would be compared to other dreams I had of him. That thought was doing nothing to keep the embrace innocent.

Our food came, and I was sad to have to move, but I knew that we both needed to eat. We made idle chit chat as we ate at his table. But I was surprised that after we finished, he picked me up out of the chair I had claimed and carried me back to the couch. I noticed his limp was less pronounced as he did, and it made me wonder how much was psychosomatic. That was a hornet's nest I'd likely poke another time. For the time being, I would just enjoy being back in his lap as he turned on some random anime I knew nothing about. It didn't matter. I was enjoying being cuddled in his lap as he shifted the blanket over both of us.

One of his hands found my hip, rubbing gentle circles over the sensitive skin, his fingers brushing over other curves that I wanted far more contact with. All his touch did, besides shifting my mind to sinful thoughts of him, was to remind me what I didn't have available to wear beneath the shirt. The last thing I wanted was to make him stop touching me so willingly, even those idle touches. So, I didn't comment. I did something else instead. Unable to completely resist the close proximity to him, especially after seeing him in a light that I had long denied, I leaned my head up to steal a kiss. It was a gentle kiss, testing the waters.

We'd kissed when he met with me, but I knew that I had trials ahead and didn't know what would happen. He'd kissed me before I began each trial so far. But this was a kiss just to have. I just wanted the taste of his lips on mine, the brush of those coarse hairs scratching my face. I didn't need a reason to kiss him other than the fact that I wanted to. My eyes fluttered shut as I reached a hand up to cradle his face, pressing my lips more firmly against his. After a moment, I pulled back, wondering if I had crossed a line.

He looked stunned. I had expected anger with how his hand had stilled and his body had tensed. But his eyes were wide as he looked at me. Perhaps the situation had settled in. We were alone in his space, and we were both lacking several pieces of clothing. I knew my body was too weak to give him something I had long denied us both, but there were other ways to make up for lost time. The question was if he'd allow me the chance to do any of them.

My lips parted to ask him if he wanted me to move. I never had the chance. Heph moved me so quickly, I couldn't contain my gasp as my back hit the couch cushions. The plush toy flopped off the side as he threw the blanket to the ground. Before I could react, his body was pressing mine into the couch, his mouth claiming mine. It was like he'd been a starved man for so long; he was finally able to devour what he'd craved. I didn't know what he had planned, but I had no intention of stopping him from feasting on me in any way he desired.

CHAPTER IX

His hand on my hip was firmer this time, dragging those calloused fingers over my skin as he explored my mouth with his tongue. Heph's other hand was tightly gripping the back of the couch to keep his weight from completely pressing into me. My tongue tangled with his, one of my hands rising to grip his fiery hair, the other dragged my nails up his back. As his hand trailed up along my side, the shirt I had borrowed bunched. I arched my back, lifting enough off the couch to help him slide it up as far as he wanted it to go. His hand hesitated on my ribs, the barest touch of the tip of his fingers against the lower curve of my breast. It was maddening. Pulling back from the kiss, I panted as I looked up into his stormy eyes. The darkness and hunger in them had me shivering, but I could see the doubt on his face.

I smiled and drew my lower lip between my teeth as I moved my hand from his back to rest atop his on my ribs. "I am yours to touch in any way that you might wish to," I reassured him, guiding his hand up over my breast, the shirt rising to bare me to his gaze. It wasn't comfortable on my wounds, but the pleasure of his touch against my nipple was enough to flip the switch for me to make that pain into ecstasy. I couldn't stop the moans that escaped as I urged his hand. It didn't take much. My hand returned to his back, exploring his skin, and leaving red lines across it. His hand kneaded and explored the generous curves of my chest. It was wonderful but doing nothing for my control. My body was throbbing with need but I wouldn't be selfish. It was about him.

If he wanted to pull away and have a moment to himself, I would never stop him, but I would also do everything I could to take those fears from him. I never wanted him to hesitate again when it came to touching me.

His growl sent a shiver down my spine as he shifted on top of me, leaning back on his legs, taking the delicious weight of him from my lower body. But I knew what he was doing. The hand that had been holding him up joined his exploration of my chest, shoving the shirt further up out of frustration. I was tempted to take it off. His gaze raked over my bare chest before trailing down the flat planes of my stomach.

The tension in him confused me, but I followed his gaze, the naked skin of my lower body all that I could see. Was there something wrong? "Heph?" I asked, voice breathy from the pleasure. His hands were still on my chest as he stared, his gaze slowly working back up to my face.

"If you want me to stop, this is your moment to tell me to do so. My control won't last long." I knew what he really meant. He wanted to give me an out in case I still had any reservations about us. It was understandable. But I didn't want that, I didn't want an out and I wanted all those thoughts of me leaving him gone.

"I might not be up to finally consummating our marriage, but other things are possible. I want you, any way that I can have you. And I want you to do whatever you want. Within reason," I added with a smirk. My hand on his back moved to cradle his cheek as I rose up from the couch to give him a tender kiss. The pain searing my chest with the movements and his shirt rubbing my healing skin were reminders that I couldn't get too out of hand just yet. "I am cursing your mother for the injuries that are keeping me from having you every way possible. But I would not do something so special while healing. I want every moment to be perfect." Nipping playfully at his lower lip, I pulled back and watched the conflicting emotions that battled on his face. It was his fear duking it out with his desire and centuries of being denied.

Heph lowered his head to whisper against my ear, the brush of his beard against my neck and cheek sending a shiver through me and adding to the dampness pooling between my thighs. "Safe word," he growled. That was probably the best way to keep things from going too far and to allow me to end things without him thinking I didn't want him.

"For tonight, I would rather use the stoplight method. I will give you my true safe word another night." There would come a night where we could talk about what we wanted, enjoyed, and wished to explore together. If he had a list, I wanted to hear everything he wanted to try with me and maybe teach him things he might never have thought of on his own.

"Green to continue, yellow to slow down, red to stop," he clarified, wanting to be sure there were no misunderstandings. I appreciated that. Most of the time I would top, but I would give control over to him for the moment. I was curious about what he would do with it.

"Or yellow to yield, yes," I replied.

He growled playfully, his head ducking down to lick over the curve of my uninjured breast. Those intense eyes rolled up to meet my gaze as he took my nipple into his mouth, sucking gently before biting down. It wasn't a harsh bite, but it was enough to throw my head against the cushion beneath me and arch my back as I cried out his name. The sound of his name on my lips brought a growl from him against my skin, his hips dropping and pressing his clothed length against me. It brought more whimpers and moans from me, my hips rocking against his to try to get some sort of relief for the aching at the apex of my thighs. The rough material of his jeans would leave me sore, and I wanted that. Desperately. And though his jeans were thick, I could feel the promise held within. I had a feeling that once we crossed every line left, I would be left sore and sated.

His hips moved harder against mine, making my cries louder as his mouth released my breast and moved up to bite and mark my neck. I gasped out at the sensation, my legs wrapping around his waist tightly as I trembled, my hand in his hair pressing his head to my throat. He was claiming me, very obviously, and I was loving the thought of wearing it for as long as it took to heal.

Heph pulled back from my throat and grinned deviously down at me. His mouth slanted over mine, his rough kiss mirroring the movements of his hips that were driving me insane. Both of my hands went to his back, clawing at his skin as I felt that pressure building higher, that coil tightening low in my belly. My body trembled as I felt that release approaching. As he shifted his hips, driving him harder against my clit, I screamed into the kiss as I bucked and writhed beneath him. My nails dug into his back as I found that release, his movements shoving me into the abyss of ecstasy. It wrapped around me, smothered me, caressed me, and I never wanted it to stop. His hips stuttered as he tore his mouth from the kiss. He cursed and moaned out my name before stilling above me. Our chests rose and fell heavily, panting in time with one another and sharing lazy, satisfied smiles.

"Love goddess indeed," he growled, peppering my face and neck with kisses. I shivered as he licked the mark he left on my throat with long strokes of his tongue. "I don't know the last time I messed my pants like this." That made me laugh with him, my hands rubbing soothingly over the scratches I left on his back.

"I am very proud that I could help you create the sticky mess in your pants," I teased.

"Careful or I'll make you clean it up." His words were teasing and confident, but the look on his face wasn't.

I grinned up at him, pressing a kiss to his lips. "I would be happy to."

He paused. It was easy to see how much he wanted to accept my offer. But he pressed a kiss to my lips and helped tug the shirt I was wearing back over my body. "Thank you, little dove, but I think we should hold off on that. You're still healing, and I think I've done enough damage to you tonight. Thank you," he murmured, brushing his fingers over the mark on my neck as he leaned down to give me a gentle kiss.

I really couldn't believe he was refusing, but I understood why. And I thought it was sweet that he wanted to take care of me like that. "For what?"

"This. Guess I wasn't really sure if we'd even do this much or not. I'm not saying you didn't mean what you said before. I just couldn't really believe this part of it. Not until now," he added. I sighed and leaned up, wincing slightly at the pain of my wounds and the ache settling between my thighs. It was worth it.

"We have plenty of time to make sure there is no more doubt about us. It could take years, but I am willing to spend each night in bed with you to be sure that you never doubt again."

"Just bed?" he asked, a devious grin on his lips.

I shook my head. "No, anywhere we please. But I will request a special necklace next time."

His eyes widened to comedic proportions as he looked at me. "You want me to collar you?"

"No! I mean, I would consider it once we figured out our dynamic, but I really have not been a bottom for anyone. I meant something more like this," I explained, tapping his hand.

Understanding dawned on his face after he thought a moment, looking down at his hand and back at me. "Next time," he promised. "I'm gonna go shower. Make yourself at home. I'll be back." Heph settled me on the couch, wrapping me in the blanket and giving me the plush toy once more. He brought another bottle of water to me before pressing a kiss to my head and heading for his shower.

While I didn't know how long I had until Hera decided it was time for my next trial, I wondered how much trouble I could get into with Heph. And more than that, I wondered how long we could resist finally consummating our marriage. Chewing my lower lip, I looked down at the plush in my arms and decided the toy would have as good an answer to that question as I did.

It was going to be a long few days, or however much time I had. And I had a feeling, after his concerns about my health, they'd be frustrating ones.

CHAPTER X

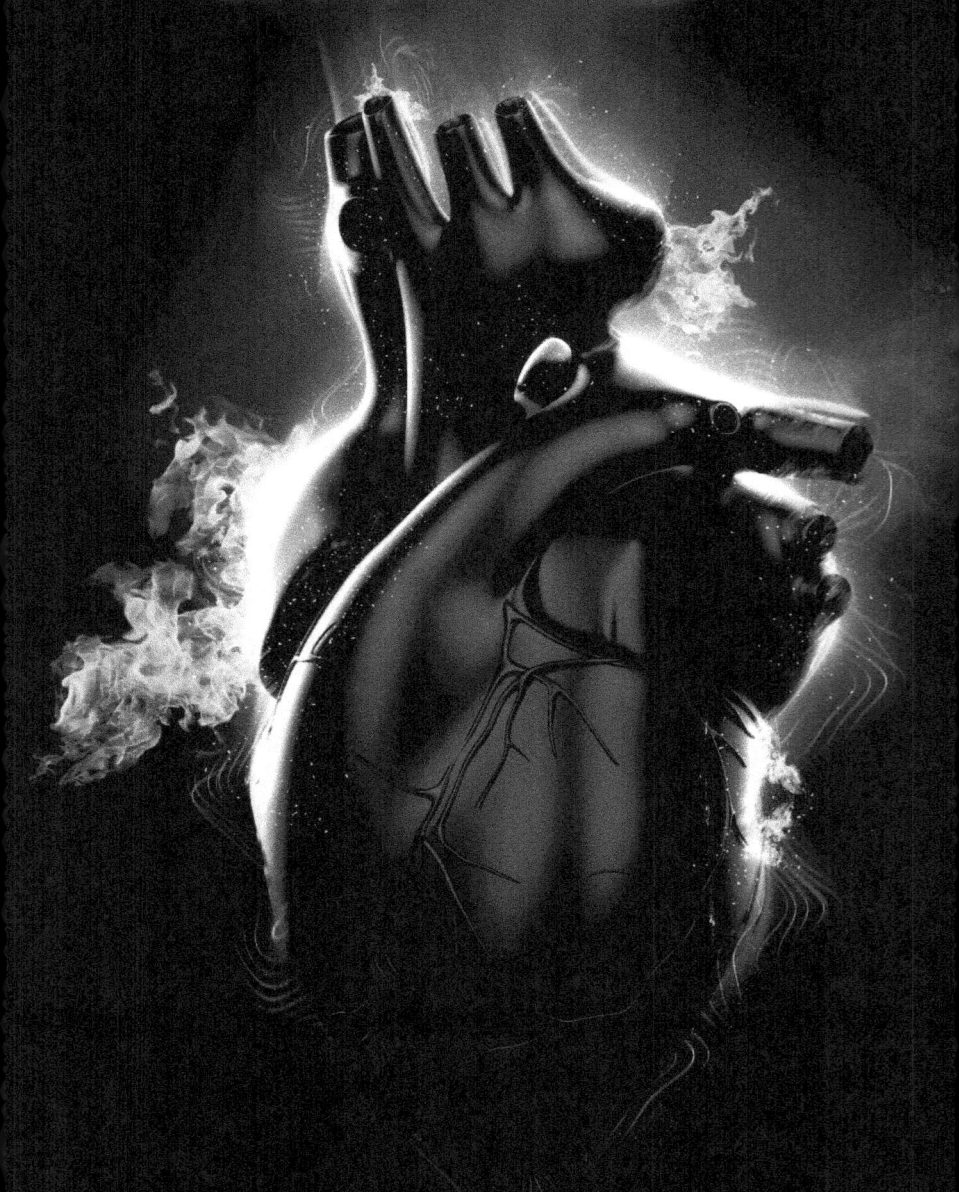

It was less than a week before I was done healing, and my powers were back at the level they had started at. They weren't really working, but I could control my aura and could attempt to flash somewhere. I had an embarrassing moment when my powers first started to go haywire, and I flashed to a meeting without clothes on. It was better to err on the side of caution.

During those days of healing, Heph didn't give into my attempts to seduce him. It was frustrating but we were able to talk. I learned that we were in Maine, and I was indeed married to a very big anime fan. We shared a love of fantasy books and movies, but I thought his addiction to anime was precious. I even perused his manga collection to try and understand a bit more of the interest.

I wasn't ready to leave him, but I had gotten some ideas and put things in motion while I was in his home. While he worked on some projects he had, I was explaining everything and apologizing to the people in my life. Lola was relentless but she explained what she'd meant about Ares. Apparently, they had been training together off and on. And I knew that she could give him a run for his money. For once, I felt no jealousy. There were no possessive feelings towards him anymore. He wasn't mine.

But Ares was the least of my concerns. Once I was healed, I convinced Heph that I was well enough to go to Hera as she asked. He was reluctant but he finally agreed. I hadn't told him why I couldn't back out or break my word to her yet. I couldn't upset him more than I already had. It wasn't as though I wanted to leave the little bubble we'd been living in, but I knew that his mother was not a patient goddess. She would eventually come for me, whether I was healed or not. It was better to go to her. The one thing I couldn't do was convince Hephaestus not to come along. I could understand given the state I was in after the last two trials, but I felt that he had already experienced enough of my pain. He didn't need any more of it.

"I was starting to think you weren't coming back," she stated without looking up at me. Hera sat behind her desk, working, and refusing to stop even to give me my next trial. At least she was efficient. She didn't raise her gaze as she motioned to the chalice that was sitting on the edge of her desk. "Your next trial. I hope you appreciate the favor I had to call in for this." Her tone was one of disgust, and I could only wonder who it was that had made whatever was in the gilded cup.

There was no clue on the chalice itself. It was gold with intricate abstract designs. That was it. Cursing to myself, I started for her desk, but Heph grabbed my arm with his free hand and stopped me.

"What's in the cup?" he growled. His voice did make Hera look up. A look I couldn't read flitted over her features.

"Does it really matter? This is her trial. She will drink this and let the effects of it take over her. Or she can quit." Hera's voice was softer with him, but I could still hear the edge of her frustration. What was in the cup that was upsetting her so much? Why would something she wanted me to drink cause her such discomfort?

My hand went to Heph's, squeezing gently before stepping away. He released his grasp, but I knew that he didn't want to, that he rather drag me from her office kicking and screaming. "Whatever it is, I will be fine." It could be anything, and I didn't know if it would be fine, but I had to say it and hope it was true. The last thing I wanted was to share my panic with him and cause him more worry. Whatever he was going to say, I silenced him with a tender kiss before quickly walking towards Hera's desk. The liquid within seemed innocuous enough. All I could smell was Heph and I thought it was just because I had to borrow his clothes, that his scent was just clinging to me. It didn't occur to me that the scent grew stronger because of the liquid in the chalice. I gave one last look at Hera's blank face before raising it to my lips. Before I could lose my nerve, I drank it down, all of it, in two gulps. The taste was strange, but familiar- like a combination of tears and how his lips had tasted on mine.

I parted my lips to question Hera about what was supposed to be happening when the world went dark. The chalice fell from my hands, and I dropped to my knees as my mind was assaulted with memories I was familiar with, but from an entirely different perspective. *Dammit*, I cursed internally as the severity of what I was going to face registered. The favor Hera had called in was from Mnemosyne.

"Zeus! Stop this!" Hera cried. The king of the gods had wrenched my head back by my hair. He dragged me to the edge of Olympus like that, but now he was just standing and snarling. When he glanced back at Hera before looking down at me, I felt my heart pound in my ears. What was he planning?

"Don't do this," she pleaded. My sweet mother had created me as Zeus had created Athena and Aphrodite. Was that why he'd always held such strong resentment towards me?

"He will learn his place," Zeus said, suddenly calm. That was even more frightening. My breath was ragged, coming rapidly

as I struggled to get free of his grasp. But his strength was something I couldn't win against. Before I could plead or do anything else, he'd lifted me, and thrown me over the edge. My stomach dropped as I plunged down, the air ripped from my lungs, heartbeat bursting painfully in my chest. My mother's piercing cry echoed, the sound of rushing air not loud enough to drown out the devastated wails of grief that made my chest ache with every gasping breath I attempted. That panic grew as I heard my mother's wails fading. It wasn't a quick fall. It felt like hours. And each moment just made that panic rise higher and higher. I don't know if I cried, but I screamed until my voice was gone, my body feeling weaker with each passing moment.

All I remembered of the impact was the sudden explosion of pain. It was as though every inch of me had been crushed, utterly and completely demolished. I couldn't even find the strength to scream. All of the breath had been stolen from my body and I succumbed as the darkness took me. The one mercy was that I fell unconscious almost immediately.

I had gotten revenge. The resentment I had towards Zeus for all those years had spread to my mother. As I laid healing, she had never sought me out. Why didn't she help me once I was down with the mortals? The abandonment and loneliness I felt was so thick I could choke on it.

But I had found my way back to Olympus. I could punish both Hera and Zeus for what they had done and how they had failed me. I made her a throne, one fit for the queen of us all. As she sat in the gilded seat, glowing with pride, she soon found she couldn't stand back up. A satisfied smile played across my face, and content that my revenge was done, I ignored everyone's pleas and returned to my place at the forge on Olympus. I had other things to finish. Their panic and cries for her release would still be there, my anthem, as I fell into the familiar rhythm of my work.

The smug smile I had as I forged faded when I saw the figure of Zeus darkening the doorway to my workshop. "If you've come to plead for her release, it would be useless. Anyone but you would have a better chance at convincing me," I growled.

"So, we can skip my asking for her release. Good. You will release her." The crown had gone to his head. He believed all should answer to him and bow and kiss his feet. It was revolting.

"Forgive me if I didn't phrase it before, so your miniscule brain could understand. I don't bow down to cheating cunts that leave their lovers to the mercy of their ruthless bitch of a wife." The edge of that smirk returned as I crossed my arms over my chest, refusing to betray my true feelings to him. It did pain me to call her that, even with how she'd left me, because there was a time that she had been a wonderful mother. But that didn't make up for leaving me broken and wounded in

the care of mortals. "I have work to do. If you get lost trying to find the door, it's the large opening in the wall. Run into the wall a few times and move to the side. I'm sure you'll find it."

I heard his roar before I saw him move. By the time I realized what he was doing, it was too late. He snatched the sword I had been working on from my hand and shoved me back. Pain erupted across my face as he slashed the searing, glowing blade over my left cheek.

"You still didn't learn your lesson." Just like that fateful day, he grabbed my hair, and I felt that same panic erupt in my chest. My heart leaped into my throat, and I struggled to get away, doing my best not to scream frantically like I had done before. I wouldn't let him have the satisfaction. It wouldn't change anything except make him feel more powerful. And just like before, there was nothing I could do to stop him. My cheek was forced down, pressed into the hot coals, and I couldn't fight back the sounds that shamefully escaped from me.

There was a gasp of horror from the doorway, but I couldn't see who it was. I don't even know how I heard it over Zeus' laughter and my cries of agony. Was someone bearing witness to my humiliation? He pulled me from the flames and dropped me to the floor like I was garbage, something to be discarded. I hadn't yet mastered my powers. It was why I had returned to Olympus with the skills I had been taught among the mortals. But as I screamed in agony, rolling on the ground of my workshop, I was determined more than ever to never let something I was meant to control be used against me. No weapon I forged would turn on me again. I would make absolutely certain of that.

As he stepped over me, I turned over, watching him go, and felt the air get knocked from my lungs as I saw a dark angel standing in the door. Her tan skin, sharp cheekbones, full lips, and large umber eyes were mesmerizing. Panting and whimpering, I quickly glanced over the rest of her, needing to free myself from the cage that face could put me into. Her body was as mesmerizing as her face, curves dragging the eye down her frame, I realized in that moment who it was. She turned to leave, a wave of dark curls fanning out. She was beauty incarnate, Aphrodite. I'd heard tales of her, but I had never seen her in the flesh. Zeus had a grip on her arm as he led her away from me. She wasn't running away? That was the last thought I had as my pain won the battle for consciousness. I was cradled by darkness, with the memory of her face bringing me peace.

When Zeus realized that bullying, beating, and berating me wasn't going to free Hera, he finally came to me, resigned to the fact that he would have to ask me for something after all. "What do you want? What will it take?" He was tired, I could tell. Somehow, he had finally turned into a doting husband, staying at Hera's side, and trying everything possible to free her. Or perhaps he just wanted his queen free since it would make others question what kind of king couldn't protect his queen. Either way, he was desperate.

"Aphrodite." It was the only answer I had for him. She was all that filled my mind, ever since I had seen her standing there with horror and sympathy on her features. Even then, she was everything I had heard of and more. There was no one that could compare to her beauty in any world. And for a moment, I glimpsed a kindness in her that made me want her even more.

"Come again?" Of course, he wouldn't just hand over his beloved daughter.

"I want her. Her hand in marriage. I want her as my wife." That was my price to release Hera, the only thing I would ever want. I wanted those lithe hands to hold my face, those perfect lips parting to say my name. I wanted to wake and see her face every morning, and for it to be the last thing I saw as I fell asleep.

He started to say 'no', but as he looked at Hera's exhausted and panicked expression, he hung his head in resignation. "Fine," he ground out.

We were wed immediately. The sooner to free Hera, after all. I stood, waiting for my bride, longing to see her radiant face again. But as she walked towards me, she had shrouded herself in black. Her face looked pained, the expression shifting to disgust as she met my gaze. Her eyes were like daggers that pierced through me, slashed at my heart. A stab of pain went through me, but I wouldn't back down. She just needed to be around me. She'd learn to love me in time.

Those dark eyes wouldn't meet my face, and all I wanted was for her to look at me. I wanted that kindness I had seen before. That pain in my chest was making it hard to breathe, but I wouldn't stop the ceremony. As I leaned in to kiss her, she turned her head, my lips pressing to her cheek as she denied me her mouth. Her skin was like silk against my lips, and I wanted to wrap myself in her, to hold her and experience that sensation forever. But as she raced away and flung herself into Ares' arms, it felt like my gut had ripped open. Her ever-falling tears made me feel like I had been thrown back in the fire that scarred my face. But she was mine. Zeus had kept his word, so I did what he had asked. With my pain souring my mouth, I released Hera.

I waited for Dite that night, but she never came to me. Our marriage bed was as cold as the look she had given me before running into my brother's arms. It seared through me, a burning cold, like ice spreading through my veins. Painful, freezing, and like my world was going to shatter just when I was putting it back together.

My hand erupted in pain as I punched my fist into the nearest pillar with all my strength. The stone crumbled with the force, but it wasn't enough. I had suspected something was happening between Ares and my wife after she sought his arms for comfort at our wedding, but actually receiving word that it was true was too much for me. Helios backed away in fear, as though I would turn my anger towards him for alerting me to her infidelity. The throbbing in my hand was nothing compared to my heart feeling as though she'd physically reached into my chest and shredded it with her perfect hands.

The roar that erupted my throat burned. I needed the pain, it would fuel me, keep me grounded. Without thinking, I walked to the shelves lining my shop and grabbed a golden net. It was an unbreakable chain-link that could hold anything beneath it. I bunched it in my hand as I stalked towards Dite's chambers, a place that I had never been welcomed into or seen for myself.

I hesitated for a moment, not wanting to look at the bed. Instead, I looked around at the white and crimson she'd decorated her space with. It infuriated me. It was a paradise I longed to share with her. As much as I didn't want to, I finally looked at her ornate bed. There they were, Ares fast asleep with Aphrodite cradled to his chest beneath her scarlet sheets. Keeping quiet physically pained me, I wanted to scream and rant with the fury that burned me from the inside. But I didn't, I managed to keep silent.

Ripping the sheets off their naked forms, I threw the net over them. They woke with a start, Ares promising retribution, and Aphrodite screaming for mercy.

"I look forward to it, brother," I hissed as I dragged them from the bed in the net, taking pleasure in their bodies hitting the floor hard. They screamed and cursed me as I dragged them through Olympus before depositing them in Zeus' throne room. I stood with my back to them, watching the other gods' surprise and then amusement at the predicament the two found themselves in. I reveled in the laughter that was aimed at them, even as the sting of realization hit that I was also a target for how I had been cuckolded.

Before walking away, I looked back and saw Dite's tears, the way she buried her face in her hands as Ares tried to comfort her while swearing that he'd make me pay. His threats amused me. But the sting of guilt for how she was weeping washed it away. All I felt was our combined pain and I needed to drown it. That agony made it difficult to breathe, and all I wanted was to beg her forgiveness, even with how she had wronged me. I still loved her, and that was the greatest form of misery I would ever experience.

Someone was screaming, nails were digging into my head, pain blossoming through my mind. I could feel the ichor pouring over my face and burning my eyes. It took a full minute to realize that the screams were coming from me. I'd taken Heph's memories, his greatest sources of agony and despair, and experienced them with the pain magnified tenfold. Gasping, I looked up at Heph through my tears and ichor as he fell to his knees in front of me.

"What did you do?!" he shouted at Hera as his hands gripped my shoulders, trying to gather me into his embrace.

My screams didn't stop as I tried to push him away. I wasn't worthy of his love, I wasn't worthy of his touch. The pain on his face echoed in my chest as I realized he thought I found him revolting. Gasping, I shook my head. "I am unworthy of you," I sobbed out, trying to push my back through Hera's desk. I needed to put space between us. It wasn't just that time he'd seen my affairs. There were so many slamming into my mind, ones I never knew he'd experienced. Sometimes I hadn't cared if Heph saw after that, but there were times that he saw even when I did try to hide. How could he still love me? How did he still want me? No wonder he refused to touch me after that first initial moment of passion.

"She is experiencing all of your pain for herself. I just had Mnemosyne increase the amount of pain she would feel." It was torture, but Hera wanted me to know just what I had put Heph through for so long.

"Mnemosyne? You? *You* swallowed your pride and asked her for help?" he spat out, still trying to pull me against him. My hands dropped and I let him crush me to his chest, sobbing and trembling in his grasp. How could he touch me? I was the revolting creature in our marriage, not him. That thought, something so far from what I normally would think, brought a little bit of myself back to me. I was an advocate of self-love. It took me time to relearn to love myself, but I would never think of myself as garbage. I knew what I had done was disgusting, but just the fact that I tried to atone meant I was bettering myself. Anger chased away the pain and my sobs slowed, the tightness restricting my breathing eased and I panted as I clung to Heph.

"Of course not," Hera replied. "I asked Nyx to retrieve it for me." That was surprising. Since when was Hera so close with Nyx? And when had Nyx left her realm of darkness? There were so many questions I knew I would never get answers from Hera for. Perhaps I could ask Thanatos when death season ended again, and he wasn't busy. Once Seph was able to go back to Hades, he'd shut the gates of Tartarus to new souls and Thanatos would have time to answer questions.

Heph didn't say anything in reply as he gathered me into his arms, his cane disappearing as he stood and carried me towards her office door.

"Where do you think you're going with her?" Hera asked, following after us.

"Home. She's in no shape to do the next trial," he replied, keeping her at his back and unable to reach me.

"One day. She gets one day to prepare for the next trial. And she will need it. She faces Ares at sundown tomorrow." *What?* My eyes widened, and my body tensed in Heph's arms. The queen goddess had gone insane.

Heph must have had the same thought because he finally stopped and turned to look at her. "No. It's still the death season. What is all this for if he kills her? We have two months left until she is safe to face him." I loved that he wanted to protect me, but that was the whole point of having me face Ares. There were only two outcomes. Hera had no intention of me finishing the last three trials after it. Either I would fall into Ares' arms, or he would kill me. Those were the only two outcomes she was expecting.

"What danger would there be if we waited until the death season was over?" Hera had a point, and I knew where she was coming from. It was the best way to protect her son from me. She'd remove me from his life one way or another.

"No. We wait. You want her to face him, fine. But not until it is over." Heph was trying so hard to protect me, and I loved that he was. That made my heart race, my body tensing again in his arms. I felt the first stirrings of love for him. To die with that knowledge would be horrible beyond all words or measure. How could I die when I had just begun to love him back?

Hera hummed in thought, and I hissed as a wicked grin spread over her lips. "Then she shall face him on the final eve of the death season. If she can last until Persephone goes to Hades at midnight, then I will consider the trial complete. She must survive from sundown until then." It was far fairer an option than facing him the following day.

"I accept," I quickly answered, ignoring the look from Heph that was asking me if I had lost my mind. I could survive six or seven hours. That was what I told myself as I looked up at Heph's face. "Trust me. I will always return to you." It was a promise I had every intention of keeping.

"Very well. Enjoy the reprieve." Hera started to say something else, but Heph carried me away before she could. I knew she hated the idea that Heph would keep me at his side for two months, but it was something she couldn't change without hurting him even more. He was suffering as much as I was through these trials.

But he was powering through and trying to make them as safe as he could for me. I loved him and it made what I had prepared to surprise him even more important. Suddenly, I couldn't wait another day to tell him. As soon as we were home, I would share my plans and hope that he wouldn't turn me down. After experiencing his memories, the fear that he might refuse me felt more like reality.

CHAPTER XI

I SAT ON THE floor of his bathroom, rubbing at the ichor staining the shirt I had borrowed from him. He was understanding when I said I needed to be alone for a little while. My plan had been to burn the guilt away in a scalding hot shower. I got as far as removing the shirt before I crumpled to the ground and let my tears fall again. Was I crying over the stain or the pain I had caused him for so long that I could still feel echoing through my mind? The answer was both. He was so good and caring, and I was the stubborn and heartless creature staining his life with my darkness. His memories were still there. I could feel them, see them, and I hated how long he had felt like the monster in our story.

Throwing the shirt down, I pushed myself up, stripping off the last of the borrowed clothes. I needed to breathe through it. I swore I would spend the rest of our existence making it up to him. But could I ever really fix what I had broken?

That was a question I had no answer for and shoved it aside as I turned the shower as hot as it would go and stepped under the spray. It was cold at first, sending a shiver through me. It heated up quickly enough until it felt like my skin would melt off. My hands were pressed to the cold tile as I struggled to catch my breath. There was so much swirling around in my mind, but I needed to sort through it. Would my plans hurt him? Would they bring up past hurt, or would they be able to replace some of those painful experiences?

I groaned in frustration. Why was I allowing myself to doubt? If I crumbled, everything I had been through would be for nothing. I sighed and looked down, watching the sparkling gold ichor swirl down the drain as I tapped my chipped nails against the tile. All I needed to do was suck it up and go ask him a question. Nothing else had been done that couldn't be undone. All the plans could be halted if he didn't like my idea. The thought had my stomach churning, but I quickly rushed through my shower and wrapped a black towel around my body. I didn't care about doing anything more than wringing out the water from my hair before I went out to where Heph was sitting on the couch polishing a sword. It was one he had made to keep in his private collection, and I thought it was beautiful, even if I wasn't familiar with the anime it came from.

"Heph," I started, not sure how to get the rest of my words out. Biting my lip, I moved to sit beside him, my body turned to face his. He set the sword on the coffee table and shifted to face me as well.

"What's going on?" he asked, his hand reaching for my bare knee before pulling back. I immediately let go of the towel and grabbed his hand, pulling it to my leg.

"I wanted to ask you something. Maybe I should have asked first, before I went and started planning things, but I wanted to make sure I did not waste any of the time we have left." I was losing my nerve. Maybe he sensed that, his hands reaching for me to pull me against him. The towel was stronger than I was, staying wrapped around me as I held onto him.

He sighed, resting his chin on the top of my head. "You don't have to be scared. I'd give you anything you wanted. Ask, it's yours." It wasn't hard to feel his fear; the fear that I might have changed my mind. It was there in how his embrace tightened, crushing me against his powerful chest, those muscled arms restraining my movements. It was a pleasant sensation, it was even calming to the turmoil I felt inside me. But I couldn't just sink into it, I needed to ask him something before it was too late. There wasn't much time until I had to meet Ares.

Gently, I pushed at his chest until he loosened his hold just enough to let me pull back and tilt my head up to look at his face. The comfort of his arms was there, his body was still like a burning furnace against me, keeping the chill of my anxiety from taking over.

"Will you marry me?" I couldn't try to skirt around it. If I didn't ask directly, I was going to lose my nerve completely.

Heph sat quietly, just staring at me and blinking rapidly. Was it that surprising? He looked stunned. "We *are* married," he murmured.

That was about the answer I was expecting. Well, other than him possibly refusing me. "I know. I just think that our wedding day was unpleasant for both of us. We should do it right this time."

The stunned look returned to his face for a moment. It made my heart race. Would he think it was a stupid idea? As he broke out into a grin, I let loose the breath I didn't realize I had been holding as I awaited his answer. Heph crushed me to his chest again with a deep, rumbling laugh. "Yes, my little dove, I will marry you again." His arms disappeared from my back as he reached for my face, cradling it and raising it so his lips could slant over mine. Those words made my heart soar. For the first time in as long as I could remember, I was truly overjoyed, burning bright with a glee that I couldn't compare to any before it. My hands pressed to his, enjoying their warmth against my skin. He was solid and real and happier than I had ever seen him. That was what I would hold on to.

Pulling back from the kiss, I chuckled breathlessly. "I might have already started wedding plans. I was unsure if everything would be done in time if I waited," I explained.

"What have you decided on?" He asked, something coming to mind. I could see an idea lurking in his stormy eyes.

"Only my part of things, such as dress and cake and whatever else my mortals could think of to get started on." I would look the part of the joyful bride. I would finally get to be one. If I could take back our first wedding, I would. But a new wedding was perfect for the new start we were planning. "I also was wondering if we should involve your mother. Would she try to stop the wedding?" It was a fear I had.

He sighed and pressed his head to mine. "I'll talk to her. I want this." *Before I had to face Ares*. It was unspoken, but I knew we were both thinking the same thing.

"I do, too. I also want you to know that I had already started this before I knew what the trial was. A few days ago, I decided it needed to be done. It was not your memories that made me want to do this." I didn't want him to think I was doing it out of guilt. Maybe I was right because of the relief and mirth that mixed on his face.

"That makes this even easier then," he murmured, pressing a kiss to my lips as he took my left hand in his. I gasped as his power flowed over me. When he let go, there was a white gold ring on my hand. The large diamond didn't matter to me. I was staring at the intricate metal design around it. There were two roses on either side, with delicate leaves holding more diamonds. There was a small dove and sparrow engraved beneath the roses, and delicate vines curved from the roses to hold the large diamond in the center.

"It is beautiful," I breathed, wiping the joyful tears that had streaked down my cheeks. His answer was another kiss that I felt down to my toes. My hands cupped his cheeks, gently touching the scars with my thumbs as I returned his kiss with as much love and passion as he had given me. I couldn't say the words yet, but I could at least try to show him how I felt.

"Not like you. Nothing I could ever create could ever compare to you. I'm still coming to terms with the fact that you allow these hideous hands to touch you." His words made my heart soar, but also tightened it as I realized that he still thought of himself as lowly compared to me. Heph, like so many others, continuously put me on a pedestal, but in the same breath he tried to make himself unworthy of my love. I was at least partially to blame for that, having helped him come to that sort of conclusion for so long. It was just one more thing I had to work on fixing between us.

I took his hands, bringing them to my mouth. As I looked into his eyes, I kissed each finger, over his knuckles and then across his palms. "They are not hideous. No part of you is hideous, Heph. You are strong and handsome, beautiful in every way. I should be the one marveling that I get to touch you, that you do not recoil from me after everything that has transpired." For what did my beauty matter on the outside if I was incapable of mirroring it within?

Whatever else I might have said was silenced as he pushed me back on the couch, kissing me hungrily. It was a familiar position, and one I could enjoy more without the aching of my wounds. As he pulled back, he growled as he reached for the towel, but paused. "No." My face fell, and I started to turn away, but he gripped my jaw and made me look up at him. "I want to wait. We're doing the wedding over. I want our wedding night to be the first time I get to be with you," he murmured, pressing a sweet kiss to my lips. It was my turn to be completely stunned. It made sense, though. He wanted a proper wedding night. I nodded in agreement and watched him get up off the couch before heading out of the room.

Sighing, I sat up and adjusted the towel. Heph limped back into the room with one of his shirts, handing it off to me. "You're going to need this," he said. I was going to ask what he meant, but the knock at the door made me stop. My brow arched as I looked up at him questioningly. "Answer it." He grinned at me as he sat beside me while I took the towel off and tugged the shirt on, hurrying to the door.

The inhuman scream that escaped my throat as I opened the door made Heph jump, dropping the sword he'd picked up. I heard his laugh as I squealed and pulled the three sobbing and squealing mortals at the door into my embrace. "Way to block the door, bitch," came a familiar voice behind me. Lola had flashed into the house and hugged me from behind. I missed her, I missed them all. Laughing, I leaned my head back to kiss her cheek.

I looked over at where Heph was kneeling on the couch, watching us with a smile. "Did you do this?"

"I knew you missed them. And I'm glad I did this since there's a wedding to plan." He had a point.

"Where are we doing this?" Tori asked as she nudged us all in, shutting the door behind her. We all separated and moved to the living room where I curled up next to Heph, Lola dropping down beside me.

"I have a farm in Scotland," Heph offered. That was an idea. It was better than anything I had planned. "Secluded, nice scenery, and the house has enough room for all of you to stay."

"Don't worry about anyone staying. We don't need to hear your wedding night activities. I'll flash them back home when everything's over," Lola chimed in.

The blush that spread over Heph's face was perfect. I couldn't resist leaning up to press kisses to his flushed skin. How could he be so rugged and strong, yet look so completely adorable? It was a gift he had that I wanted to witness forever.

We spent the day chatting and planning the wedding, catching up. I had butterflies in my stomach as

I thought about our wedding, trying to drown out the voices telling me everything that could go wrong. Micah was surprisingly quiet throughout everything. He made only the barest attempts at small talk when we all ate dinner. Heph fixed up the guest rooms for my mortals, Lola hugged me and told me she'd return to help with wedding preparation. As the girls went to their rooms, I grabbed Micah's arm and pulled him aside.

"Is everything alright?" I asked, hoping nothing had happened to him while I was gone that no one had filled me in on yet.

"Yeah, I just...I think your husband doesn't like me. He looks at me like he's wondering if I'm more than just your driver and fix-it guy." That was insane. Or was it? I looked up at Micah's face and sighed. He was handsome, devistatingly pretty. There were times he'd gotten offers to model and he brushed them off. But I could see what Heph saw.

I wrapped him in a hug, like a million times before, but I felt a presence to our right. Heph was in the doorway of his room looking at us. He looked possessive, and it would've been a nice sight except it was accompanied by a flash of jealousy. When he noticed me looking at him, he looked guilty. "I think you are right. I will explain things to him. Go on," I told Micah as I pulled away and went to Heph. Immediately, I leaned up to wrap one arm around his neck and kissed him deeply. He tensed, surprised, before wrapping his arms around my waist and pulling me tight to him, returning my kiss.

Heph lifted me, wrapping my legs around his waist as he stepped into the room. The door slammed shut as he moved his hands to my ass, holding me up. There was no chance of me falling with how tightly I clung to him. We fell to the bed with a grunt from him and a sharp exhale of air from me as I pulled back from the kiss, his weight pressing me back into the black covers. "Heph," I murmured, nudging my nose against his. "There never has been, nor will there ever be anything, but platonic love for Micah. He is mine to protect, and I care for him as I do Callie and Tori. They depend on me, I would never do that. And you are the only one I want."

His face shifted through emotions. He was trying to believe me, but his face as I said the last words showed me it was what he really needed to hear. "You're all I want, too, little dove." While I knew that, it felt wonderful to hear him say the words. It made my chest feel light, my stomach flutter.

All he would allow me were gentle kisses before we fell asleep, his arms cradling me to his chest. I couldn't wait for the wedding so I could show him everything I should have shared with him before. There was so much time to make up for, and I wasn't sure how much time we would have left. I was going to fill that time with love, and I was going to find a way to survive the next trial.

THE TRIALS OF APHRODITE

First, we had to get married.

CHAPTER XII

We decided on having the wedding in two weeks. It would give Heph time to finish up his projects and push everything else until after the next trial. We would have a month and a half to enjoy married life before I faced off with my former lover. Neither of us wanted to wait longer than we had to. My mortals were incredibly efficient, and Lola helped plenty as well. Her powers were working at full capacity. She was able to transport herself and the girls wherever they needed to go. It made things so much simpler.

A week before the wedding, we all traveled together to what Heph had called his little farm. It was a huge expanse of land with animals and a sizable house, hidden from the road with a large wrought-iron gate. I was in love with it the moment we got there. It was a massive yet cozy craftsman, but it was made with dark stones that felt true to Heph.

He led us inside. It had been decorated similarly to his other home. It made me smile as we walked through his home. Callie and Tori got settled quickly and started figuring out where to set everything up. I tried to remind them we really didn't have any other guests coming. Unless they knew something I didn't. It didn't matter much to me, I just wanted to give Heph the wedding he deserved.

Somehow, that week was even more frustrating than the weeks before. I ended up sleeping in a room down the hall from Heph's because I didn't trust myself not to maul him in my sleep. I couldn't remember the last time I had been so desperate for another person. It was getting out of control. There was a touch of guilt that my yearning and frustration was making me irritable and desperate for my wedding day to come. But I wouldn't push him to do anything until he was ready. With how long he'd been waiting, I could handle a few more days.

"You came." I enjoyed being the one to say it as Hera flashed into the room the girls had chosen for us to get ready. "The question is whether you came as a guest or to stop us from getting married again."

The look on her face was unexpected. She wasn't angry; she was a little sad, and I wasn't sure why. "I won't stop you. He's happy, and that's all I've ever wanted.

Make him happy. Survive the trials, prove you are ready to build a life with him." I would've sworn that the world had just entered a new ice age. Hera embraced me, I was frozen for a moment before my arms just wrapped around her without my thinking about it. I was still processing the fact that she had reached out for me in an amicable way. While she was my stepmother, we had never been exactly close. Maybe if I finished the trials, that could change. If I survived.

"He will be glad you came. And I will make him happy. I will spend whatever time I have left fixing his heart. Whether I have a month or an eternity, I will spend it giving him the life he deserved all along," I swore. Her hand patted my back as she pulled away from the embrace.

"That is all I ask." Her hand raised to my face, and I flinched, but she just caressed my cheek before turning to leave the room. My heart was still racing when Lola grabbed my arm, asking if I was alright.

Nodding, I turned to her and smiled. "I am. A little confused, but I suppose she agreed to his request to officiate."

"Who knew she would be able to stand you long enough to get through it. Took me months to get used to you," Lola teased.

"Hush." I chuckled and shoved her shoulder as Tori approached with a veil. It was as long as the dress, cascading down my back. I had chosen it because the glitter in it shined like the sparks from Heph's forge. It was a wonderful contrast to the dress we had settled on. We, being Callie, Tori, Lola, and myself.

It was strapless and hugged my body perfectly. There was a line of large pearls that started by my left breast and formed a sweeping line across my stomach to my right hip and down my right leg. The sheer lace material and decorative applique that spread up over my cleavage looked like waves of seafoam. Its train made me feel like I was dragging the ocean of my birth behind me. Perhaps that was why I fell in love with it.

The wedding was going to be more like that of a human wedding ceremony. We were wedding our mortal personas while having a ceremony just to make up for the one that went oh so wrong all those centuries ago. The normal ceremony we would've had on Olympus wasn't necessary. And that meant that we didn't actually need Hera or Zeus to oversee it. Heph had just wanted her to because he wanted her to be a part of it. Our first wedding wasn't exactly a joyous occasion for Hera, either. She'd been bound to a gilded throne and was only released because of the ceremony taking place. She was forced to sit and watch from that seat.

We'd both made mistakes, Heph and me, and we'd take the time to fix them. Lola handed me a bouquet of dark peonies and red anemones. I smiled down at the bouquet, the white roses scattered among our flowers as accents. They were ours, mine and Heph's, and the girls had decorated the aisle and makeshift altar with them as well. The warmth in my chest eased the butterflies in my stomach. If Hera was going to stop it, she would have. Lola swore Ares wasn't going to come and ruin the ceremony, and I couldn't think of anyone that knew that would try.

Lola led me out of the room we'd gotten ready in, Tori trailing behind us to fuss over my train, all my mortals clad in shades of red as well as Lola. My heart skipped a beat as we stepped outside and I saw Heph standing at the end of the 'aisle' they had made. The material they'd laid out was crimson and complimented the red flowers tied to the white chairs. In the chairs were Micah and a few faces I hadn't expected to see.

Eros sat between a mortal that was speaking with her hands, literally, the sheer sleeves of her pale blue dress flinging around as she signed along with her words; and a tattooed male with dark sunglasses on that matched his solid black suit. I didn't care who Eros brought, I was just glad that he was there. To the other side of the mortal was Adrestia, my other sweet child, in a simple black dress that made her fair skin seem even brighter. She was as beautiful as ever and I felt a pang as I realized that I hadn't exactly kept in contact with my children either. We texted occasionally, but I needed to fix our strained relationship.

Nyx was out in the daylight, a brunette human male beside her holding a black parasol over her head. It was an amusing sight, but I expected nothing less from her. Her skin was as pale as milk, and I feared what would happen if she spent too long in sunlight. Amphitrite's blonde hair drew my attention away and over to where she sat alone, a bright turquoise gown wrapped around her. That was a surprise. I hadn't thought she would come given how we'd left things decades earlier. I wasn't sure if that was a relationship I wanted to mend, but I appreciated her attendance.

Bright red hair signaled Persephone's appearance. Her freckled face smiled at me as I passed her. It was rare to see her without her mother when away from Tartarus, but I was glad to be without Demeter's presence. And she wouldn't have approved of the deep maroon dress her daughter wore, overlaid with black lace. There were gods present I didn't recognize but I knew I would meet sooner or later. I couldn't identify them by the power circling them either. Were they Heph's friends? He'd been rather busy if he'd befriended other pantheons.

My brows rose when I saw who was standing beside Heph. I'd been so focused on him and then on Nyx's appearance, that I didn't notice the one person I didn't want there. My heel nearly caught on the cream-colored carpet lining the aisle as I saw Ares' face. I looked over at Lola who was just as surprised to see him. I stopped at the altar, facing him and Heph. Ares looked livid. He exuded his anger so strongly that I could choke on it, lips pursed and fists balled as he stood there, staring. Heph was blissfully unaware. Hephaestus was beaming at me, and I refused to let Ares drag me down on such a joyous day. I returned Heph's joyful smile, my heart fluttering at how handsome he looked in his black suit. Even his shirt was black, but his tie was silver with red roses. It was his tie pin that made me chuckle. A small silver dove.

"You look beautiful," I murmured as he kissed my cheek.

"That's my line. And I asked him to be here. For me," he whispered. I swallowed and nodded. This wedding was for him as much as it was for me. Heph wanted his brother at his side. I understood that. And I wouldn't take that away from him. Nodding, I kissed Heph's cheek, my scarlet lipstick doing its job and remaining on only my lips. Perhaps later I would don one that I could smear over his body. The thought made my smile grow as we turned to face Hera so she could begin.

She looked between our smiling faces and nodded, starting with the usual wedding opening before looking to where Lola and I stood side by side with Heph on my right. "Who presents the goddess of love and beauty to be bound in matrimony?"

"Itzpapalotl of the Aztec pantheon. I present the goddess to go forth in love and happiness with her bonded beloved." Lola hugged me before going to stand beside

Ares on Heph's side, Tori and Callie stood across from them on my side.

Hera went through the usual mortal wedding speech as Heph and I turned, clasping hands. When the time came for vows, I leaned my face into Heph's and whispered, "can you produce a small flame for me? Please?" He was confused for a moment until I pulled a small blade from my bouquet, realization crossing his features. "Dite, you don't have to." But I did.

"Please," I repeated. Tears brimmed his lashes as he held his hand out, a small flame appearing on his palm. "I vow, by the blessed ichor, to love and cherish you. I will be true to you, love only you, and protect you as I would my children." I didn't hesitate, making a small cut on my forearm and letting the gold liquid drip into the flames in his palm. Tori carefully took the blade from me and wrapped a white satin ribbon around the wound as I lowered my arm. "I love you, my sparrow. I cannot promise to never hurt you again, because even the best of intentions fall short. Instead, I will always reach for you over my pride, I will warm you, heal you, seek your forgiveness and work to always be worthy of it. I will walk through flame and darkness to make you feel the same joy that you have given me. I choose you, over everyone that may come into our lives. I choose you." My tears fell at the same time as his, laughing through the mirthful show of emotion on both our parts.

Heph closed his fist, putting the flame out. "I vow to love you, my little dove. I will cherish you. Nothing before your return to me matters. Each morning I awake by your side is a blessing that I have not and will not take for granted. You are my world, Dite. I will protect you from any threat that comes our way, like cylons." A surprised laugh escaped, mangled with a sob I couldn't hold back. Of course, he had to add a bit of my nerdy secret. "And I will love you. Even if you are one." He just had to use my love of sci-fi against me. "I could thank you for loving me and fixing me, but instead I want to thank you for showing me that I deserve to be loved, that I was never truly broken. Every day with you by my side is far better than any dream I've had of the life we could've lived together. I look forward to putting every dream, every fantasy, to shame with you, one day at a time."

I pressed the back of our hands to my head as I tried to breathe past the tears. Chuckling, I kissed his hand and looked up at him again. "Do you have rings?" Hera asked. Lola moved past Ares to hand the band Heph made to match my ring to him, Tori handing me a band I had made for Heph as she took the bouquet flowers from me. His band was gunmetal gray, darker than mine, but not quite black. It would've been lovely, but I wanted them to match a little. There was a vine that was etched into his band, similar to the one he created on my diamond ring. His band also had 'dove and sparrow' engraved inside. My hand trembled as he slid my band on, and then as I did the same for him.

Even though I hadn't expected Ares' appearance, I was glad that Hera skipped over asking if anyone objected to our union. Instead, she announced that Dita and Heston were married, our human personas. I had forgotten that was why we'd done a mostly mortal wedding ceremony. "You may kiss and let your bond be reforged in love."

My breath hitched as he grinned, grabbing me and dipping me. I didn't know he'd want to do a dramatic kiss, but it brought laughter from those present. This time, I didn't turn away. I slid my arm around his neck, leaning up to meet his lips in a tender kiss that warmed me completely. Whispers from Heph's side could barely be heard over the cheers of our friends, family, and those that had come with them to bear witness. Whatever Ares and Lola were arguing over quietly wasn't important. I trusted her to deal with it. And she did, flashing the two of them away as Heph took my hand and Tori returned my bouquet. We walked back up the aisle with Callie and Tori at our backs. They'd convinced me to take some pictures, and I agreed because I wanted to have pictures of us at our wedding in whatever home we decided on. It was something a normal mortal couple would have after all.

Everyone left as we took a few photos to treasure. Eros promised to catch up soon. The mortal apparently was needed back wherever they had traveled from. I understood, and I had every intention of learning about his new life and those that he surrounded himself with. Adrestia flashed away after a quick greeting. It made my heart ache, wanting to spend time with them, but I knew they had lives of their own. I would find a time when they were free and could catch up. I would mend our relationships. I had to.

Heph pulled my attention back to him and I smiled sweetly, squeezing his hand. Lola returned to flash my mortals home before going to find Ares again and calm him down. He had apparently stormed off from wherever she'd taken him earlier. "I am sorry you had no time with your brother," I murmured, leaning up to press a kiss to his lips.

"It's alright. I knew it'd be hard. I didn't think he'd accept it." But I had a feeling that Ares had accepted the invitation to see whether I would go through with the ceremony or not. I don't think he ever expected me to fall in love with Hephaestus.

The pain that started to fill his eyes made me quick to change the subject. "You understand that I will have to find events for you to dress up and attend now, right?" This time, the look of pain was exaggerated and completely in jest before he let loose a boisterous laugh.

"I can live with that. As long as you are on my arm, I would gladly bear this torture again for you." Chewing my lower lip, I tugged his hand, trying to lead him back towards the house. As much as I enjoyed him in his suit, it was time to get him out of it. "Oh, no you don't." Without waiting for a reply from me, he lifted me into his arms and carried me into the house. I expected him to put me down once inside, but he kept walking, up to his bedroom and kicked the door shut before finally setting me down. "I want to do this right," he whispered, his hands going to the bejeweled comb that held the veil to my head. I don't know if I had ever been nervous going to bed with someone before, but I was with Heph. It was an important moment that we both had been waiting for. Him longer than me, but it was something we'd both craved and needed.

He dropped the veil and grabbed my face between his hands, kissing me hungrily as I gripped his waist. There was nothing left to say. I didn't have any more pretty words to prove my feelings to him. All that was left was the one thing I had withheld from him for centuries and couldn't bear to forgo for another moment.

CHAPTER XIII

THE AIR WAS KNOCKED from my lungs as my back hit the bed. I couldn't help the grin that spread over my face as I watched Heph strip his jacket and tie, tossing them aside before ripping his shirt open. Years of frustration and denial had his self-control crashing down into rubble. The feral glint in his eyes sent a shiver through me as he stood at the edge of the bed, looming over me. He didn't bother removing my dress, just pushing it up, the sound of seams ripping filling the silence with our heavy breathing. Right then, I didn't care. The dress was meant for the ceremony. He could do as he pleased with it. His breath came out in a hiss as he saw my lower body was bare. I felt my core tighten, dampness pooling between my thighs from the hungry look he gave my body. The calluses on his hands sent a shiver up my spine as he dragged them up my thighs. "Later," he growled, leaning down to press a kiss to my mound. My breath hitched at the visual of his face buried between my thighs, leaving a beard burn on my thighs. I was excited for that to become a reality.

Heph shifted me up the bed, dragging the dress up until it was bunched completely around my waist. He quickly unbuckled his belt, nearly ripping his pants to get them open before kneeling on the bed between my legs. Pulling his length free, I whimpered seeing it for the first time. I knew from how it felt through his clothes that he was rather endowed. It was different seeing it for myself. "It is truly wonderful that you have remained untouched. If another woman had ever seen this part of you, I would be bound by the absolute need to remedy the fact that she was breathing." I would've truly deserved a reputation for having a wrath like Hera's then. If anyone had seen his body bare as it was then for me, I would have earned that reputation with the blood of each woman that came before me.

The blush on his face was precious, but that intense look in his eyes, the hunger and lack of control accompanied it. He gripped my thighs, pulling them up around his hips as he dragged my body to him. The tip of his length brushed my swollen lips, rubbing at the moisture there. I whimpered, writhing against the bed. His hand moved from my thigh, wrapping around his length to position it at my entrance. My gaze met his and that first push into me pulled a cry of his name from lips. It was painful, the way he stretched my walls, like he might tear me, but that switch in my head flipped and it just made every sensation turn to pleasure. There was the edge of pain still, but it fed into my arousal, heightened the sheer delight I got as he pushed his hips forward. I wanted the sore ache that would be left when we were finally sated. Heph shuddered, his breathing ragged as he leaned forward, caging me in with his arms. "I don't think I can hold back," he growled, voice strained.

My hand rose to cradle his face, a gentle touch that didn't echo what I craved for him to do to me. "I would never ask you to," I murmured. Leaning forward and kissing him deeply, I pushed the torn shirt off his shoulders. Heph shifted his weight from one arm to the other, letting it fall to the floor before settling over me once more. He hesitated for a moment, like he was doubting my words, his body trembling with how he was attempting to hold back. I rocked my hips up to his and watched all that careful control shatter completely. His hips snapped forward, and I gasped, my hands going to his shoulders, nails digging into his flesh as he started a brutally quick and rough pace that I couldn't keep up with.

It felt like all the breath was stolen from my body as I barely managed little mewls and moans, writhing beneath him against the bed. In that moment, I realized that it had been more than a decade since I had shared my body with anyone. Never before had I gone so long without the touch of someone, something to ease the aching and dripping need that consumed me. No wonder I was as overwhelmed by all the sensations as much as Heph was.

One of his hands rose, gripping the top of my dress and tearing it down. The force of the motion ripped the bodice of the dress, pearls skittering off the bed to the floor. It was a beautiful sound, and I loved the hunger on his face as he stared down at me. I expected him to turn his attention to my exposed chest, but his hand slid up to trail his thumb over my lower lip before wrapping around my throat. The promise of his strength was there, but he only squeezed gently, my eyes widening and breath hitching.

The slapping sound of skin against skin was loud in the still room, punctuated by our moans and cries. My legs slid up his sides, angling my hips so that each vigorous thrust had him hitting my cervix and rubbing along that little ridge that heightened my pleasure. Each thrust had white bursts exploding behind my eyes, his name like a desperate prayer on my lips. I must admit that I had wondered if he would last very long given his 'innocent' state. But he was doing better than I was at that moment. That pressure was building, and my body flooded with warmth as I writhed beneath him. Between one thrust and the next, that pleasure broke over me. It felt like electricity flowing through me, causing me to twitch and thrash as I cried out his name. Warm liquid touched my fingertips, and I realized that I'd punctured his skin, but his groans just grew louder. His hips bucked, movements growing less rhythmic before he gave a few last hard thrusts and stilled above me. The warmth of his release left me shivering beneath him as I came down, the world edged with a hazy afterglow.

Our panting breaths echoed one another as we mirrored each other's lazy grin. I reached to brush sweaty red tendrils from his face, pressing sweet kisses to his lips. "Next time, you can squeeze harder," I purred.

The devious glint in his eye made me shiver as he did just that, his hand tightening around my throat and cutting off my air. My body reacted, tightening around him, pulling a curse from his lips. "I don't think I'll be giving you back for those trials," he murmured, loosening his grip and kissing me sweetly. "We're never leaving this bed again."

What a wonderful thought it was, to stay like that with him for the rest of eternity. But I knew it wouldn't be possible. One way or another, I would have to finish the trials. Hera was supportive of our second wedding for Heph's sake, but I had to make good on my word. For the moment, I could just pretend that it wasn't true, that I didn't have to leave him far too soon. We had a little over a month until I had to continue. For that long, I could try to pretend as though our existence would turn into one of marital bliss and nothing would stand in our way.

Neither of us wanted to move away, to separate our bodies. I hadn't yearned for that physical connection for nearly as long as he had, but I was just as reluctant to let him go. His hand moved from my throat, down to caress my breast, and he groaned at the sensation, rocking his hips forward. A moment before, his length had been softening, but all the movements of our bodies' reactions to one another had him hardening once more, filling me again. It was tempting to take control, but I would give him his time to have me however he wanted. He'd waited long enough, and I was curious what fantasies I could fulfill for him, how he had wanted me over the years. Never before had I craved to submit to anyone, had I wanted to let someone use my body for whatever pleasure they craved.

What I didn't expect was him pulling free of me, separating our bodies with a grunt. I whined in protest, trying to tighten my legs around him once more. But he just smirked down at me and shook his head. "You'll get me back, little dove." It should've bothered me that it felt like our roles had switched, but I was so caught up in my desire for more, it really didn't matter. His firm hands unwound my legs from his waist and he twisted me over, flipping me onto my stomach before I could protest. Heph ran a hand down the back of what remained of my dress before gripping it and tearing it open. A gasp escaped my parted lips as my hands grabbed at the sheets beneath us. "You don't need any of this," he growled, ripping along the seams of the dress until he'd bared my body completely.

Every pull of the material, the jerking force that he used, made the arousal coating my thighs even more intense. The renewed anticipation of what else he had in store for me overshadowed the emptiness I felt. It was strange to me, giving up control, but I couldn't deny how wonderful it was to let him take it. Would it be the only time? I wasn't really sure, but I knew he needed it more than I did after waiting for so long.

The feeling of his coarse beard hair brushing over my skin as he trailed kisses over my exposed back sent shivers through me. They were so gentle compared to the way he was yanking the material from my body. I raised my hips just enough to help him get the remains of the dress off me before he shoved me flat to the bed once more. Vaguely, I heard the dress hit the floor before his hands were on my skin once more. Soft pants and little whimpers escaped as he slid those calloused hands over my sides, the barest brush of his fingers against my breasts before they were gone. He repeated the action down over my hips, grazing the curve of my ass and sliding them to the backs of my thighs. It was frustrating, my body screaming out for him once more, to resume what he'd started. How was he not in as much agony as I was?

I truly thought he'd completely get off the bed to continue his torture, but he gripped my thighs, forcing my legs apart, and settled between them. One of his hands moved between us, sliding down to my core and pushing his seed back into me, his head lowering to pepper kisses to the crook of my neck. I thought he'd do more, that he'd pleasure me properly with those thick digits, but he pulled them free after only a few moments. I couldn't stop the whine that escaped as my hips rocked back, eager for more. His shushing calmed me, not wanting to spoil anything by rushing him. The other source of my frustration was that his pants were still on, just open and baring his member. At the same time, there was a thrill in being completely naked to his gaze while he still had something to shield the part of his body that he was most self-conscious about. His glistening fingers pressed to my lips, our mixed juices on his skin. I couldn't help how eagerly I parted my lips, drawing them in, suckling and licking them free of every trace of us. Each lick of my tongue, every pull of my hollowed cheeks, drew a groan or curse from Heph.

As soon as his fingers slipped out of my mouth, his hand moved to the back of my head, tangling his hand in my hair. The grip on my hair tightened, wrenching my head back. Heph slanted his mouth over mine as he lifted his hips, his other hand guiding his length into position at my entrance. The force behind that first thrust took my breath away, my eyes watering as my hands clawed at the bed. It was wonderfully painful, more than I had hoped he'd give me once the initial rush of passion had worn off. Would he always be so desperate and demanding of my body? I could only hope so. "More," I gasped out, breaking the kiss. Movement was as difficult as drawing breath right then I learned as I tried and failed to rock my hips against his.

"You're not making demands," he growled into my ear, pulling my hair harder. It wasn't a comfortable angle, but it heightened the pleasure that had my body trembling beneath him. Heph shifted and moved his legs over mine, pressing my legs together as he started a ruthless pace. Each thrust pushed me up on the bed, his hand holding my head back so I could see him and kept pushing me back to where he wanted me. It was a painful dance that I craved more of. I wanted more of his eagerness, that yearning. It was so rough and raw, I needed all of it.

My gaze met his wild eyes, and I made the slightest movement to try to steal a kiss before my face was suddenly buried in the mattress. The hand that had been gripping my hair was suddenly at the back of my neck, pushing my head down and making the struggle to breathe even more difficult. It wasn't at all what I expected him to do. His lips brushed my ear, his hot breath pulling another shiver from me. "Is this what you wanted, little dove? For me to use you? I saw that desperate look on your face the first night I brought you home with me," he growled, giving a particularly rough thrust that had me crying out into the sheets. "All wounded and offering yourself up to me."

Degradation was never a kink I would've pegged him as enjoying. Not that he was being as cruel or insulting right then as he could be. But I could feel that he was holding back. I didn't need my abilities to know that much. One of my hands unclenched from the sheet and moved to brush over his leg, scratching at the material hiding him from me. It was enough to make him grip the sides of my neck and lift my head. Before I could explain anything to him, that pressure that had been building, that high I had been chasing, suddenly erupted. As I drew a gasp of air, it broke and crashed over me. Searing light, electricity, however one wished to describe it, it set my body on fire and left me bucking under him as I screamed his name with my release. He cursed, his thrusts becoming sloppy with how my body pulsed and clenched around his endowment. Heph rested his head against my shoulder as he shuddered, muttering my name in a low growl. The warmth of him filling me was fast becoming a favorite sensation, as was the way his body rested heavily atop mine. This time, he did draw his body free of mine after a few moments.

Rolling onto his side, Heph pulled my body to his, cradling me in his embrace with my back pressed to his chest. He whispered sweet nothings, pressing kisses to the side of my head for a few moments, until my breathing evened out and I stopped trembling. "What were you going to ask for?" he murmured.

"I was going to say that you could say anything to me, and I would enjoy it." It was true. If he was going to take control like that, I wanted him to take it completely. And I wanted everything that he could give me. I turned my head to look at his face when he didn't answer, and I saw a look of confusion and hunger there. "I mean it, my sparrow. Perhaps you do not understand how truly kinky I can be," I teased.

That earned me a laugh. I turned over in his embrace to rest my face against his chest. I longed for as much physical contact as I could get with him. Who knew what would come of my next trial? There would be no more regrets between us. Turning my head, I smiled at the sound of his heart racing in time with mine.

"I will take that into consideration," he replied. I didn't point out that I didn't particularly enjoy bottoming most of the time. That wasn't the moment that I wanted to break with reminders of anyone else that had been in my bed. It was a conversation that could wait. Besides, I was thinking that I might be shifting into the 'switch' category with him.

If anyone could continue to change me for the better, it was definitely him. There were many roles and behaviors I'd likely settle into after spending so much time running from something that was the best path for me. While the way we came to be wasn't the greatest, especially by human standards, I ran from the potential happiness that could've been found with him. Never again.

CHAPTER XIV

IT WAS NEARLY AN hour before either of us wanted to leave the bed. We laid there, my head pressed to his chest, just listening to his heart as his hand made idle paths along my back. When I finally made a move to break free of his embrace, he chuckled and told me to lie still as he released me and carefully set me on the bed. Heph got up and tucked himself back into his pants before limping to the bathroom. He returned with a warm damp cloth, surprising me since I hadn't expected him to clean me up. I grinned up at him as he tossed it aside in the general direction of the bathroom once he was done. "Where are you trying to escape to?" he asked, handing me his discarded shirt.

I slipped it on, buttoning a few of the remaining buttons before sliding to the edge of the bed. My legs were a little unstable, but I could stand without falling over. Though Heph lingered like he would catch me if I tried to lose my balance. "I think I saw a gift from Callie in the kitchen." His brows furrowed in confusion, and I just motioned for him to follow me. Instead, he lifted me, draping me over his shoulder, and carried me laughing into the kitchen. My gaze drifted to his legs, though it was so tempting to stare at his well-formed butt. However, I was more interested in how his limp would disappear whenever he carried me, like his body didn't want to risk dropping me. Was it worth talking to him about? Would it be cruel to point out that the defect he thought he had was entirely in his mind for who knew how many centuries? That was probably a discussion better left for after the honeymoon. If there was an after.

Heph set me on the counter and looked around. "Alright. Where's this gift at?" My silent answer was a glance at a plain white box on the island. It was innocuous enough compared to the other boxes that had been piled in the living room and even a few in the kitchen. I knew there was likely food stuffed in the fridge from her, but the box I had my eye on was one I was familiar with. Whenever I was especially upset, it would appear in whatever room I had barricaded myself in. Without further questioning, he picked up the box and handed it to me, obviously curious at the contents within.

"She always leaves me my favorite treat," I explained, opening the lid, and showing him the variety of macarons within.

"These are your favorites?" I could tell he was filing the information away for later.

"They are. I never quite figured out why, but I fell in love with them the first time I tried them," I explained. Grinning, I picked up a raspberry one with a chocolate filling and held it out for him to try. Though I rarely liked to share them, I wanted to let him have everything I did. Even something I had once been so greedy over, that I refused to let another sample, I wanted him to enjoy it as well. All the things that brought me joy, I wanted them to warm him in the same way.

He took a bite of the macaron, his tongue swiping out to tease along my fingers before standing upright once more. I watched his face, curious about whether he'd enjoy them as much as I did. "Want to take these back to bed?" he asked, his hands resting on my hips. All I could do was nod. I took his question as him enjoying my favorite treat. Without further conversation, he lifted me, and I held the box of treats as he hurried back to the bedroom. Our bedroom. 'Our' was a strange concept to me.

Hopefully, I'd have plenty of time to get used to it. Then the smallest bit of doubt trickled in, wondering if he'd want to keep things separate from one another. What would happen once the honeymoon period was over? I had to remind myself that he wanted me with him, that any time I wasn't in a trial, he would keep me by his side. His embrace, his love, it would have to be enough to drown out that stupid little voice of doubt. For now.

We spent a few hours like that, working our way through Callie's gift and introducing one another to our favorite shows. He was surprised once he started watching mine, and I was amused at how easily he was able to get me into anime. Little moments like that were what I had been dreaming of when I finally realized how much I wanted to make our marriage work. There had been plenty of fear that we would remain married in name only. Or perhaps we would see each other from time to time, maybe scratching an itch, but not trying to build a life together. That was what I wanted with him, to build a life with him, to make a home with him. I wanted to share every passion and secret desire with him, and for him to do the same with me.

My hand played down his stomach as another episode ended, my fingers dipping below the waist of his pants. "Why did you keep these on?" It was something I'd been wondering. While I had an idea, I needed to hear him say it for sure. His gaze met mine before he turned his head away, a soft pink tint to his cheeks.

"You were there when my face was scarred, and they're not really something I could hide if I wanted to," he murmured. I had a feeling that I knew exactly what he was going to say, and it was something that I had feared. Even after everything, he was still hiding from me. "My leg-" he started before I cut him off with a kiss. It was a tender press of my lips to his, silencing whatever self-deprecating thing he was going to tell me. There wasn't an inch of him I could find ugly. Scars were just the story of his painful past etched into his skin.

"Show me. I think I have proven that I am not going anywhere ever again." *At least not by choice.* I didn't add the last. We both knew the possibility that was looming over us. "Please, Heph. I never want you to have this kind of doubt." Despite my plea, he made no move to show me his other scars. I reached for the fastening on his pants and undid it, my gaze going to his face. Each movement was slow, and I paused to give him a chance to stop me. But he didn't. "What is your safe word?" I asked him, though it wasn't the sort of situation one would need it for. I still believed in sharing it, for any time that the experience became too intense for one person or the other.

"Iron." It was simple enough. Though it wouldn't work well if we ever had a 24/7 dynamic. For now, it would do just what we needed. "Yours?" His voice sounded a little strained, his breathing labored. If it hadn't been for the panic in his eyes, I would've thought that he was just excited by my undressing him. My hand brushed his length as I carefully lowered his zipper, perhaps it was a bit of both considering the firmness that nudged against my knuckles.

"Kobol." It was a tie-in to my nerdiness, and I likely wouldn't forget it if I had a moment of panic.

"Kobold?" he asked. Of course, he'd make the connection to a certain tabletop game.

"No. Kobol, no 'd'. It is less fantasy, more sci-fi," I explained with a grin. The conversation was at least relaxing for him. The tension in his body eased, an amused smirk on his lips as he lifted his hips and allowed me to drag his pants down his legs. As I reached his knees, his breath hitched, but he didn't ask me to stop. I kept my gaze on his face as I pulled them free of his body and tossed them to the floor with my ruined dress. All that tension that I had helped him ease was back, his hands trembling as he grabbed the sheets. Slowly, I lowered my gaze, lingering on his half-hard erection, enjoying the fact that he was all mine and I had free rein to touch him. When I glanced down at his previously injured leg, there were a few thick scars decorating his thigh, growing larger and more numerous as my gaze trailed down to his calf. They tapered off into thinner scars around his ankle and over the top of his foot where they were fainter.

For a moment, I considered touching them with my hand, but as soon as I raised it, he flinched. Instead, I gave him a reassuring smile before leaning forward to brush my lips across his scarred thigh. My tongue darted out, tracing the smooth edge of each one before I moved my mouth down to do the same to the rest of his scars. As I made my way down to the top of his foot, he relaxed more and more, gifting me little grunts and sighs of pleasure. I rolled my eyes up to see his expression as I pressed a kiss to the scars atop his foot, my gaze not able to move past how hard and thick his length had gotten. "All for me?" I breathed against his skin. I'd hoped to ease his anxiety over showing me the physical trauma of his fall, and I had succeeded. At least for one night. It was our wedding night. The last thing I wanted was for him to feel any shame.

Then again, it was also my wedding night. I sat up and back on my feet, a mischievous smile playing over my lips. "Can you make a set of restraints for me?" I asked, my fingers playing over his scarred calf.

"Why?" he asked, suspicion dripping from the question.

"Because I wish to try something with you." I figured he might have thought it a trick, but I hoped that sharing my preferences for such times with him would help ease that. Perhaps something simpler than I might normally choose, until he could fully trust me.

"I need more information than that, Dite." That was fair.

My teeth worried at my lower lip as I got up from the bed and went to his dresser. Would I find what I needed? Barely, was the answer. He had two ties. It would be enough. "How about these until you trust me with something sturdier?" Though he would've been able to remove the restraints with his powers more easily than I would've, I understood the hesitation.

He eyed the ties in my hand before nodding slightly. It was the best I was going to get. "You can stop this at any time," I reminded him as I crawled back onto the bed and he sat up against the headboard. I settled in his lap and claimed his lips as I reached for one of his hands. He didn't fight me as I broke the kiss and lifted his arm to tie the decorative material around his wrist. The tie wouldn't truly restrain him, not with his strength, but I still didn't bind it tightly to the headboard. It took an immense amount of trust for him to let me restrain him like that, trust that I hadn't earned properly. Yet.

I repeated the action with his other wrist, giving him a tender kiss after as thanks for letting me. "Tell me your safe word again," I commanded softly. I shifted forward, letting him feel my arousal against his shaft, teasing both of us with a shuddering sigh.

"Iron," he growled between clenched teeth. His length twitched against the apex of my thighs, his hands clenched into fists. I met his darkening gaze and was relieved that there was no more anxiety left in his expression.

"Good boy," I murmured, as my hand came up to grip his chin. The coarseness of his beard tickling my hand just made my smile widen as my fingers dug into his flesh. It earned me a moan from him. My other hand slid between us, pumping him a few times as I kissed him, eating the groan that had left his throat. The kiss was as rough as the grip I had on his face, all teeth and tongue claiming his mouth. I knew that our lips would be swollen, my face burned from his beard, and I longed for it. My body still ached from how roughly he'd taken me the last round. Yet I needed more. I wanted to never let the ache of his body in mine fade. I needed that constant reminder that he could and would have me whenever and however he wanted, and I him.

As much as I might want to tease him, I didn't want to draw out my own torment. I lifted onto my knees and guided his member into position. My hand on his length released him and tangled in his fiery hair instead. I loved that it was long enough to grip, to bury my hands in. With a shift of my hips, I took the head of his length into me, breaking the kiss as I wrenched his head back with a tug of his hair. The hand I had on his chin moved down, dragging my nails in harsh lines down his chest. "I always knew you would look so pretty tied up," I purred, my body lowering slowly to take more of him in.

His answer was a frustrated growl, his arms tugging at the restraints. Apparently, I was moving too slowly for him. That was the point, of course. Though it was growing irritating for me as well. I'd only taken half of him so far and I needed more as much as he did. I moved my hand from his chest and gently gripped his throat as I dropped my hips roughly to take the rest of him into me. My hand stifled his pleasured sound as it tightened around his throat, my lips parting to let out a cry of his name. The burning and stinging pain was exactly what I had wanted. For a moment, I wondered if I had hurt him with anything I was doing, but his hips bucked up impatiently. "You are not in control," I growled at him, reminding him of what he'd told me earlier. We both knew it wasn't true, both times. The submissive always held the power. At least as long as the dominant wasn't a piece of shit.

He stilled his hips. As much as I wanted to ride him roughly, I rocked my hips slowly, raising them slightly as they made a lazy circular motion and dropped back down. It was a pleasant sensation, but I knew it wasn't what either of us needed. It was a pleasurable form of torture for us both. I slid my hand from his throat, down to the scattering of coarse, dark red hair decorating his chest. My lips slanted over his again as the hand I had in his hair tugged roughly as I gave into what we both wanted. I wasn't one for self-control, apparently, not like I usually would be. So, I rode him hard, my hips rising and falling at a quick and relentless pace. Each rotation of my hips dragged my clit against the trimmed rough curls that decorated around the base of his cock. A light sheen of sweat coated my skin as I wrenched his head back harder. Our moans and curses mingled together as I broke the kiss. I wanted to see his eyes, I wanted to watch his face as I pleasured him.

"Dite, wait. I'm not gonna last," he ground out, but it just made me smile at the admission. He knew that if he wanted me to stop, he could say his safe word. So, I took it as what he meant it to be: a warning. My answer was to lower my head and mark the skin at the crook of his neck, biting down and sucking at the tender flesh. His hips bucked up, his head falling back against my hand that cushioned it from hitting the headboard. My name was a ragged sigh on his lips. I moved my hips so my clit was pressed to him more firmly with every movement of my hips, chasing my own building release. With a cry of his name, I followed him over that precipice, my vision going white for a few moments as my body stilled against his. I didn't register that his hands were free or that he saved me from falling back. All I knew was that he was cradling me against him, and he'd slid down in the bed so he was laying completely beneath me rather than sitting up against the headboard as he had been. Panting, I gave a lazy smile as I nuzzled my face against his chest, not wanting to move off him in any way just yet.

His hand rubbed in gentle circles over my back, his lips pressed to the top of my head. "Next time you ask for something, I'll give it to you," he said, the smile on his face creeping into his voice.

"Thank you," I murmured. My body was tired, I was tired. So much had happened in such a short time, and I had finally worn myself out.

Perhaps he sensed that I didn't want to let him go just yet, so Heph gently rolled us over and slid his softening member free of my aching core. He cleaned me up once more and tucked us beneath the covers before turning off the light. The TV was on, volume low, and something I couldn't recognize or care about at the moment was playing. His body wrapped around mine, drawing me back against his chest. I had never been a big fan of spooning, but we fit together perfectly. Heph made me feel small and dainty in the curve of his body, cradled with a thick muscled arm across my stomach. The warmth radiating from his body, the firmness of him at my back, the safe feeling I had every time he held me, lulled me to sleep. I was home, at long last.

CHAPTER XV

My hands trembled as I pushed the earring backing against the back of my ear and let out a shaky breath. Heph's strong calloused hands slid over my shoulders, smiling at me in the mirror. "Want me to come with you?" he asked as he ducked his head to press a kiss to my cheek. "I'm sure they're happy to see you, no matter what." What he wasn't saying, thankfully, was that he could tell that I was being overwhelmed by my nerves.

We'd spent a week in bed, creating our own little nerdy paradise sprinkled with all the spice and nefarious fun we could think of. And when I'd asked if he minded me going to see my children, he'd been more than happy to pause our honeymoon for me to do so. Even though my children were a physical reminder of everything that had happened between us, he wanted to accompany me. How was his heart so full of kindness after what I had put him through? He was ever thoughtful and doting. I could only imagine the type of father he would've made had I given him the chance. A pang of regret stabbed at my stomach, the taste bitter on my tongue. I couldn't live in what might've been, could've been. There was no changing it. Heph seemed to let it go. I needed to do the same.

"Dite?" he murmured, his arms wrapping around my waist from behind. I realized I was so caught up with my thoughts that I hadn't answered him yet.

"Yes, please." I managed a smile as I turned in his arms and rested my hands and cheek on his chest. Was it cowardly to depend on him to help me? Perhaps. "Only if you will not find it difficult to do." It wasn't fair to ask him to spend all that time searching out for and with my children that I'd had with his brother.

He sighed, one of his hands rising to cradle my face and turn it up to meet his gaze. "I know what you're afraid of. I came to terms with you having them a long time ago. If my going with you today helps you, then I'm more than happy to do it. Besides, they should get used to me being around more. Eros is the only one I really know."

That was not what I was expecting him to say. "Eros? You spend time with Eros?" Heph seemed to enjoy the surprise on my face.

"Yes, little dove, I do. I ran into him at a convention. We've stayed in contact since then. Occasionally, he'll drag me online to play games with him." Was that why Eros hadn't stayed to talk to either of us? While he'd said that the mortal with him needed to return home, I couldn't help but wonder if he had wanted to keep his friendship with Heph to himself.

"I never knew." I wasn't ashamed to admit when I wasn't aware of something, at least not anymore. It wasn't a blow to my ego anymore to have to admit that I was wrong. "I am glad that you two have some sort of amicable relationship. Perhaps that visit will be the easiest," I murmured. And it happened to be the visit I had planned to make first.

It would've been so much more difficult without Heph by my side. My palm was sweaty against his as we approached the darkly colored door. Was it too late to beg off and drag him back to bed? Probably. As much as he would enjoy that, I knew he wouldn't let me. So, I raised my free hand and knocked on the door. It was the only option and something I should've done a long time ago. I was ashamed that I had put off fixing the broken relationship I had with my children for so long. Fixing myself was important, but they hadn't deserved the sporadic messages and lack of visits.

"Breathe," Heph reminded me softly. He pressed a quick kiss to the top of my head, his other hand gripping the top of his cane with a force I was glad he wasn't using on my hand. It was the only sign I had that he was nervous in his own way. Was he worried he'd lose Eros as a friend because we'd reconciled? Or, rather, fixed our marriage?

"I am," I answered as I lifted my hand to knock again. From inside, I could hear a familiar voice cursing and some sounds of struggling. As much as those sounds concerned me, I knew Eros could handle whatever came his way. One thing I had done was ensure that all my children could defend themselves. Whether I showed them, helped them take advantage of their abilities, or guided them to sparring with their father, I knew that none of them were defenseless.

The door swung open with more force than was probably necessary. Eros stood there, his hair mussed and tangled, face red, his chest and shoulders decorated with red lines, and wearing pants that were too tight and far too short to be his own. The borrowed pants were practically indecent, and I had to look away quickly. Perhaps my face showed how hard I was trying not to burst into laughter because he looked down and cursed. "Aleister!" he bellowed over his shoulder. A masculine laugh sounded and a feminine face with messy strawberry blonde hair peeking around the corner. As soon as the first giggle came from her as she ducked back from view, I couldn't stop my laughter. It was an amusing sight, and I could feel all my nerves wash away with the laughter that had me struggling to stand upright. Clinging to Heph, I gave into the boisterous and mirthful sound until I could barely draw a breath.

"Nice pants. I don't think that's really the style. Most people don't want to risk getting the cops called because they can't fit their dick in their pants," Heph teased beside me. His face showed just how much he was struggling not to laugh with me. Though he did lose the battle as a few chuckles escaped that he tried to hide with a cough.

"Man, shut up. Come in," Eros grumbled as he turned and walked away. I assumed he was in search of wherever his pants had been left behind. We stepped inside, closing the door behind us. I couldn't help looking around, seeing what had changed since the last time I had made a brief visit to Eros's home. It was still dark and simple, masculine. But there were touches of a darker almost Victorian taste, and a feminine one that enjoyed cool pastels. Interesting combination, but it somehow worked.

I had let go of Heph's hand to look around a bit more. The sound of clothes rustling preceded Eros's return. The mortal female and tattooed male I had seen with him at the wedding followed behind him. I set the pale blue pillow I'd been admiring back down on the couch and smiled at my son. "It is lovely to see you in clothes again," I teased him. He grumbled as he walked over, pulling me into a hug. If Heph dwarfed me, Eros made me feel like an absolute child with how tall he was. Heph was closer to 6'3" while Eros was around 6'8". They dwarfed me and the other woman in the room. Even the third male was just a couple of inches shorter than Heph.

"Still as funny as ever, mom," he huffed. "I didn't get to introduce you at the wedding." Was he nervous? As soon as he released me, he'd started rubbing at the back of his neck and tugging at the plain black tee he was wearing. All signs were pointing to him indeed being nervous. My gaze flitted to the two at his back that each put a hand on his arms to try and calm him. The male at his back was wearing the pants that Eros had tried to pour himself into before. I heard Heph cough to cover his chuckle when he noticed the same thing. "This is Aleister," he murmured, motioning to the male that stepped up to his left side.

"Pleasure," he drawled in a voice that was so deep it seemed as though it should be painful. "You're even lovelier than the rumors said you'd be." The male was definitely charming, but I could sense something about Aleister that I knew would anger quite a few people in our family. Still, I let him take my hand, giving a polite kiss to my knuckles that made me believe he was older than I originally thought.

"A pleasure for me as well, Aleister. And this lovely creature?" I took my hand back and motioned to the strawberry blonde still behind Eros on his right side.

THE TRIALS OF APHRODITE

Aleister and Eros drew her between them, each taking one of her hands. "Mom, this is Perdy," Eros introduced her. I smiled at the three of them, especially when a deep flush spread over her pale freckled skin.

"Perdita," she corrected softly as her fingers twitched against their hands. That reminded me that I had seen them signing with her at the wedding.

It wasn't something I had done in a long time, but I could manage well enough. I signed as I answered her, hoping I wasn't too rusty. "Perdita, a lovely name for a lovely mortal." I couldn't help a laugh when her flushed cheeks darkened even more. "Perhaps we should sit and talk about why we interrupted your...fun?" As I finished my sentence, I truly thought that Perdita was going to pass out with how dark her skin had flushed in embarrassment.

The two males on either side of her chuckled and did their best to reassure her, guiding her onto the couch between them. Heph and I took our seats as well, and I was back to being nervous about the visit. The warmth and comfort that Heph's hand provided helped me to catch my breath. By the time I was ready to speak, Perdy had calmed down and each of the men sitting with her had wrapped an arm behind her on the back of the couch. I bit back a smile at how Aleister played with Eros's hair. I couldn't remember the last time I had seen my son so relaxed and content with another person. For the happiness that the two seemed to bring him, I could forgive Aleister for his origins.

"What's up, mom? I'm happy to see you, but I figured you'd be on your honeymoon still. You're not really one to drop by unannounced." Eros wasn't wrong. I normally would give ample warning. But I needed to get there quickly before my nerves won out. How could I tell him what was about to happen?

"I know. I apologize for interrupting you, all of you. But I need to see you and your siblings before the last day of the death season." That got his attention. Even Aleister had managed to pull his gaze from their mortal lover to look at me curiously.

"Why? What's going on?" Eros wasn't calm any longer. He was doing his best to conceal the panic that only his eyes and breath showed. I didn't fault him for his concern. Mentioning death season generally meant something tragic was going to happen or had happened.

How could I tell him? I couldn't back out though. I was in his home, and I had shared enough to make him worry. It had to be done. He needed to know, all my children did. And perhaps it was better since he had his lovers there to help him. "You know how I have been undergoing trials?"

"Yeah, though I don't know why you're still doing them. You've proved to the rest of the pantheon that you're serious about Uncle Heph." It was a strange title to hear, but I wouldn't be distracted.

"I appreciate hearing that. But I agreed to seven trials. Even if I have managed to prove myself, I am bound to the contract that was struck. If I tried to end things now, I would have to let Heph go." Heph's hand tightened around mine and I reached with my other hand to pat his. That caused enough of a reaction that I wouldn't share the other outcome that would happen if I tried to back out. "I apologize, did I need to sign for Perdita?"

"Oh! It's more of a habit. I still have some hearing left in my right ear, so I can follow along. But my ex was completely deaf, and I still sign whenever I talk," the mortal explained. That eased my concern and a bit of guilt as well.

My lips parted to ask why neither of them had done anything to heal her ears, but it wasn't my place. Besides, they all seemed happy with how things were. The love I could feel between the three of them comforted me. Even if something were to happen to me, his two loves would be there for him. "The next trial is going to be especially difficult."

"It's not like you to drag things out like this, mom. What is it?" Eros's voice rose a bit in pitch, the panic peeking through.

"I have to face your father in combat. We begin on the last day of the death season. I have to survive until midnight, when the gates of Tartarus close." Defeating Ares wasn't even an option. Maybe once upon a time we might've tied, but I was not the warrior I once was.

All of the color drained from Eros's face. Perdy seemed confused for a moment, as did Aleister, but when they looked at Eros, understanding seemed to dawn on them. "His father is Ares, right?" Perdy asked as Aleister got up from the couch and knelt in front of Eros.

Once more, Heph's hand tightened, and I glanced over to see his jaw clench. "Yes," I murmured in reply, squeezing his hand.

"Why? Why didn't you back out?" Eros growled. He gently nudged Aleister away and stood, walking around the coffee table to stand in front of me. Just as I was getting ready to stand, he fell to his knees and buried his face against my stomach, his arms wrapped around me. Heph released my hand that he'd been gripping. I placed one hand on the back of Eros's head and the other made small comforting circles on his upper back. "Why would you risk this? I wanted your blessing when we figured out. . ." His words were cut off with a sob. My large, strong, handsome son had been reduced to tears at the thought of my facing his father when the possibility of death was still a very real risk.

"The agreement was always that I would do whatever task Hera wanted without question. I believe her original plan had been a battle to the death. It would have already taken place if she had had her way. Heph convinced her to change it." Still, it was a difficult thing to do, to face off in battle against Ares of all people.

And Hera hadn't been happy about the compromise. It was one reason I was still surprised that she'd let us get married, or have another ceremony at least.

"You can't do this," he sobbed out, his strong arms pulling me to the edge of the seat as he buried his face against my blouse. I shushed him, trying to comfort him, but I was at a loss. The last time I had seen Eros so out of sorts, he was a small boy and had watched Ares storm out after we had one of our usual arguments.

It wasn't fair to him, to any of my children. How would they be able to face their father if he was able to kill me? I thought I was being merciful by going to them first, in case the worst happened, to give them a warning. Would it have been kinder to not tell them? Would it have been easier for them to go on blissfully unaware unless the worst came to pass? It wasn't an easy decision to make. Every time I thought I was doing the right thing for my children, I seemed to fuck something up royally.

Perhaps I looked as lost as I felt because his two lovers came over to kneel at his back, helping me to comfort him. By the time Eros lifted his head, his tears had dried, and his face was back to its usual stoic expression. If the news reduced my powerful giant of a son to a blubbering mess, I could only imagine how some of my other children would fare when they heard.

I looked over at Heph and saw the pain in his face; the sadness filling his eyes. He was worried, and my concern was that he would do something foolish. That was a problem for later. Right then, my concern was Eros. "Shush. My sweet boy. I will refresh my skills by training with Lola. You have forgotten my past battles already?" My voice was light, a faux smile on my lips. But I was doing my best to appear calm, like I wasn't terrified at the prospect of leaving everyone I loved behind. Eros still looked upset, but he shook his head. He remembered I had once been a warrior. Hopefully, it was enough to bide my time until death season was over. "Now, tell me all about your two loves," I demanded softly, wanting to focus on happier things. Hearing the story of how my son had come to love a mostly deaf mortal, and a demon was much more important than my impending doom.

And that was what we focused on. The reason for my visit was still lingering over us, but we were able to try to pretend it was a normal day of catching up. With how tightly Eros hugged me as we tried to leave after hearing all about Aleister and Perdy, I knew he would likely warn his siblings and try to formulate a plan. It wasn't something he could stop, but I really hoped he wouldn't cause himself trouble by trying.

I was right that he had warned his other siblings. Adrestia had fallen into my arms sobbing when I went to see her and Harmonia. Phobos and Deimos had tried to keep their stoic faces, a habit that took after Eros, but they'd dissolved into tears and smothered me between them. Aeneas had just quietly hugged me, unable to find the words to express his anguish. Pothos, Anteros, and Himeros had similar reactions to their other siblings. It pained me to cause them so much turmoil, to cause them such worry. I was still torn over whether or not I had made the right decision. There was a good chance I could survive, I didn't have to worry them over something that was not likely to come to pass. Then again, with how furious Ares was at the wedding, the chances of my impending doom were increasing by the moment. I wouldn't let regret cloud the memories of one last visit with each of my children or the rest of the honeymoon I still had with Heph.

It wasn't how I wanted to patch my relationships with my children, but it was a start. If I survived, when I survived, I'd see them all again and fix what I broke between us. I couldn't leave them with doubt about my love for them, and I refused to miss out on the important events still to come in their lives. Any of them.

CHAPTER XVI

"Dammit, Dite!" Heph slammed his cane down on the table before turning to face me. We'd been arguing since we got back from seeing the last of my children. Apparently watching the tearful reunions and their worry over my going up against Ares had reignited his anger. He wanted me to back out, to call Hera's bluff. I believed that she would do everything in her power to separate us. Heph didn't. That was not the hill I wanted to die on, but I couldn't back out. Not if I wanted to keep him. And then there was the part I had yet to share with him. It would just cause another fight with him, but I rather try and soothe him, not to let him know that there was a risk of death whether I faced Ares or not.

"You know that I cannot do that! If I do, she will do everything she can to make sure that I never see you again. This was the deal. You knew that from the beginning. If I could stop this, if I could prevent you from suffering through this with me, I would. Perhaps it would have been kinder to go through this alone, to reconcile with you after," I murmured. I watched Hephaestus, watched his slow steps over to me, the trembling in his hands, the anger clashing with the pain on his face. He stopped just out of reach, like he didn't trust himself to touch me. I wondered if he did touch me, that he might whisk us away to hide from Hera and the set date for the next trial. "I know I have not earned your trust, but I will do everything I possibly can to make sure that I return to you once more. As much as I do not want to spend a moment away from you, I will do some training with Lola to ensure that I am able to at least fend him off until midnight." Would I take the coward's way out and merely run from him? No, I wouldn't dishonor Heph like that. He hesitated for a moment before grabbing me, crushing me to his chest.

"You're my only weakness, little dove. I don't fear falling again, I don't fear the flames that scarred me. All I fear is losing you or you waking up tomorrow and realizing that this was all a mistake. I look at you sometimes and I fully expect you to tell me that all this between us has been a form of punishment for humiliating you or sullying something of yours. That you made me believe I could finally taste paradise, wrap it around myself, and then you would take it away. But that moment passes, and I realize that you really care about me, you're here. And I would slaughter every pantheon if it meant that you would stay here with me. I would annihilate anyone foolish enough to try and take you from me."

My chest felt heavy, aching, and tight with all the emotions his words stirred in me. I didn't blame him for not fully trusting me yet, for having those doubts. I earned his suspicion. But I was glad that he was able to work through those on his own, that he realized just how much I wanted to be there with him. "I do not care for you, Heph." His face fell and I shushed him, my hand quickly moving to cradle his cheek. "That word will never be enough. I love you. I die every time I think of the pain that I caused you. And every touch, every kiss you grant me, breathes life back into me. While I have spent years washing away the doubts I had about myself, you managed to burn the last traces from me. Self-loathing, regret, jealousy... It all fades away with you. Every day it is easier to breathe, to look in the mirror, to think about the future we will have together. And never doubt me, Heph, we will have that future. I will face Ares. I will stay alive until the death season has passed, and we will continue building our future together."

"You can't go. What if he was to... No. If you lose, I will shatter the doors of Tartarus, deathless season or not. Let Hades or Than put me in a cell beside you. But I will not lose you again. I will not let you go without a fight," he vowed, his large hands gripping mine and placing them over his chest.

"Foolish sparrow. You think I will go into Than's embrace without a fight?" I tried to smile through the silent tears, my hands clinging to his shirt.

"If you lose, I will slaughter my brother. I will crush anyone that stands between me and getting you back." While I knew he meant it, the gods didn't really return after their death. Hades' presumed death and return had been out of the ordinary. Then again, there was a story there that was far too complicated to even think about at the moment. He was back and Seph didn't have to bear his responsibilities alone anymore. It was partially the reason that the deathless season had been enforced. While it had happened occasionally before, their reunion cemented it.

None of that meant that I would be able to be brought back if I were to die at Ares' hand. "I know you would. Just as I would rip apart the heavens to find you. There is not a space anywhere that I would leave unsearched if you were to be taken from me. Let the universe crumble as all the gods are slaughtered for coming between us. Let the stars fall from the heavens, let existence cease. It is the only way that I will be kept from you again." I watched his face, let him search my expression for all the sincerity I felt, the truth behind my words. My chest ached as the tears he'd been struggling to hold back fell, my hand trembling as I wiped them away, caressing the scarred skin. "There is something I have been keeping from you though."

He stiffened against me, suspicion clouding his expression once more. "What is it?"

"There is another reason I cannot back out besides your mother swearing to tear us apart." I felt his breath quicken, that anxiety taking over again. If I had kept it from him for as long as I had, it had to be truly terrible. "The day I went to her office, to beg her to help me find you, she had me prove my sincerity."

"How?" he growled out. But there was only one way at the time. I knew that he knew. He wanted me to say it, to admit what I had done. Aloud.

Chewing at my lower lip, I let out a shuddering breath. "I swore by the ichor." Heph immediately stepped away, his fist put through the nearest wall as he roared in frustration. "It was the only way, my sparrow. As much as I suspected she would try to kill me with the trials, I refused to back down or give her a reason to keep you from me." But I didn't go to him. I didn't think he'd hurt me, I just didn't want to upset him more by touching him before he was ready for me to. His body trembled with rage as he hit the wall again and again. With one sentence I had shattered his hope that he might be able to drag me to safety, that he might be able to talk me out of facing his brother in a potential battle to the death. Whatever hope of being my hero that he'd had was gone. And I felt worse for having taken it from him. "I wanted to keep you from worrying even more. If you knew, I feared that you would be even more upset. I should never have kept it from you for so long."

He held a hand up and anything else I might have said was silenced. We stood there, his ragged breathing the only sound as I waited for his decision on how things would go from there. Either he'd allow me to beg forgiveness, or he'd take his leave. The latter scared me, but I knew that he'd return. I just wouldn't know when. Though perhaps there was a third option I hadn't thought of yet. "After everything we've shared, that we've moved past, you still didn't trust me enough to tell me this last secret. Is there anything else you haven't shared?"

"No." It was true. I shared every dark secret I held with him, every detail that he could stomach. We laid everything bare. And yet I had withheld something from him even then. He was right to be furious. Especially given the gravity of the situation. I'd kept a vital detail from him. What if he'd given into his desire and hidden me away? My death would've happened anyways because I'd broken my vow to Hera. His reaction was completely justified.

I refused to squirm under his gaze as he turned to look at me. "I want to believe you. I need to if this is ever going to work." Just when I began to earn his trust again, I proved that I truly was unworthy of it. It was truly fitting, very like me. "But I won't waste what time we have left being mad at you." There was a slip of the tongue, but I wasn't going to correct him or point it out. I was just grateful that he wasn't going to walk out and leave me wondering if he was going to return or not.

Wrapped up in my relief, I was late to react to his approach. Without warning, his hand grabbed a fistful of my hair and yanked my head back. I couldn't hold back my gasp or whimper. It was like everything was moving quicker than I could register. Like every other time he'd chosen to dominate me, I quickly was able to switch into the headspace for it, the pain heightening my pleasure.

His other hand grabbed my face, his fingers digging harshly into my cheeks. "Open your fucking mouth," he growled. There was no hesitation as I quickly obeyed. It wasn't just that I was reacting to his anger, it had been that way every time he wanted to dominate. He made me submit in ways I never had before. Every other time, not that there had been many, I didn't play the role well. With him, bratting didn't even occur to me until after the fun had ceased. Perhaps that would change going forward, to resist his commands even a little, but I wasn't ready to do it just yet. It was strange for me to enjoy submitting so completely, but I did. Just as much as I enjoyed when it was my turn to make him submit.

I knew what was coming but I was thrilled by the idea of him doing it. No one had dared to do such a thing before after all. I watched him with bated breath as he nudged his nose against mine, drawing out the anticipation. It was just another way to exert his control, but I would stand there like that for as long as it took. Just as I was resigning myself to it, he spat into my waiting mouth, fingers digging harder into my skin. "Swallow it." As soon as I did, he released my face and hair, picking me up and turning me to the wall. His hand cradled the back of my head as he pushed me against it, using the surface to help him brace us as he ripped at my clothes. "Don't think that's the end of it. I plan on making you very sorry for what you did for the rest of the night." A thrill went through me at the idea of him drawing out the small bouts of kinky sex we had had. I wanted him to tease me, to punish me, to leave his lessons on my skin.

Just as quickly as he'd started, he stopped. Half my clothes had been ripped and thrown to the floor when he suddenly let me go , a devious glint in his eyes. I couldn't help wrapping my arms over my bare chest.

Wordlessly, he grabbed my arms and shoved them down before turning me to face the wall, pinning them to my sides. He roughly pushed me against it, his body pressing into mine. "I don't think you understand your situation yet," he grunted against my neck.

"Help me understand," I breathed in answer.

I felt the smile that briefly curled over his lips against my skin. "Oh, I plan to, princess. You think you understand pain and exhaustion? Not even fucking close. I'll show you the true meaning of those words," he promised, the gruff sound of his voice sending another shiver through me. I wanted him to make me truly understand, I wanted him to use me until I was a blubbering mess barely clinging to consciousness. And that didn't scare me in the least. It felt freeing. I had never trusted someone enough to give them that much control or freedom with my body before. But I trusted him with that and so much more. It wasn't something I would second guess. It just was.

He did something that I couldn't see, one of his hands releasing my arm before running his fingers between my cheeks, something cool and slick coating them. It drew another gasp from me, my hips instinctively trying to push back. "Stay still," he commanded. I didn't want to, but I pressed my hips forward against the wall, willing them not to seek out his fingers. One of those thick coarse digits gently nudged and rubbed at the puckered entrance he'd yet to try before. I was surprised for a moment given all the other ways we'd had one another.

More of that cool liquid slid down my lower back and down to meet his exploring fingers. I didn't notice the whimpers that were escaping as he slowly worked one finger in. While he'd wanted to be rough and show me pain, I understood why he was taking his time prepping me. He'd never done it before, and I could appreciate him wanting the first time he did it to be pleasant for us both. The last thing I was going to tell him right then was that he didn't need to worry about prepping me so much. But I didn't, for two reasons. One, he was supposed to be in control for the most part, and two, I wasn't going to remind him of any past lovers when he was vulnerable like that. Even afterwards, I would be careful with how I told him that I would enjoy the pain of it should he want to give it to me.

All I could manage were little whimpers of his name and pleas for him not to tease me. Soft apologies sounded as I braced my hands against the wall, my nails scratching at the gray paint. It was torture, him being so attentive and sweet. And I knew that he wasn't just doing it out of care, it was also so he could drag out my need, make me beg him for any sort of relief. Was that it? Did he want me to beg? There were worse things I could try. He managed to fit one finger inside me, barely pressing the second against my entrance when I decided to do it. "Please, I need more."

He stopped, his hand that had still been on my other arm rose to grab my hair again, wrenching my head back. "You need more? You're in no position to be making demands, little dove. But amuse me. Tell me what you need."

"You," I gasped out, low moans crawling up my throat.

"Not good enough. You'll have to do much better than that or I'll tie you to the bed and make you watch me take care of myself. Would you like that?"

"No, please." The image was incredibly hot but was just too much torture to bear right then. I didn't want him to stop touching me. That particular punishment could wait for another night. "I want you inside me."

His exasperated sigh made me worry he'd stop working that second finger into me, that he'd step away and make good on his threat. "Last chance. Ask properly or you won't be getting anything." He was far more forgiving than I had anticipated, or perhaps he didn't want to make good on his threat either. I wasn't going to test that theory.

I had no choice but to give in. "Please," I whimpered. "I need you, your cock, your fingers, everything. Fill me, fuck me, tear me, own me." Whatever else I might have added to my plea was cut off with a scream as he replaced his fingers with his length. I could tell he'd coated it in the same liquid, but there was still searing pain as he pushed into me. Not far, but enough to give me just what I wanted. Involuntary tears sprang to my eyes, but I wanted that. I wanted him to use me until mascara ran down my cheeks and what was left of my makeup was smeared to ruin.

"Don't cry when you asked for it," he murmured, but I could see the concern on his features. He was suddenly worried he'd gone too far. I didn't want to shatter the moment by reminding him that I hadn't used my safe word, but I needed to reassure him all the same.

"Thank you, sir. I can take more." That was probably the best way I could share those bits of information with him. He took them at face value, slipping back into his rougher persona and shoving his hips forward. The hand that had been prepping me was resting on my hip, but as he pushed and shoved his way into me, he slid it between me and the wall, finding the apex of my thighs. While he was making good on what I'd asked him for, he did indeed want me to enjoy it still. That caring part of him didn't seem to be able to be suppressed completely when he went into dom mode. His fingers slid between my folds, rubbing along them, and barely brushing my clit. Perhaps I had given him too much credit, the torture would continue apparently.

As he fully sheathed himself inside me, he pinched my clit, the dual sensation causing me to cry out his name. "Good fucking girl. But you made me work so hard for it." His hand between my thighs slapped that bundle of nerves, bringing another cry from me. But he knew that it wasn't a pained cry from the way my body soaked his hand as it returned to torturing me with idle touches. "You're not supposed to be enjoying this," he growled. The hand in my hair lowered to my throat, pressing on the sides with a firm steady pressure he knew I loved. Breathing wasn't an option but I didn't want it, I wanted him to manipulate my body in every way he'd figured out and every way he wanted to try.

Without warning, his hips pulled back before slamming forward, starting a vigorous and ruthless pace. The hand between my thighs pinched and rubbed at my clit, his hand on my throat squeezing down harder. All the sensations were swirling together and I wouldn't last long. He used the grip on my throat to pull my head back enough to claim my lips. The sting of his beard on my skin was pushing me over the edge. Whether it was the lack of oxygen or the cacophony of stimulation, as soon as that building pressure exploded, I lost consciousness. I was taken from that wonderful combination of pain and pleasure, and given a thrilling and electric abyss to drown in.

As his hand released my throat, or perhaps it was a few moments later, I wasn't sure, I gulped and choked down as much air as I could take. My body was aching and yet, I craved more. It took longer than I cared to admit for my eyes to readjust. When I was capable of coherent thought once more, he was carefully walking us back to our room. Were his legs unsteady? Later, I could revel in that. I was too preoccupied with the memory of him telling me that he had every intention of dragging out my punishment for the rest of the night. I wasn't sure if I'd be able to move, let alone walk the next day, but I wasn't sure I cared either. Losing all use of my body at his hands seemed like a pleasant way to go.

Hephaestus set me down on the bed before discarding the last of our clothing that had managed to survive his initial wave of ferocity. I wasn't sure what else he might have in mind, but I was eager to find out, to offer up every bit of myself. He could have my body, my soul, everything. I just wanted him to continue touching me, using me, taking out all his frustrations on me. But I also knew that these were new experiences for him that he would have to take some time to work up to more extreme activities. Until then, I wanted to encourage him to explore the things he was comfortable with attempting. I just had to carefully do so; I wouldn't want to risk taking him out of that headspace again. So, for the moment, I enjoyed watching him looming over me, taking in the look of concentration and admiration on his face.

He took a quick break from venting his frustrations on my body to clean us both up a bit before he grabbed my arms and shifted me further up the bed. Before I could ask what he had in mind, Heph flipped me onto my stomach. I was sensing a pattern. "Safe word?" he grumbled against my ear as he pressed his body to my back. Since he hadn't confirmed it before, a thrill went through me with the confirmation that he was raising the intensity level.

"Kobol," I quickly replied, unable to keep the smile off my face. The mirthful expression earned the barest tap to my cheek. The hesitation he showed, the insecurity, I wanted to erase it all. Perhaps I could unleash a little of the brat that I had picked up over the years. "Your mother hit harder than that. Sir," I added with a challenging tone. As if to imply that he might not deserve such a title. It had the desired effect, though he did stop to look at me first to gauge whether or not I was still trying to play the twisted games he'd started. Whatever he saw on my face seemed to be the right thing because he pulled my head back by my hair with one hand as the other smacked my cheek. It was harder, but not quite as forceful or painful as what Hera had done. Not that I minded completely, I just wanted to get enough of a rise out of him so he'd stop questioning himself. He knew what I was okay with, but it felt like he wasn't sure if he was allowed to do those things to me. "Thank you, sir. May I have another?" It was worth the deep rumbling laugh he gave as he smacked my cheek once more.

"I have a better place to hit you." With that, he released me, practically shoving me forward and disappearing from view. Anticipation and excitement thrummed through me as I waited for him to return. After a few moments, he returned and knelt on the bed between my parted legs. His power brushed over my bare skin, raising goosebumps as it moved towards the head of the bed. I loved feeling that warmth spreading from him through the air. He hadn't used restraints on me since the trial under his forge, but it seemed as though it was time for him to try and do so. The golden shackles appeared, quickly capturing my wrists and pulling my arms up towards the headboard. His grip on my hips was all that kept me from crawling forward. He wanted my arms outstretched it seemed. The position became a bit more difficult as he raised my hips, forcing my knees under me. I could bear the discomfort for him. Though there was something thrilling about how he had me situated so that nothing was hidden from him. I was completely bare, open, and on display for his viewing and use.

A shiver of excitement went through me at the knowledge. His hands shifted my legs and hips until he was happy with my position, his breath grazing over every delicate part of me. I couldn't hold back my whimpers, and I knew that he could see how my swollen lips glistened with need. It didn't take much for my body to prepare itself for him. I craved him, needed him.

His beard tickled the back of my thigh as he pressed a gentle kiss. For a moment I thought he was going to let his comment about somewhere better to hit me go, but he wasn't one to disappoint. Just as quickly, he rose from the bed with a gruff command not to move from how he'd placed me. It was tempting to disobey but I wanted to see just what he had planned, not what he would have to do should I try to brat again. There was plenty of time for that later, I hoped.

I felt Heph brush the edge of the bed, a calloused hand reaching out to rub over my asscheek. The rough sensation sent a shiver of pleasure through me. A soft whine sounded when he stopped but quickly was replaced by a cry as he brought something down hard over where he'd been rubbing not even a moment before. And then his hand was on me once more, rubbing gently at the throbbing red spot he'd left. "You'll be counting these, little dove. Lose count, and you won't get any relief tonight." Oh, he knew how to play the game. While he hadn't laid in another's bed, I wasn't going to assume he wasn't familiar with the scene. Whether from research or from his own experience, he knew how to play. Our brief encounters with any sort of kink play before hadn't really shown his depth of knowledge. While I regretted hiding anything from him, the whole situation did seem to have an upside.

His hand that had been gently rubbing roughly grabbed my skin, digging his fingers in until I knew that they'd leave a bruise. "I don't hear counting, princess." I had gotten lost in thought and hadn't done the one thing he wanted me to. Before I could get the word out, he brought what I figured out to be a riding crop down over my skin again.

A strangled cry of 'one' was ripped from my throat as I pulled at the gilded restraints, trying not to lose the position he'd set me in. That wouldn't please him in the least and his happiness was all that mattered right then. It was all I wanted. The arousal that coated and dripped from my core with every strike didn't matter, the throbbing need wasn't important, the fact that every breath grew more difficult to draw wasn't even a factor to me. All I wanted was to make him happy with me again. And it was a wonderous feeling.

After six more strikes, he paused long enough that I thought he was done. I risked a glance back over my shoulder just in time to see him strike once more with the crop. But his strike landed between my legs. My body pitched forward as an inhuman cry left my lips. All I could do at that moment was tremble against the sheets and pray he wasn't going to start over and deliver all the strikes against my mound. "So that was what it took to break you?" he murmured as he crawled onto the bed, laying his body over mine until his face was beside mine. Tugging my head back, he licked at the tears that coated my cheeks, his other hand waving and removing the restraints. "You're even more beautiful with tears in your eyes. Thoroughly fucked and ruined will be a masterpiece, I'm sure. But we're not there yet. You still have to apologize properly."

I wasn't sure what else he had in mind, but the promise of leaving me sated and ruined was one that I was looking forward to. At least Heph gave me a few moments to breathe as he got off the bed to prepare something else. It'd been a long time since I was taken to my limit in the bedroom. Never before my abilities began waning, but since then, I wasn't sure anyone had managed to do so. I wish that I was at full power to see if he could manage even then.

My trembling had ceased for the most part by the time he returned to help me off the bed, apparently happy with what he'd prepared. The most concerning thing to me wasn't the small metal table with candles and ice, it was the rough woven mat on the ground beside it. I had an idea of what he might want with that, and I also knew that he was moving me slowly closer to it so I could stop everything if I needed to. Meeting his gaze, I gave a slight shake of my head before pushing away from him and kneeling on it. It dug into my skin, but I knew that was the point. I was on my knees, begging forgiveness.

As he stepped in front of me, I reached out to run my fingers over his thigh, trailing light touches over the scars. He gave me a few moments to do so before grabbing my wrist, his other hand smacking my untouched cheek. "Do you have permission to touch? I'm not your toy tonight, little dove. You're mine. Mine to break, to twist, to mold and reshape exactly how I want." Still, he leaned down to kiss my fingers. There was still hesitation in him, and I knew it. "Pause," he murmured as he knelt down in front of me. "I know that you are okay with everything here, but I'm about to take away your use of safe word and your hands. Are you okay with this?"

"My sparrow, I trust you implicitly," I quickly replied, my hand reaching out to cradle his cheek. "That is why we had that discussion, setting our limits. I appreciate you stopping to check on me, but I owe you a proper apology."

His uncertainty showed for a moment more before he nodded and took my hands. "Then I'll make sure you can break the restraints if you need to get free." That would mean that I had to be careful with them. But he was giving me a way to stop things if they went too far. Heph leaned forward to settle my arms behind my back, restraints appearing as he released my wrists. As he stood, his expression shifted and I knew that he was going back into the headspace he needed once more. His gaze moved over my bare form, kneeling and bound at his feet, the rug beneath me digging into my skin.

A few more moments passed like that, and I savored the discomfort of my bound arms and the mat digging into my knees and shins. It helped me get back to where I needed to be, a contrite submissive wife that withheld important and deadly information from her husband.

One of his hands fisted my hair, pulling my head back as the other gripped the base of his cock. The tip rubbed at my lower lip as he glared down at me. "You don't know how to use this mouth to tell me things, I'll find a much better use for it." A shivering went through me as I parted my lips. He took little time in pulling my head forward and sheathing his length in my mouth. He tugged my head forward, forcing me to take the entirety of his endowment into my mouth and throat. I choked only for a moment, my body shuddering as I fought the need to breathe and to push him away. He'd learned quickly after our wedding night, how easily I could take all of him into my mouth. But he was looking to push those limits as he held my head in place against his body. Breathing was the only thing my body wanted to do and just when I thought I might lose consciousness, Heph yanked my head back and off him. I gasped in as much air as I could, choking slightly, trying to clear the fuzziness that had started to take over my mind. "You take my cock so well, princess. It's like every hole was made just for me."

If he wanted me to speak, he was going to be sorely disappointed. Words were beyond me for the time being. Whether he was pleased or not by that, I wasn't sure. Rather than shoving himself into my mouth once more, he picked up one of the candles by his side and trickled the pooled wax over my chest. My breath left in a hiss. The heat added another stimulant to my already over sensitive body. Perhaps I should be grateful that he hadn't seen fit to use that wax anywhere else earlier. Setting the candle down, his hand in my hair forced my head forward and I quickly opened my mouth without instruction to take him once more. Rather than holding my face to his body, he pushed completely into my mouth again and pulled his hips back, thrusting into my mouth as he would any other part of my body. Only that first thrust was gentle, testing the waters. But when

I didn't break free of my restraints or offer any sort of resistance, he found a rough pace, fucking my mouth with the same vigor and abandon as he knew I loved him to do with the rest of my body. Every thrust was for his pleasure alone, but my body was still dripping and thrumming with my denied need. Tears and snot coated my face, spit dribbled out of my mouth and down my chin as I struggled to suck and add to his mounting pleasure.

I was grateful that he didn't seem to have much endurance left. The taste of precum coated my tongue and I savored that salty sweetness. Perhaps having me restrained and not touching or using me how he wanted was just as enticing and torturous for him. Whatever the case, I was glad that he wouldn't take long enough for me to either pass out or my jaw to really start hurting. One thing about endowed men was that the longer they took orally, the more discomfort there was to be had.

When he pulled my head back, freeing his length from my mouth, I was confused. There was no chance to ask because his other hand quickly pumped his shaft and his release coated my face, mouth, and the hardened wax on my chest. I didn't mean to laugh, but the mirth just bubbled out with the surprise of the action. As he wiped my face with a damp towel, I quickly sobered up at the displeased expression on his face. The corner of his mouth curled up the slightest bit. It amused me that he was struggling not to join me in my laughter. But according to him we weren't done.

He didn't release my wrists from their bindings as he picked me up and carried me over to the bed. At least he knew as well as I did that my legs were completely useless. The relief of being off that mat was wonderful, but I wasn't sure just what other limits he might try to take me to. As he set me on the bed, he once more had me on my knees with my torso pressed to the bed. Rather than releasing my arms and putting them back how they were, he left them behind me and instead bound my ankles to the bedposts.

"Be a shame, princess, for this ice to go to waste. That sinful mouth of yours just made me lose control and I couldn't stop." He leaned forward, pressing a kiss to my soaked center before pulling away. The back of his hand brushed my thigh as he brought it to my core. I couldn't stop my yelp as he pressed a frozen cube to that sensitive flesh, sopped and burning with need. My reaction made him laugh, his fingers running the ice between my folds before pressing it to my entrance. Surely, he didn't plan to do what I thought he did.

I didn't have a chance to issue such a challenge as he pressed just enough to push it inside me. The sensation wasn't something I'd ever felt before. I bucked against the bed, unable to keep still. How could I? He was driving me crazy in ways that I had never experienced before. There were new heights and limits that he was dragging me towards, and I was suddenly able to understand why my body was so ready and willing to submit to him at every turn when I would never have done so for another person.

Heph was quick to push down on my restrained arms, using them to press my hips to the bed once more. His other hand pressed between my thighs with more ice, urging another cube into me. It was a race against the heat he ignited in me, to fill me with the ice before I melted it all. And it was a challenge he took seriously, pressing cube after cube into me while I writhed and cried out incoherently. "Poor little dove. You can't take anything more," he murmured, pressing his chilled fingers to my abused hole. "Guess I'll just have to help you. There's something else I want to fit in here," he growled, pushing one finger forward. I felt the heat of his hand intensify, moving from his finger into me.

It only took me a moment to realize that he was using his powers to melt the ice he'd filled me with, that he was ridding me of it and evaporating the water left behind once it melted. The heat just pulled more mewls from my throat as I was dragged from one extreme temperature to the other, his powers trying to burn me up from the inside. Still, I refused to give in. I could take more. I wanted more. "Good, princess," he rasped. His finger didn't pull back once he had finished removing all evidence of his temperature play. Instead, he pushed a second into me, thrusting with enough force that only the restraints holding my ankles in place kept me from moving up to the headboard. A laugh sounded as he knelt on the bed, pressing his body over mine as he worked a third finger into me. "But I'm not sure you're sorry enough yet. Are you?"

"I am!" I cried out, his hand thrusting against my core with a bruising force that would leave me even more sore the next day. It was everything I'd wanted him to do, but so much stimulation was sure to do me in. "I am so sorry. I beg forgiveness!" The words came out strangled by the moans he was forcing out of me with the way he was driving his fingers into me, like he was hurling me headfirst towards release. Just as I was about to find the relief I'd wanted for hours, Heph stopped. My clenching walls wept with the loss of his fingers. Even the weight that had been suffocating me was something I missed, needing anything to keep me from losing what was left of my sanity. "Please, no," I whined, my hips trying to rise up in offer, but I couldn't find the strength to move. Fresh tears coated my cheeks as I waited for what fresh torture he was going to give me.

"You don't want this? I don't think you have any say in the matter," he gruffed out as he leaned over me. Heph braced one hand on the bed beside my head as he shoved as much of his endowment into me as he could, tearing a scream from my throat that I knew would leave me unable to speak above a whisper for at least a day or two. The tears didn't stop even as he found the same brutal pace that he'd used on my mouth. All the stimulation, the edging, the need, it was mounting faster than I could keep up. My entire vocabulary was wiped from my mind with his hips hitting my ass, his body smacking roughly against my sore folds.

But as much as I craved my release, needed it, I could feel it like it was just on the other side of a thin wall. It was so close, I could almost grasp it. And yet, it refused to come. A choked sob of frustration punctuated the cries he was pulling from me. Maybe he could feel what was wrong because he shifted after a few moments. His new angle was just as wonderful as the last, the way he slammed his hips into mine sending shots of pained pleasure through me. But it was him forcing one finger and quickly working a second into my ass that had me able to finally find that release. The last bit of pain he thought to give me finally slamming me through whatever wall had been keeping my orgasm from me.

The intensity of it tore me from my body, the electric heat searing me until I couldn't think, move. My walls clenched down on his length with such force that for a moment, he had difficulty pulling back. That was the last thing I felt, knew, losing consciousness for a few moments again. Once was impressive, twice was unheard of. Then again, everything that he could do to me and make me do, it was all unheard of.

THE TRIALS OF APHRODITE

If there was anyone in the universe able to make me fully submit and happily give up control, to be a collared sub, it was the man that I had married. Twice.

CHAPTER XVII

FOR DAYS AFTER, I was sore. Moving was a true difficulty. And I loved every moment. Heph was wonderful at aftercare and doted on me when I couldn't get out of bed. All that soreness and aching did nothing to impede our activities. We still were ravenous for one another. But it also helped us to talk things out about everything that happened. Communication was something we were getting better at, and he was helping to break me of my habit of playing things close to the chest. That meant being honest with everyone in my life that depended on me.

With Heph's help, I sat my mortals down and was honest about the likelihood of my demise. They reacted as I thought they might, wails of despair and pleas to back out. And that led to my explanation of how I couldn't back out of the trials, refuse a trial, or fail. They did ask why my life wasn't truly in danger when facing the gorgon or when I was under Heph's forge, especially with my powers sealed as they were.

"The only thing that can kill a god is another god. Especially one wielding a weapon forged by one," he'd explained to them. And he knew better than most given that he forged all our weapons. It was something he told me he'd regretted more than once, but never more than then. He hated that something created by his hand would be wielded against me. Especially since it could end the life we were building before we got started.

As much as I hated the thought of doing so, I talked to Lola about increasing the amount of training time together before I had to face Ares. It would take time from our honeymoon, but Heph insisted, and he was backed up by the humans I treasured. Lola agreed and said she'd just have to shift some things around, but she wanted me to survive the encounter so she would prefer I train longer if that was what it took for me to get through the trial with my life intact.

A few days more of honeymoon bliss passed far too quickly. Before I knew it, I was standing in Lola's personal arena, a mortal forged sword in either of our hands.

"I never thought I'd get you to spar with me. I'm sorry that this is what it took to get you here." Lola tapped the flat of one sword against her leg as she watched me get the feel for the ones that she'd given me. It'd been my preference to dual wield once up on a time, but I lost my taste for it quicker than I lost my taste for battle. It wasn't challenging enough.

"I am as well. I hoped to never do this with you, truly." And she knew that as well. It wasn't something that our friendship was built on. She didn't care that I didn't want to hold a sword. Strangely enough, we had a friendship that mirrored some mortal ones. We bonded in ways that my humans did with me. Our talks just happened to also turn to pantheons, battles, and things that no mortal in my life would ever understand.

"Get through all this shit and I'll steal you from your husband for another marathon." She enjoyed torturing me with as many action movies as possible. And in return, I tortured her with sci-fi. We had nights where we shared a love of fantasy movies, but it was more enjoyable to torture one another.

"I will hold you to that. You should know that Heph has been introducing me to anime and I fully intend to subject you to them as well." That drew a groan from her as she lunged at me, our swords clashing. I knew she wouldn't be pleased about being forced to watch some new form of 'torture'.

Lola dropped beside me on the ground as our cuts healed over quickly. We'd both managed to land a hit at the end and earned a break. "I missed being able to heal quickly," I couldn't help muttering as I let go of the swords in my hands. "It has been some time since I was injured by a mortal weapon. Everything else I have been injured by has been making me feel like the mortal."

"Quit bitching," Lola replied, her gentle tone didn't match the words. I knew that it wasn't about my complaining but about my lingering on the past trials. I was getting into my own head. She didn't want me to think about being injured, bringing that sort of reality into being. Every sparring session she told me to only visualize being whole and uninjured and back in Heph's arms at midnight. Perhaps she was right. I was already handicapped with my abilities being what they were, I didn't need to psyche myself out either. "Let's talk about something happier. How are things with moody, scarred, and handy?"

Between her and Heph, I wasn't sure how I was standing. They both exhausted me, drained me of every bit of energy until I couldn't move. And I just kept coming back for more. "He is still upset but he is better at not showing it. He just saves it until we go to bed."

"So, you really submitted?" Like mortals, we also shared such things. Though it'd been some time since Lola had shared details about her love life. I thought it was because of my decade or so of celibacy. But even more recently, she hasn't shared. And I knew that she had someone, I could feel it. I also knew that pushing her to tell me before she was ready would never work.

"I did. It was rather freeing, shocking, and thrilling. I honestly have never thought I would enjoy doing the things to me that he does. They are usually things I would do to another." Which was true. I loved to manipulate another being's body, to wring every ounce of pleasure from them. But with Heph, I could count on one hand the number of times I had taken control. It was something I still needed to wrap my head around.

"Guess you just needed the right partner to get you out of your head." That, it did. Letting him have that 'control', it eased my mind, took away every worry and concern. And the more comfortable he got with exploring my body however he wanted, the more it worked for me. I was grateful to him for that.

"You just enjoy always being right," I shot back. It was something she'd pointed out years before when I stopped sharing my bed any way but platonically.

"It's a gift. One of many of mine that you love to make use of."

"You should not have so many gifts if you do not wish for your friends to make use of them."

"Shut up." Chuckling, she shoved my shoulder before moving to lay down and rest her head in my lap.

As much fun as it would be to shove her off, I couldn't resist running my hands through her dark tresses, playing the silky strands between my fingers. "Should I not be the one resting on you? This is an activity that you partake in every day after all. My poor weary, old bones still have not grown used to it."

"Well, you are old. But you don't need to rest too much. How else will you survive later when your man has his way with you?"

"What sense does that make?" I asked, tapping her forehead with my finger. "I should rest up before you deliver me back to him."

"Nah. I think you should be sore and crying already so he doesn't have to work as hard." Of course, if she did bring me back to Heph sore and crying like that, he wouldn't want to dominate me the way he really enjoyed. He'd want to care for me, dote on me, ease my agony before causing some of his own.

"Never. I would never forgive you for ruining his fun like that."

"Dee, you didn't say 'our' fun. Isn't it fun for you?"

"Of course, it is. I have fun no matter what we do. But I know how much he has been enjoying exploring this side of himself, and me."

Oohing, Lola reached up, grabbed my chin, and shook my head back and forth. "Does someone get upset if her man doesn't beat her and fuck her raw before bed?" Apparently, she thought I would refute her words because her eyes widened when my cheeks merely flushed. "Oh, my gods. He does? You don't always go into specifics about the kinky parts. So, he really does?"

"Not beat, but he does give me a few good hits when I provoke him enough. I quite enjoy it."

"This was something you both talked about beforehand though, right?" she asked, her hand releasing my face and instead caressing my cheek. I enjoyed how concerned she grew over my well-being.

"We did. We had a long discussion regarding things we both enjoyed, the things we might like to explore, and our hard limits. Some nights, he will negotiate or explain what he wants for the night before we start, sometimes we will just see where things take us." It worked for us, that was all that mattered. I didn't care how anyone else felt about it, we did what felt right and made us happy.

"And after?" she asked, dropping her hand as I continued running mine through her hair.

I grinned as I thought about all the ways he took care of me. "He should have been gifted the title 'the god of aftercare,'" I murmured. That drew more excited sounds from Lola as she continued to tease me about my love life. "But what about you, dear butterfly? Have you found someone to explore that sort of dynamic with?"

"You know that's not really my scene, love bug. I mean, I want it rough, but I don't think I could do the whole 'submit to me, call me sir, do as I say' thing. And I really don't want the responsibility of making someone else submit, you know?" I knew that was how she felt, but something in me believed that if she found the right partner, I knew that she would enjoy it. Especially with how she always talked about her romantic encounters.

"So, there is no one in your life?" I asked, hoping that phrasing it differently would change her answer. I knew that there was someone that was earning her affection. Such were my gifts.

Lola shook her head. "No. I don't want to focus on that kind of stuff right now. For now, I want to help you, make sure you survive all this bullshit, and then we can see about fixing my love life. I don't need the distraction anyways. You know I've been working on building up the village again."

It was a passion project of hers, creating a utopia for those women and children in need. I was reminded of the other role she played besides being a warrior goddess. "I know. And you know that should you ever need any assistance, all you have to do is ask and I will give it to you."

"I'll be taking you up on that once you're done with the trials. I could use some of your expertise or recommendations to help a few of them."

"I will help in any way I can." It felt good to plan with her for something after the trials were complete. It was different from how Heph and my children had. With her, it didn't feel like we were hoping and determined for it to happen, it felt like something we were both sure of. It was comforting in a way.

She pulled more details from me about my love life with Heph before dragging me to my feet and beating me black and blue once more. I was sore and spent and desperate for a hot bath by the time she was done with me. But instead of taking me home, she took me to his workshop that he used in the mortal world. "I just was trying to take you to him. Don't ask me. You two have fun," Lola said as she pressed a kiss to my cheek and flashed away. So much for her help.

I stepped through the door and found Heph muttering to himself as he tossed pieces of armor around the shop. "Sparrow?" I called to him. He didn't seem to hear me, and it broke my heart because I knew that it was my fault. He was suffering because of the trials, spiraling. I caught a piece of armor that he tossed over his shoulder, apparently still displeased with it. It was a piece of the armor he'd created for my battle against the gorgon. Or it looked the same, it felt sturdier. The pieces clicked into place and I stepped over to him. I wrapped my arms around him from behind, pressing my cheek to his damp back. "Come back to me."

His body shuddered as he took a deep breath, his hands releasing the pieces he'd been holding and instead rubbed at my arms. "You're done already?"

"You lost track of time." Turning in my embrace, he pulled me tight against him, burying his face against my head as he murmured apology after apology. "Why are you tinkering with my armor? It is perfect."

"I can make it stronger. I have to. It has to hold up against Ares' sword." His words made my chest ache, wishing I could take that pain away, that worry. But I knew that nothing I could say would change it. He would forge armor for me again and again until he was happy with it.

All I could do was distract him, put his mind at ease for as long as I was in front of him, by his side, in his arms. "You told me so many of your fantasies, but you never mentioned any about your forge." The sudden change of subject was enough to clear his mind and make him give me that toe-curling grin that warmed me to my core. "There you are," I murmured, leaning up to steal a quick kiss.

"Honestly, I never thought I'd be able to get you in here. I thought it'd be too dirty, hot, or grimy." Instead of contradicting him, I took his hand and led him over to one of his workbenches that was free of any instruments or projects.

"You could tell me all about your fantasies, or you could show me how you wanted me here," I offered, hopping up on the table. He didn't need to be told twice. Heph made quick work of our clothes, ripping and tugging until I was bare to his gaze, and he was revealed to me in all his glory. Looking at him like that, naked and glistening in the light of his forge, I understood those who worshiped him more than ever.

His hands gripped my hips, pulling me to the edge of the table as he pressed his body between my legs. I thought he might take his time or tease me as he often enjoyed doing, but he was as eager and impatient as the first time he was able to have me. Heph pulled me against him until I was barely resting on the table at all, my legs wrapped around his waist as he pushed his hips forward, fighting for every inch. My nails dug into his shoulders until I felt his ichor coat my fingers. His lips claimed mine, eating down the frantic pained little sounds of pleasure that he was dragging from my throat.

Every push of his hips set my body on fire, driving away the pain from training and giving me an all new wave of agony and pleasure. I wanted him to destroy me, crumble me to nothing and reforge me to do it all over again. While my body might have preferred that I try and get away, to beg for some sort of preparation, I could only cling to him. I needed to feel as much of him against me as I could. The feel of his skin against mine, his beard scratching my skin, the sweet press of his lips to mine, it erased everything and cleared my mind until nothing could bother me. I needed him, body and soul, and I would do anything to keep him.

He stilled as our bodies merged fully, his fingers digging into my flesh. His breath came in ragged pants as he broke the kiss, staring down at my face, chest, where our bodies joined. Without saying a word, he leaned his head down and bit the crook of my neck as his hips pulled back and slammed forward. Every rough thrust that had me screaming his name drove home everything he'd been feeling. As much as we did talk things out, saying it with our bodies just seemed to work through whatever was still lying beneath the surface.

And as he stole the last of my energy, leaving me sore and filled with his seed, I knew that I had at least helped him clear away some of the unnecessary thoughts that were tormenting him. All I could hope was that when I left with Lola the next day and he returned to his forge, he would be able to work with a clearer head and not lose himself in whatever caused him to spiral like that. But if he needed me, I would do everything I could to help with working through it, distract him, or be whatever he needed me to be.

CHAPTER XVIII

THOSE TWO MONTHS PASSED faster than I thought they would. It felt as though all the time I had to prepare had gone by in a blink. The last thing I wanted was to say my goodbyes, to leave behind the brief glimpse of what life could be like with Heph that I had been granted.

"Let me talk to her one more time," Heph pleaded, crushing me in his embrace. "You have already proven yourself, been living with me, what difference does this make anymore? Surely, she can release you. She could find a way around the oath if she really wanted to."

"I doubt even the queen could dissolve it. Besides, it is far too late to try that again." I loved him for trying to save me up until the very last moment. But every visit he made to his mother to try and resolve things had ended with him growing ever more frustrated and feeling more helpless. He wanted to help me, save me, and it was incredibly sweet of him. I just needed to save myself and he could pick up the pieces. With how unwilling she'd been to heal me last time; I was likely in for another slow and painful recovery. I could believe I would hold Ares off until the end of the death season, I wasn't foolish enough to believe I would come out unscathed. Returning to my husband with an injured body was an inevitability should I survive. Ares hadn't let his skills in battle be underused, he was as sharp and deadly as ever. Perhaps more so given how furious he'd looked the last time I had seen him.

"Return to me, little dove." It was such a simple request, and I wanted nothing more than to promise him once more that I would. But I couldn't. If it was the last time that I was ever going to see him, I wouldn't lie to him.

The only answer I could offer him was a kiss that I poured every bit of my love and regret into. I regretted how long it took for me to finally see him, to love him. And it was the last time I'd let myself be haunted by those emotions. He deserved better, and I needed to let those regrets go. I wouldn't let them drag me down in battle after all. I'd leave them in the dirt with whatever ichor Ares drained from me. With the end of death season, I would let go of everything that was still holding me back from him.

Before I could say anything else, I felt Lola's energy before she appeared behind Heph. He growled as he hugged me tighter to him, but I patted his chest and shook my head. "I love you. That is all that matters."

"I love you, too," Hephaestus whispered, hanging his head, and letting me go. The last thing I wanted was to leave him, his embrace, or to leave him standing there with that sorrowful expression. But I had to. Steeling my resolve, I turned my back to him and walked past him to Lola.

"It's not sundown yet. You want more time?" I loved her for offering it to me, but if I had more time with Heph, he'd wear me down and I'd back out. So, I merely shook my head and she quickly grabbed my hand, transporting us to the arena that my trial would take place in. It was familiar. "I offered my training grounds. You're both familiar with them, so it's not like it'd give either of you an advantage." Her face scrunched as she realized that he already had the advantage. "Or more of one," she amended.

"Thank you. It was kind of you to do this," I murmured, trying not to look over to where Ares stood inspecting his sword. Or perhaps it was me he was inspecting, his gaze felt heavy on the armor Heph had re-forged and then placed on me. I had a sneaking suspicion only Heph would be able to remove it with the amount of power he'd poured into every piece. It was the same beautiful armor that I had worn against the gorgon, but I could feel how much sturdier it was, how much more it'd protect me. Though I wasn't sure how well it'd do against Ares' fury. While I had faith in Heph's abilities, I had fought by Ares' side once upon a time, trained with him. He only could have gotten better over the centuries since.

"Dee. Dee!" I could tell I had been lost in thought for a while with how Lola was snapping her fingers in my face and calling to me. "Don't let him get in your head. What the fuck have I been telling you?"

Taking a deep breath, I turned to face her, blocking him from my vision entirely. "Only visualize walking away whole and into Heph's arms."

The shadows grew heavier as the sun lowered in the sky. I prayed for it to hurry and stop. Once it was gone from view, I would be faced with the greatest foe I'd ever had to battle. And one that I had hoped never to have to meet in such a way. "That's right," she said, grabbing my shoulders and pulling me away from the thoughts I was trying to get lost in once more. "Stay with me. Get warmed up. You only have a little while longer until you need to give me your war face."

That was enough to make me grin at her. She was a wonderful friend. I knew that she'd also grown closer to Ares over the years, that it wasn't fair to have her in the middle, but she was always there to support me when I needed it the most. And how could I not take advantage of that when I needed it the most?

"The sun is setting," Hera's voice boomed through the sky. "Prepare yourselves." There was no satisfaction in her voice, she sounded exhausted. Did she regret how things had progressed? I knew, from Heph's many visits, that this had been a trial that was set in her mind when I said the oath. It was one that couldn't be changed. And she'd told him that there was another that she wouldn't be able to change either. As much as I feared it, I knew her saying as much meant that she had faith I would pull through and survive the trial. But did she think I would manage it with my sword or live up to her worst expectations? That wasn't really a question I wanted the answer to.

All that was left to do was warm up and wait for the last bit of daylight to sink from view. Already, the sky had turned such beautiful colors, warming me with the memories of lying under such skies with Heph during the past couple of months. Those thoughts were what I would hold onto while I fought, wonderful memories he'd given me, and the drive to make infinitely more by his side.

My breath hitched as the last bit of light sank down beyond the horizon. "Begin," came that booming voice. I was expecting an exclamation, a triumphant tone. Instead, she sounded almost...sad. Regretful? I couldn't let it move me. I wouldn't. Instead, I held onto the fiery emotions that drove me, telling myself it was merely that she couldn't be there to watch. I had to think the worst to continue on. Lola had left us to fight. Maybe she couldn't bear to see the result, maybe she had been banned from being there so she wouldn't interfere. For whatever reason, it was merely Ares and I left in that darkened place. At another time, it might have felt intimate, but I just felt dread and fear. There was nothing warm about what he was making me feel right then.

"Never thought this day would come," Ares said as he stepped closer to me, looking over every curve accentuated by the perfectly formed armor. "Never thought you'd be able to stand across from me like this."

"I never thought it possible either. But there is nothing I will not do to prove myself to Hera."

He sneered as he drew his sword, a beautifully forged blade that was well loved. I knew Heph's work, and how much Ares treasured it. Just as he did the small shield bound to his left forearm. He wasn't in full plate armor, opting for lighter leather armor. Obviously, he didn't think me a threat worthy of his full battle regalia. Fair enough. I had no intention of trying to mortally wound him anyways, it made little difference to me what armor he wore. "For him? I love my brother but this...this is something I may not be able to forgive either of you for. All these years you played him the fool. Was it me that you both were playing?"

"No. This is a newer development. Something that I came to in the last decade while I...It does not really matter, does it? You will think the worst of me. But know that I never played you for a fool. I treasure our time together, but I cannot see it in the same way as you do anymore." I didn't continue, I wouldn't explain. Hurting him with my revelations would do nothing to help either of us.

"What does that mean?"

"Nothing."

"It means something!" he roared as he stomped closer, nearly nose to nose with me. "Draw your swords. Speak. Either with your blades or those talented lips." Ares ducked his head, a gesture he'd done thousands of times before, his mouth moving closer to claim mine.

My hands shoved at his chest as I stepped back. "I have no intention of letting you taste these talents ever again. They will never be yours to enjoy."

Fury ignited in his eyes. Despite seeing the ceremony, despite knowing I was fighting for Heph, he seemed to believe he could still make me melt into his embrace. It worked for thousands of years, why not now? But he didn't know the woman I had become; he didn't know the trials I put myself through before ever approaching Hera. He didn't even know my mortals' names. How could he still think he knew me? I wasn't sure I knew him anymore either. Had he changed? It was likely.

"Draw. Your. Swords," he hissed. Punctuating each word with a huff.

What was left to say? Stepping back, I did as he asked, drawing the swords that Heph had forged for the trial.

They were as beautiful as the armor, and I could feel his love and protection in them. It pained me to use them against Ares, to raise a weapon made by him against another he'd poured his love into.

But I would do what had to be done. As Ares slashed his sword through the air, I knew he was holding back. I could tell by how easily I was able to parry. Would he continue to hold back? That shouldn't count against me though, it wasn't as though I asked him to hold back. The answer came as I choked on ichor that filled my throat.

Doubling over, I coughed it up, struggling to breath past it. So if he held back on my account, it was still breaking my oath to do everything that Hera asked and put forth in the trials. Ares stopped his swing, watching with a slight panic on his face.

"What's happening?"

I wasn't sure if I should explain. I could always merely provoke him. No, he deserved the truth. After everything we'd been through, I could give him that much. "You are holding back. And I swore on the ichor to Hera that I would fulfill every trial exactly as it was set forth. This is a battle to death, and you have no bloodlust."

"You swore on the ichor?" he asked.

Nodding, I stood and swung at him, Ares easily deflecting. "For him? You swore on the ichor to do all of this for him? You swore on it *twice*? FOR HIM?" he roared. That was all it took for that bloodlust to ignite in him. He easily broke through my defenses, his boot finding home in my stomach and knocking the air from my lungs. I fell back, unable to catch myself. As my head hit the ground, I was grateful for the helm that seemed to soften the impact. Bless Heph.

"Yes. For him. Twice," I gasped out. Ares roared wordlessly as he stood over me. He brought his sword straight down, the tip aimed at my face. There would be no more holding back, there would be no mercy. Ares would bring about my death. Or at least injury. But as I watched his sword come down, I was beginning to bet on death.

I thought about how I might get to meet Thanatos and ask about Nyx's escort much sooner than I had meant to. At least Seph might let Hephaestus visit me. I could resign myself to death, to a quick victory for Ares.

CHAPTER XIX

A LIGHT BLUE BARRIER stopped Ares' blade just as it reached my nose, barely brushing the tip of it. The barrier pushed the sword back enough that I didn't worry about impaling myself by accident. Had someone interfered? No one should have been able to reach us or use their powers to aid me. It didn't register in my mind that it was my barrier that I had used in battle thousands of years earlier.

"A snake to the end, huh, Aphie?" Ares spat at me as he took a step back.

"I hate that name," I grumbled as I rolled to the side and pushed myself to my feet. The barrier disappeared as soon as I moved.

"You claimed that your powers were failing you. Was this your plan all along? To surprise me when it was most convenient?" I knew I had hurt him by not explaining myself when I went to make amends with Heph. The last thing I told Ares was that I couldn't continue with him anymore. And that was long before my decade of self-discovery. Or it felt like it.

"They *are* failing me!"

"LIES!" he roared, lunging at me, and swinging his sword with such force that my arm went numb as I raised mine to block it.

Apparently, he wanted my head after all. Or at least to add my skin to his collection. A shudder went through me at that thought. Even in death, I rather be given back to Heph whole and completely his. That was another reason to fight for my life, knowing that even that would be taken from my husband. And I knew that Ares wouldn't believe anything I had to say. He wouldn't believe me that the barrier happened without my thinking about it. He was hurt, and that anger and betrayal was blinding him to everything else.

I could hear the pain in his heart. I knew that he didn't want to do this, but he would. He had to, as much as I did. Not that I knew the reasoning behind that exactly. Perhaps I never would. And it filled me with despair, knowing that we would never even get back the easy friendship we once had. At least not with how things were. Maybe one day, when the pain had abated, he might be able to see me without wallowing in the hatred he shielded himself with. It was his coping mechanism, and I hoped that he found a way to work through it. I missed the friendship we once shared. And at that moment, I realized that the friendship we had ended centuries before everything else. We'd destroyed it before we destroyed what we'd loved most in one another.

That realization made me falter. Ares didn't realize I wouldn't block until his sword came down on my shoulder. It slid along the armor there and sliced at the small bit of skin exposed by the gap left for ease of mobility. The heavy material beneath the armor did nothing to stop his blade from cutting into my skin. I knew it was the hide of some mystical creature that Heph hoped would protect me. Perhaps it did, perhaps it kept him from slicing as deeply into me as he would have otherwise. But the wound still stung and ichor welled up from it. It was a gash in my skin that wouldn't heal without assistance from someone with healing abilities. At least not easily. It would heal human slow if left alone. That was the curse of weapons forged by my beloved. They made mortals of us all.

I threw myself back when he pulled his blade away, staring in disbelief at the gold coating it. Distance, I needed distance. But even in my haste to put space between us, I didn't miss the look of regret and agony that graced his features. What pained me was that it didn't really move me. Not the way it once would have. His pain didn't hurt me. Seeing the pain on Heph's face hours earlier was agony.

"We're really doing this." It didn't seem like he was speaking to me, he was staring at his blade in disbelief. He couldn't look away from it. Even as my ichor trickled down the blade and stained his fingers, he couldn't tear his gaze away. "I didn't think I'd be able to do it. I didn't...believe this would happen."

It was getting difficult to breathe again, and I worried that he wouldn't be able to go on. All I could do to ensure that he would be able to fight me was to provoke him again. I needed to truly provoke him. But could I? I wasn't sure I could be that cruel to him. *I need to get back to my sparrow. This is the only way*, I reminded myself. If I couldn't get him to battle me properly, the broken oath would do me in. I would die either way. I might as well die fighting for my life and the chance to bring a smile to Heph's face once more.

"I figured the only way I could make you get serious was to land a blow. I never thought it would turn you into a fair maiden fainting at the sight of a little ichor. How the mighty have fallen," I taunted.

Ares growled as he swung his blade with a harsh movement, spattering the ichor from it across the ground. The fire was back in his eyes, and I knew that the fight was on.

As much as I didn't want to give him the satisfaction of making me cry out, I couldn't help the yelp as he slashed an opening in the armor on my legs. Pain blossomed as I fell to the side to avoid his next attack. It wasn't graceful by any means, but I had ichor staining over half of my armor in some form of fashion. One particularly nasty blow had managed to knock the helm from my head. There wasn't even time to tie back my hair that had fallen free, to clear my gaze of ichor that trickled from my brow.

"There's the sound I like to hear. Always could get you to scream for me."

"Heph makes me scream louder," I panted, rolling backwards and onto my knees. I lifted my right sword in time to block his blow as he brought his sword down with a yell of fury. "And they say women are the emotional ones. How fragile is your ego, dear Ares?" I probably didn't need to keep provoking him. He was well and truly incensed, but I didn't want him to hold back either. The angrier he was, the less likely he'd go easy on me.

"As fragile as your untrained body," Ares growled as he swung at my neck. Dropping to the side, I kicked out, surprised that I managed to connect my foot with his knee. The loud crunching sound, followed by his scream of agony told me that I had done damage that might cripple a mortal. It wasn't my intention, but it bought me enough time to wipe my face, pushing my hair back. The ichor coating my hand held it back enough that I could see without the dark strands in my face.

"That would be quite offensive if Lola heard you call me untrained. She has been very helpful."

"You devious little..." he trailed off, groaning in pain. I watched in horror as he shifted his weight, his hand glowing as he brushed his shield over his injured leg. When had he learned healing magic? Ares tested it, shifting his weight back and forth. It wasn't perfect, but he would be able to stand and move without too much difficulty. He had yet another advantage over me apparently.

I sighed as I finally made it back to my feet, wiping at my brow though I knew it was useless. "Now who was deceiving whom? You were never able to heal before."

The only answer he gave was a shrug. Perhaps he no longer saw the supporting magics as lesser than anymore.

Before I could ask anything else, Ares was once more on me, raining down blow after blow, so quick that I was barely able to keep up. Heph's armor was all that kept Ares from landing a death blow. Or perhaps he was still holding back, just a bit. He could have gone for my exposed head or neck. His blows were focused on my body though. There was bloodlust there, I could practically taste it, but I don't think he wanted an easy victory. Or perhaps if he killed me, he wanted it to have at least looked more like a fair fight. He was rarely one to go for the head and end a fight early.

"Come, Aphie, you've yet to land a single blow with your sword."

"I thought it was I...that was supposed...to provoke...you," I gasped out. He'd managed to hit the piece of armor on my sternum hard enough to dent it in. The protective piece did its job but impeded my breathing a bit.

The tip of his sword touched under my chin, guiding my head up to look at him from where he'd left me crouched on the ground. "You used to love it when I called you that." He wasn't wrong, I did love it. But there were others that had called me that and I hated it. The ones that I asked to change their nickname for me had been kind enough to do so. Except for him and one other. But seeing how I had cut them both from my life, for the most part, it made little difference. I had no intention of seeing Ares for a long while after we were done with our battle. Not just because of Heph, but because Ares deserved to have all the time he needed to heal as well. The time I had taken for myself to heal emotionally, he'd apparently spent it believing that I would return to him once more. One regret I would likely carry for a while longer was that I didn't do him the kindness of driving home the fact that we would never reconcile again.

"Can't take it? Aphie?" Ares was doing it intentionally. He deserved to, but it was still annoying me.

"Never imagined you could be so childish," I answered.

He didn't answer with words. His blade came down and would have granted me another wound if I hadn't rolled backwards at the last moment. The ground was all he hit as I pushed myself to my feet. It was my turn to swing. All I had managed to hit so far was air, wall, his shield, and his blade. At least with my blade. I only seemed to be able to kick him successfully. That would do little to stave him off. Not that I could tell how long had passed. It felt like we had been fighting for days, but it could have been hours or merely minutes. All I could focus on was his blade against mine in the dark.

The moon was full and the only light we were able to fight by. It glinted off our armor and the ichor that decorated us and the arena. My ichor.

"I love the temper tantrum," I spat through gritted teeth as the flat of his blade connected with my side. That was insulting, turning his blade. But it extended the fight, something that he would do against any opponent he was enjoying battling. And that he thought weak enough to need it.

"How long can you keep up those witty remarks, Aphie?" he hissed, swinging at my midsection. I dodged the blow and swung, finally my blade made contact with his arm. It wasn't deep enough to cut into his flesh or draw blood, but I landed a blow. It was gratifying in a way. I had a renewed hope that I would indeed survive the night with him. Not that I knew how much of the night was left. Did he? Could he feel how long we'd battled for?

"As long as you need encouragement not to go soft on me. That was an embarrassing night, was it not?" A low blow that earned me another trip to the ground as he kicked me in the stomach. All my breath was knocked from lungs again. Somehow, I managed to roll out of the way as he brought his sword down, gasping for air. I got my feet under me as I watched him seethe. Though I could tell his face was red with more than anger, he was embarrassed. It hadn't been his fault; he had been drunker than I had ever seen him that night. It was the only time he had ever had that issue. That I knew of.

That was probably one of the only things that I should never have said to him. "You truly wish to die tonight."

"It was something I hoped to avoid, but I have made my peace with the likelihood that I will die by your hand. I have made amends with our children, Lola, and my husband, and said my goodbyes. Whatever the outcome of this battle is, I can take solace that I had the time and presence of mind to do so." Perhaps that wasn't the answer he sought or expected, his face unreadable for a few moments. But without warning, his blade narrowly missed my face as I threw my head back.

The time for talking was over, and I was closer to death than I had ever dreamed possible. But I was determined to hold out until midnight. Even if I didn't know how much longer I had, or if I could avoid any more wounds, I would hold out. I had to.

CHAPTER XX

I HAD TUNNEL VISION. All I could see was Ares' sword. Without warning, an unfamiliar black blade was deflecting my blow as another swept his aside. I blinked a few times as I realized it was Lola. What was she doing? She couldn't stop the fight! We weren't done. Were we? "It's midnight," she explained as she dropped her swords. They dissolved into the darkness around us as she pushed us both back by our chest plates. "You're done. You lived. Now back the fuck up."

The pain of every wound and the soreness of every part of my body hit me at once. I dropped to my knees just as Heph appeared and ran to my side. He frantically inspected every inch of me, checking how deep the wounds were, the absolute panic and worry practically radiating off him. I loved how concerned he was. Hera's presence didn't even register for me.

I didn't know when I dropped the blades, but my hands were empty and shaking as I raised them to cup his face. "Hello, my sparrow," I murmured, meeting his kiss.

Perhaps it was a sight that was too much for Ares. I gave Heph the kiss I had denied him. As Heph pulled me against him, wringing a painful whimper from my lips, I gave him the kiss he needed. Neither of us noticed Ares approaching. He hadn't laid down his sword and he hadn't let go of that fire in his eyes. As he swung his sword down, Heph must have felt the call of his own work. It was an insult to use something he'd forged against him.

Ares jumped back as a wall of flames appeared between us and him. I pulled back from the kiss, looking at Heph with confusion and amazement. It was an impressive sight. "Rest," he murmured as he stood, letting me sink down to the ground once more. I didn't have much choice.

"Getting bold, brother. Never knew you had the desire to be humiliated by me in a fight," Ares called through the flames.

"I will do whatever it takes to ensure my wife's safety. You had your chance to take your anger out on her. You're done. You'll never touch her again. You'll never look at her. Don't even think about her when you're sad and alone tonight." Was I rubbing off on Heph? He was taunting Ares in the same way I had. Not the wisest move on my husband's part, but it was effective.

The wall of flames died down as Heph launched himself at Ares. I didn't even have time to be amused that he hadn't limped once since the fight began, that he'd limped less and less over the last couple of months. All I could do was watch him rain down blow after blow with the impressive warhammer that appeared in his hands. It was Ares' turn to be on the defensive. As furious as he was at Heph's words, he was having some trouble against Heph's expert blows. The blacksmith was used to wielding such a weapon day in and day out after all. He knew how to use the weight and force of it to its fullest extent.

When Ares' sword dropped from his hand, Heph tossed aside the hammer in his. I blinked a few times as it disappeared while soaring through the air. My husband had hidden talents that none of us knew of apparently.

"Here," Hera said softly, kneeling beside me. I didn't have time to ask why she was dirtying her chic white pantsuit for me; her hands were already glowing and the pain I was wallowing in ebbed away. "A belated wedding gift." That was a strange way to explain herself. I wondered if it was her way of telling me that she was finally warming up to me.

"Unnecessary. But thank you," I managed. "Are you going to stop them?" My head nodded towards the brothers that were pummeling each other with their fists. At least Ares had shed his shield at some point when I was focusing on Hera.

"They need to fight it out." She refused to look at them. Her back was to the confrontation as she continued to heal me. I thought perhaps she'd just do a little, but she intended to get me back to the state I was in prior to the battle. It was a kindness that I never thought I would receive from her. Perhaps something had started to change her as well. For so long, I had felt nothing but pain and coldness from her. Not necessarily towards me, but since her husband had given her a reason to despise him. Many reasons, really. She'd tried to nurture a love for him, for all our sakes, but it had died long ago. That was why I was so surprised to see something, a new ember of affection growing brighter and stronger within her heart. But I wouldn't be the one to piss her off and tell her what I knew or saw. That was a way to break whatever was slowly building, not only between us, but potentially between her and whoever was making her feel that way.

I looked past her as Heph struck Ares across the face. Ares quickly answered by kicking at Heph's bad leg. "No!" I cried, hoping that I might be able to stop him from doing something so cruel. Everyone stopped as the light blue barrier returned, Ares foot stopped against the soft glow as Heph moved his leg away from it. Obviously, it was something that I couldn't control, as much as I wished I could.

That was enough for Lola to step in though. Just as Ares stepped back, preparing to lunge at Heph again, she grabbed the back of his armor. "*Déjalo*," she commanded. "That's enough. You got your temper tantrum out. We're going." Lola wasn't at all bothered by how Ares flailed, trying to free himself. She just dragged him along behind her. "I'm glad you survived, Dee. Just give me a few days to calm this one down and I'll come check on you, okay?"

I nodded as she turned and transported herself and Ares away. Whatever was going on between them, it was better I did not know. I refused to look at it and decipher it. If something was going on, Lola would tell me when she was ready.

Hera had finished healing me at some point, I wasn't sure when. It didn't matter. My only concern had been Heph and his safety. She stood, dusting her pants off as Heph made his way back to me. "You both fought well," she said as she stepped away. Though we all knew Heph was never in any danger.

Death season had passed. As midnight struck, Persephone had disappeared into the night and gone back to Tartarus with the help of either Hekate, like normal, or perhaps even Nyx, since she'd made her way out from her realm of shadows. The gates of Tartarus were firmly shut. No soul, mortal or immortal, would be allowed through. It was a time of reprieve for everyone within Tartarus. I couldn't help but smile as I thought about the passionate reunion that Seph would be having with her husband. While hers wasn't a reunion after her potential demise was looming over her head, I could appreciate how we both would have our own reunions and give ourselves over to the love for and need of our husbands.

Hera looked up at the sky and gave a little smile, the small ember in her chest flaring a little brighter. I was wise enough not to comment on it, of course. "I have something I must attend to. Take a week then come and see me for the next trial. The sooner you complete these last few, the better. I long for a time when I won't have to see your face." Her voice was mild as she said it though. Something was making her happy.

"I shall be there. Thank you for the healing and the break." Though from the look on her face, I was wondering if that break was actually for my benefit, or if she had something she would rather tend to herself.

Before I had the chance to foolishly ask, she was gone. "Let's go home," Heph murmured, pulling me against him. "I'm glad I don't have to be careful with you after all."

"Were you planning to be gentle?" I teased.

"No. Just not as vigorous as I had planned." That was a fair explanation. I nearly asked why we didn't just make use of the arena, but I saw how he glanced at the ichor still decorating the ground and thought better of it. Besides, it wasn't my space to make use of.

"Take us home." My words pulled him from whatever thoughts were plaguing him and he lifted me into his arms, doing as I asked.

THE TRIALS OF APHRODITE

As we were transported back to the house, the ichor covered armor disappeared. I half expected him to just bare my body completely to his gaze and have his way with me. But that gold still coated my skin, and he winced as he looked at it. Instead, he set me down long enough to remove his shirt and put it on me before lifting me once more. I wasn't sure what he planned, at least until he carried me through our room and into the bathroom. "I would rather clean you up first," he explained.

It was sweet, how he carefully did just that. I loved that he stood in the shower with me, so focused on washing away the ichor and inspecting every inch of my skin that he didn't give into the psychosomatic limp. As the last of the ichor was washed away from my body, I watched his expression shift. It sent a shiver through me, knowing that he was finally ready to take out all those concerns and fears on my body. And I was more than happy to let him.

CHAPTER XXI

THERE WERE NO WORDS between us, they weren't necessary. They would have just been in the way. His lips claimed mine as his hands went to my hips in a bruising grip. I could only hope that they would mark me, that I would have a lingering reminder of how much he'd craved me upon our reunion.

A wonderful feature of the shower in the home we picked out together to settle in after the wedding, was a bench that ran along the shower wall. I gave myself over to him as he moved me, laid me back on the smooth surface, and knelt between my legs. He wasted no time as he moved over me, breaking the kiss to look down our bodies as he guided his length to the apex of my thighs.

With how often he enjoyed my body, I knew that he didn't need to look, that he could do it by touch alone, but I also had learned how much he enjoyed watching our bodies become one. Sometimes he would have a look of disbelief, just for a moment, like it still wasn't real to him that he was free to have me any time that he wanted, that he could at all.

I couldn't stifle my sounds as he pushed his hips forward, working for every bit of my body, wrapping me around him. His gaze didn't meet mine, and I had no intention of taking it from the sight it seemed he needed most. My fingers played over the scars on his face as I let him have my pleasure, giving him every sound that he craved, that he skillfully drew from my throat. His gaze remained fixed on my mound, as he pushed his hips forward until our bodies were flush to one another. It was his way of consoling himself, I supposed, proving that I had made it back to him, whole and his. For a moment, I had to wonder if he had worried that Hera's other possible outcome might be true. Did he worry that I would forsake everything I had done for him, with him, and fall into Ares' arms? A small part of me told me that the thought was always in the back of his mind that I would pick Ares over him once more. I would spend the rest of our lives proving to him that it would never be the case again. He was all I wanted. The only one that I needed.

Heph raised his head, slanting his mouth over mine as he drew his hips back before driving them forward, his lips devouring my cries. My hands moved to his back, digging my nails into his skin as I wrapped my legs around him. He took me, hard and fast against the bench. There was nothing kind or loving about it, it was frantic and passionate, desperate. Our bodies craved to be together, needed to feel whole with one another. All the fear and anticipation flowed out of me as I writhed beneath him, moving with him the best I could. Heph shifted us, just slightly changing the angle until every thrust had him hitting my cervix with uncaring abandon. I was always grateful when he did that. I loved the sensation, that it drew my pleasure ever higher as it took my breath away and made lights explode across my vision. My nails raked down his skin, leaving harsh red lines as I tore my mouth from his and cried out his name. In such a short time, he'd learned the secrets of my body, knew exactly how to use his own to make me give him exactly what he wanted.

I tried to hold out, but what little control I had left was wrenched from me with ease. My lips parted in warning but all that came out was a wordless scream that echoed off the shower walls. His cry echoed mine as my walls clenched down on his member, my nails piercing his skin. My head fell back against the bench, but the pain didn't register as I bucked and thrashed, lost in the pleasure only he could inflict on me. It wasn't until he stilled above me, and I drew a shuddering breath that I registered the burning in my lungs. He'd taken my ability to breathe for I don't know how long.

Heph made no effort to move, and I had no intention of asking him to. We laid there, his body pressing into mine as I wrapped myself tighter around him. "I hate how difficult all of this has been for you. That was never my intention," I murmured, pressing kisses along his collarbone.

"I know, little dove. I know." Through everything, he still tried to reassure me, comfort me. What had I done to deserve his enduring love? No, I wouldn't say I didn't deserve it anymore. I'd promised myself to leave those regrets and thoughts behind once my battle with Ares was done. Heph deserved better after all.

"Can you ever forgive me?" I whispered, nudging my nose against his when he turned his head to look at me.

"I already have. But you can make it up to me if you really wish to."

"I can?" He nodded in reply, and I nearly melted at the devious grin that he gave me. "I look forward to your instruction on how I can do so." Licking my lips, I decided to share something with him that I had discussed with Lola, but I wasn't sure how to tell him. It wasn't as though I was finished processing it myself. "I realized something recently." By that, I meant a few weeks prior.

"What's that?" he mumbled, dragging his mouth and beard along my neck, sending shivers through me.

It was effectively distracting. But I wanted to tell him while I still had the courage to do so. He was special, in every way. "I have only ever willingly submitted to you." Heph paused, raising his head to look down at me with a curious expression. "I never have wanted to submit to anyone before. It has always been a fight for dominance, or I was always in control. But I have never wanted to let someone take me from the very beginning, to put myself in their hands the way I do with you." He deserved to know how special he was, that he alone changed my preferences. We both knew the truth of such a dynamic, who held the power. But it came from a trust that I had only ever felt with him. He made me feel safe enough to go there with him.

Heph was quite for a few more moments, and I couldn't help squirming under his gaze. "You're serious?" I nodded, averting my gaze. The vulnerability of the moment was starting to become too much. "Look at me little dove." Without waiting for me to do so on my own, he grasped my chin and turned my head, his intense gaze burning into me. "I have never wanted to make someone submit to me before. I knew things because of clients, but I never wanted to participate before. But you ignited something in me that I never knew was there. There are no words for what you've done to me, Dite."

I wasn't sure what to say to that. The only thing that came to mind was, "perhaps you can show me then."

The wicked smile on his face told me that I was in for a very tiring night of him showing me exactly what he meant. That mirthful expression set me ablaze. It was like all the energy I had spent in the battle with Ares had returned, and I was grateful because I was sure that he would take everything I had and more before the sun rose.

Heph took great care in cleaning me up and greater care in drying me after carrying me out of the shower. Even though he'd seen Hera heal me and looked over my body repeatedly for any sign of a wound, he did it once more. Every brush of the towel over my skin, he inspected my body, like he was worried either he or his mother had missed some fatal injury. I didn't bother trying to dissuade him from doing so. I knew that it would give him peace of mind. Or at least I hoped it would. I knew the toll that months of waiting had taken on him, the time that he spent thinking only the worst of what could happen in my battle against Ares. Why would I deny him whatever gave him comfort?

I saw his demeanor shift a moment before he turned me to face the large mirror in our bathroom. After everything, I had expected him to drag me to bed, to wear both our bodies out until we were utterly spent and exhausted. That was how it usually went at least. Not that I would complain about Heph being impatient enough not to move us back to bed.

A shiver went through me as I watched Heph through the mirror, his gaze raking down the reflection of my body. One calloused hand rose to cup my breast, roughly massaging it as he teased the nipple with his fingertips. His touch made my head fall back against his shoulder, soft gasps and whimpers escaping my parted lips. Heph slid his other hand down to rub at my mound before moving it to tease along my inner thigh. It was infuriating, the way he'd barely brush his knuckles against my lips as he ran his fingers over my skin, avoiding the one place I really wanted him to touch me. My whimpers grew louder, a wordless plea for him to give me the attention I needed.

"Patience, little dove. You still have to be punished." His voice was low and rumbling, my body tightening in reaction to that tone.

"Why?" I breathed.

"Because you let this beautiful body be injured." We both knew that it was an inevitability, but I could play along with him.

"It was an accident," was the only argument I had. "I am very sorry."

"Not good enough." His hands on my body were suddenly gone. No more stimulation, no more maddening touches. I lifted my head to see what he was planning but he moved first, his hands grabbing and lifting me. Instinctively, I put my feet on the counter, trying to offer any assistance I could to him. The pleased smile on his lips told me that was the right move. "Good little dove," he purred, shifting us so my weight was resting on him. He used his hands to position my legs exactly how he wanted, bending my knees and spreading me until I was completely exposed to our gazes in the mirror. "Such a pretty sight. Look how puffy and needy you are." His words sent a flush across my skin, but he reached up to hold my chin in place when I tried to look away. "I said look." Heph's other hand moved to teasingly run his fingers over those swollen lips with feather light touches that left me mewling and even more frustrated than before.

"I am," I whined. It wasn't a sound I was familiar with making, not before Heph, but I had a feeling he'd be pulling it from me even more from then on.

"That's not the attitude you should have, little dove. You seem not to want your reward." His fingers pinched at that swollen sensitive skin, making me cry out for him.

"I want it! I want it!"

"Then take your punishment like a good little princess." His fingers released me, rubbing gently. I let out a shuddering sigh and nodded for him, wordlessly agreeing to anything he wanted. I'd give him any and everything that he wanted, all he had to do was ask. Especially when he was pairing it with praise. I had no idea when that became something I enjoyed, but he was skilled at somehow helping me to find new kinks and enjoyments that I hadn't considered before. During my period of self-discovery, I found that I did like being reassured, but Heph had transformed that into a need for praise.

Heph moved his hand from my core, the throbbing and pulsing growing even more intense. Instead, he grabbed something off the counter. I didn't have a moment to see what it was before he was bringing the smooth back of it down between my legs. Pain and pleasure exploded in a searing light as I threw my head back over his shoulder, my body writhing against his. I would've collapsed into a screaming, dripping mess on the counter if he hadn't wrapped his other arm around my midsection to hold me against him.

A low rumbling laugh shook his upper body as he murmured against my ear, "that was a very good reaction, little dove. Now you're starting to get it. I'll completely destroy you before we're done. I'll break you down and remold you until you only know the pleasure that I can give you."

His words did nothing to help the burning desire that was ripping me apart, that was driving all reason from my mind. The only thing I could think of was him making good on that threat. It was a promise that I needed him to keep. I knew he could do it; I knew that he could drive me insane with pleasure and then wrap me around his finger, fill my head with only thoughts of him. Just as I was ready to voice that, to tell him how easily he could do it, he brought that object down between my legs again. It took a few moments for my breath to return and my eyes to clear enough to make out that it was my hairbrush. "Wha-" I never got to finish the question as he struck me again, slapping the smooth back of it against my dripping core until I was screaming his name, and my vision went dark.

"Little dove," Heph murmured in a singsong tone. His nose nuzzled against my ear. I was still propped up on the edge of the low counter with my legs spread in front of the mirror. But I lost at least a few moments. Maybe longer given how he was affectionately trying to rouse me. "There you are. It's too soon for you to give out on me." But the concern in his eyes told me that he worried he might have gone too far.

"Forgive me. I was overcome by your skill." He'd given me the chance to use my safe word, to stop things entirely, but I didn't.

The proud look on his face made me glad that I could hold out and continue. "You are even more impressive than I imagined, little dove. I wonder just how much more you can take before I break you beyond repair."

"I can take everything," I murmured, rocking my hips slightly as he rubbed the back of the brush against me once more.

"I'll put that to the test." Heph pulled the brush away and shifted it in his grasp. I was curious what he had planned but I didn't have to wonder for long. He teased the handle between my swollen lips for a moment before pushing it into my center. I cried out as he pushed the entire handle into me, giving me a mere second to breathe before pulling it back and thrusting it back into me with enough force that I knew my lips would be terribly sore in the morning. Or, rather, delightfully so. Whatever soreness he left me the next day was absolute bliss because he knew just how to put it to use. I knew in the morning, he'd explore every inch of my skin with his fingers, seeking out anything that might still be tender from our previous activities. And I loved what would come after, how he'd go from being so tender to releasing his ruthless side so he could make the soreness even worse.

My hands grabbed onto the arm that he was using to maneuver the brush. Not to stop him, just because I needed to hold onto him, I needed to ground myself. I felt like I was falling and floating while being wrapped in the most vicious pleasure possible. I was so lost in the sensations that I couldn't decipher the filthy things he was whispering against my ear, just that his breath was hot on my skin. But just as I felt that pressure building and I knew that one drop more would send me over the edge, the brush was gone. I had never before screamed in despair during amorous activities, but I couldn't stop the sound from escaping.

The sounds of my misery and denial amused him as he removed my hands from his arm. He looked incredibly pleased as he raised the brush to his mouth, his tongue flicked out to lap up some of my juices coating the smooth surface. With him distracted, I thought, foolishly, that I might just be able to take the edge off. As discreetly as I could, I slid a hand between my thighs, running my fingers over the aching flesh. I'd barely managed a single pass down my slit before Heph dropped the brush and grabbed both my arms, wrenching them back and between our bodies.

"That was very foolish, little dove. Now it seems like I just might have to punish you more." His hands flowed with power before smooth metal wrapped around my wrists, holding them in place. I thought that was all, that he'd just restrain me. But one of his hands wrapped gently around my throat, more energy flowing from his skin and wrapping around me. When he pulled his hand away, I could see a gold collar left behind, a thin chain coming from the front, a slightly thicker one going down my back. From how it brushed my spine, I could tell that it connected to my manacled arms he had pinned between us. Not for the first time, I wondered about collaring, that he might just enjoy having that sign of possession over me. Of course, there were plenty of ways to collar someone, the most common discreet one being a necklace. Would that be something we might explore? We had eternity to do so, to figure those things out. And I just had a few more trials until we were free.

Heph didn't give me a chance to answer. He lifted me and carried me from the bathroom with his hands under my thighs. The throbbing and dripping need between my thighs weren't getting any better, and there was something incredibly arousing with how he kept me exposed and helpless like that. I knew what he was doing, and I loved it.

As he reached our bed, he set me down on my feet, so I was bent over the edge of it, wrapping the thin gold chain hanging from the front of my collar around his hand. Heph pulled it tight, wrenching my head back as he brought his face down to mine. His other hand disappeared from view, but I could tell from his movements and his hand brushing the back of my thighs that he was stroking himself. "I hope you're ready, little dove. We aren't stopping until you learn your lesson." I knew from experience that there didn't seem to be a limit to how many times Heph could take me. Never before had I met someone that could keep up with my libido, not the way he could. Some nights it felt like I was the one struggling to keep up with him.

I had nothing to say, and he didn't need me to. He pushed his cock into me with a vigorous thrust, slamming his hips forward and tearing a cry from me. Heph would be as good as his word, and he'd make sure that I was overflowing with his seed from every orifice and begging for mercy before he was satisfied. And then I would enjoy aftercare, the likes of which I had never had before. I could take any punishment he meted out, and I would crave more of it.

CHAPTER XXII

It nearly took me having to chain Heph to our bed to keep him from going with me to see Hera. I just wanted to spare him from more torture, more pain. Besides, I faced Ares and survived without loss of life or limb. Nothing else Hera threw at me would be nearly as difficult. Or at least I hoped it wouldn't be. How could anything ever be more trying or life-threatening than facing off with the god of war himself?

Hopefully, that thought wouldn't be a curse I cast on myself. The last thing I needed was for Hera to change her mind and suddenly think of something worse. Then again, she did say that there was going to be another difficult task that she'd already set. Was that what I was walking into?

Once more, I'd forgone heels. I doubted that anything the queen goddess set for me would be able to be done in heels. Boots would be better. Maybe. I had to hope that I didn't mess up by leaving Hephaestus at home, that I wouldn't need my armor. Though if Hera was kind enough, she'd bring Heph to us if I did. What did she have planned for me? The nerves roiled through me, churning my stomach as I opened the door to her office. My hand didn't shake as I did. Yay for small victories. I wondered if any others would be coming my way.

Hera looked as chic and polished as she always did. Like a busty wet dream that was cleaned up and set in the most professional office possible. Not that I would ever describe her as such to her face. I'm not quite sure whether she would be flattered by that or not.

"Would you like to hear the good news?" She had good news for me? That was incredibly shocking. All I could do was nod. "The trial I wanted to set for you, I heard from my son that you've already done it. Congratulations. I will count this trial as passed."

"Is this the other difficult one that you had set for me?" I wouldn't celebrate yet, not until I knew how much trouble was ahead of me.

"No. That one, I think I will save for last."

"What did I already achieve?"

For the first time, Hera set her pen down and sat back in her seat, smiling at me with a look in her eyes I couldn't decipher. "You reconciled with your children."

I blinked, not quite sure that I heard her right. "That...that was my trial?"

"I know the pain and difficulty that comes from trying to do just that. So I am glad that you already took the initiative and did it. Celebrate. Be grateful that I didn't

THE TRIALS OF APHRODITE

At least Heph had grown less distrustful of Micah, he accepted that there never had been and never would be anything between us. But I still brought Tori along to make Heph more comfortable. Besides, I liked whatever was blossoming between my mortals. I wouldn't pry, but I found it precious. Callie had stayed behind at our home to fix dinner. My mortals were going to help me convince my beloved that tonight would be a sci-fi marathon. It would be a welcome break from the countless anime that he'd put on for us over the last few months. I loved that he worked to find ones that I would enjoy, but all the characters and stories were starting to mix together in my head. I needed a dose of sci-fi, it was something I desperately craved. And while I was certain that I could convince Heph to watch what I wanted on my own, it was far more enjoyable when we had my mortals over to back me up. Plus, I loved it when Callie made us a feast. Food was more enjoyable when shared with a crowd. And my found family, as well as my beloved, were my favorite crowd.

CHAPTER XXIII

THERE WEREN'T WORDS TO express how happy Heph was to hear that I had one less trial to do. I could see the joy and need bubbling up under the stoic expression he kept around everyone else. No one else could see it, but I could. I knew him better than anyone else. It was something I could proudly say, something I loved. And I knew that he was ready to let all that happiness out the moment we were alone.

As soon as the door shut, Heph laughed and lifted me by my thighs. "You marvelous woman! Your inherent goodness and motherly love is even more impressive than I thought." I had never been lifted and spun before, but Heph did it. The limp that he'd had in front of the mortals was gone. Like he didn't need something like that to hide behind when it was just us. I treasured the fact that he was so comfortable with me, that he didn't fear my judgement any longer. He finally seemed to accept that I loved him, that I craved his body as much as I did his company. And I was his, wholly and completely his.

"I take it you are pleased by the fact that your mother has given us another week of peace?" I asked as I grinned down at him.

"Very," he replied, carrying me from our front door and over to the couch. As he sat, he lowered me into his lap and crushed me against his chest. "One less trial. There is nothing that could make me happier. Well, unless she said that the other two had already been passed as well."

I didn't want to break the happy moment; I wanted him to beam at me like that for as long as possible. So, I didn't tell him what I knew, what else had happened in Hera's office. At least not regarding the trials that were left. "Did you know that she still has the penis I threw at her?" The look on his face amused me. He leaned his head back to stare at me with wide, unbelieving eyes. "The next time you go to her office, look at the display cases. There is a scaled penis that should seem incredibly familiar."

"I will keep an eye out," he promised with a chuckle. Sighing happily, he brushed my hair back from my face, gazing fondly at me. "This is starting to feel like a dream again, one I never want to wake from. I would tear the world apart if someone tried."

"That will be unnecessary, my beloved. This is reality. Dreams of you pale in comparison to everything that I have gotten to enjoy with you. None of my dreams did you justice, they could never show just how beautiful you are, every inch of your body surpassed everything I had hoped you would be." I loved the slight dusting of pink across his craggy cheeks. It just made him even more beautiful in my eyes.

"Now who's the sweet talker?" he grumbled, swatting at my bottom. I couldn't stop the moan and giggle that escaped, but the grin he gave me was worth it. "I just want to love you tonight."

I wasn't sure what he meant by that, but I was happy to let him show me. Though I had a slight clue. It would be a first if I was right. "Love me, Hephaestus. Show me every ounce of your feelings. I can hear them if you let me. I can watch them dance across our bodies like the most beautiful array of lights ever to exist." Wordlessly, he stood up, lifting me but wrapping my legs around his waist this time so that our faces were closer together. I took advantage of it, a tender kiss, a small glimpse of the affection that I was sure he was going to drown me in.

Sightlessly, he carried me through the house to our bedroom. He was gentle as he set me down on the dark coverlet. Every move was tender as he peeled my jeans down my legs, lifted my crimson blouse and pulled it over my head. He touched me like I was a delicate treasure as he removed every piece of fabric that was blocking his view of my body. I loved it when he was affectionate just as much as when he was rough and domineering. The loving actions were rare once things turned nefarious usually. He was quite affectionate when we were alone in our everyday life or once he began the aftercare, but gentle lovemaking wasn't something we usually partook in.

But I could tell that tonight it wasn't just him that needed it, I did, too.

As he reached for the bottom of his shirt, I pushed his hands away, taking the olive fabric in hand as I got up on my knees on the bed. I savored the sight as I lifted it, slowly exposing every inch of his scarred skin, the impressive muscle he'd built through years of hard work. He didn't need to have defined muscle, though his arms were well defined. Abs for vanity's sake weren't his style. And he didn't need them. The solid build he had, the strength that he used against me so often, just seeing him like that was enough to set my body alight.

"Little dove?" I didn't realize that once I removed his top that I had just knelt there, gazing fondly at his bared upper body. It was a sight that was worthy of being lost in.

"Just enjoying the view, my sparrow," I murmured in reply. His shirt fell off the edge of the bed as I released it, reaching for his pants to unfasten them. Heph had used the last of his patience though, stepping back to finish undressing himself before moving to the bed once more, crawling on it to face me where I knelt naked.

"I do the same, but I cannot wait forever. I need to feel you, be inside you. This hollowness inside me is only filled when we're one." I knew what he meant, and I hoped that one day, it wouldn't take our bodies being joined for that to be made better. For the moment, I was happy to do whatever it took to make him happy, especially when I knew it'd bring me the same amount of joy.

When he reached for me, I took his hands in mine, gave him a chaste kiss, and then moved away. The look on his face made me regret it, but I had something in mind. "Sit against the headboard. Please," I added. It was enough to please him. He did as I asked, pressing his back to the quilted headboard and looked at me expectantly. My gaze slid over him, from the fiery hair, down to his muscled body, lingering on the jutting length that twitched with anticipation.

"Aphrodite," he growled, his patience obviously gone. It was rare that he ever said my full name, so I knew that I needed to stop just enjoying the sight of his naked body.

I nudged his legs together before crawling over them, straddling his lap. My hands rested on his shoulders as I ran my lips over his face. Heph grabbed my hips, gently but firmly. I knew it was wrong to continue teasing him, but I wanted to savor the moment a little longer. Quite often we seemed to worry about foreplay after we'd finished our first round of fun, but it just couldn't be helped. I didn't even care. It just went to show how much we desperately needed one another. And I would never be ashamed of how much I needed my husband.

His hands squeezed gently, a warning as he ran his lips down to my breast. As he took a nipple into his mouth, suckling at it, I reached between our bodies and lined the head of his member to my core. Slowly, I lowered my hips, my hand tangling in his hair. Heph's sounds vibrated against my skin, pulling a pleasured shudder from me as I took more of him in. I'd never wanted to treat him so delicately, but I loved how I could savor every moment by sheathing him in me so carefully. Once I'd taken all of him in, I let out a shaky breath, stilling as I enjoyed the way it felt to have him filling me so completely. Heph raised his head, resting his forehead to mine with a sated smile. It was a bit early for such an expression, but I was just glad that he seemed to be getting everything he needed as well.

A groan escaped as he moved his hands down to reposition my legs. I got the message quickly, wrapping them around him as I shifted in his lap. My hands cradled his face as I lowered my head, kissing him lovingly. As I did, Heph pulled my body flush to his. The feel of my breasts pressed firmly to his chest made me whimper into the kiss, his mouth drinking down every sound I gave him. There was something so intimate about how our bodies were tangled, as much of our skin touching as possible, and it was incredibly comforting. It always felt like I could never get enough of him, that I couldn't have enough of his body wrapped around mine.

My hips rocked forward, drawing more muffled sounds of pleasure from both of us. One of his hands pressed to the middle of my back, the other going to my ass to help guide me. I loved that even when we were being slow and gentle, he would take control back.

Every slow thrust shouldn't have been as satisfying as it was. I never expected such a delicate coupling to bring me satisfaction. Even if it didn't, I wouldn't care. I was content to just sit there being held against him, to have him filling me up. I could sit there like that with him for hours. If only I could stop time, to remain like that forever.

When had I developed such intense feelings? I knew I loved him; I knew I craved him, but there was an intensity that was nothing like what I'd experienced before. The fighting and passion that I had with Ares; I'd thought that the most intensity that my feelings could have. But there was something in the way I craved Heph, body and soul, desperation, it was new and something that I could never put into words properly. How could I ever express something that I was struggling to understand myself?

It wasn't something I needed to figure out. I knew that if I wanted to, I could talk it out with him. Heph and I were discovering new levels of communication that neither of us had ever had with someone before. And I loved how much I trusted him, that I could be so open and vulnerable with him.

Our kiss deepened, growing more intense. While my hips were still thrusting shallowly, the pace had increased. I didn't know if it was my doing, or he'd guided me to it. All I knew was that my head was swimming as the pleasure drew that coil deep in my belly ever tighter. His hand on my ass tightened his grip, the hand on my back pressed me tighter against him, like he was trying to merge our bodies until nothing could part us. I tangled a hand in his hair as my other gripped his shoulder, digging my nails into the skin there. It was just something I enjoyed and he liked how I would care for the scratches after our fun.

I didn't mean to pull back from the kiss, taking a gasping breath before that coil snapped. A scream tore from my throat as I bucked against Heph. His hand guiding my body was the only thing that kept me moving, I was lost to everything. It was like electricity was searing me from the inside in the most wonderful way. I couldn't control the jerky movements of my body as I rode the pleasure that he extended, moving me atop him until he finally filled my clenching walls with his seed.

His grip stilled my body, pulling me as tight against him as physically possible as I struggled to relearn to breathe. My smile mirrored his, lazy and content.

"That was everything I'd hoped it'd be," he whispered, nudging his nose to mine.

"Agreed. Just please let me stay like this."

"I wouldn't have let you move." His answer made my smile widen. I was glad that he enjoyed the contact as much as I did. While I knew we'd have to move eventually, I just wanted to stay there.

It was an intimacy I'd never realized I needed, one that I had never dreamed possible. How could I pull away? "I love you, Heph."

"I love you, too, Dite."

I savored those words, the feel of his body against mine. We stayed like that for hours, just wrapped up in one another. And for two more rounds, just slightly repositioning each time. But even when we untangled our limbs and laid down to sleep, he was buried inside me. There was nothing like falling asleep with him filling me as he spooned me against his strong form. And waking like that, to him rocking his hips in his sleep, it was something that I hoped to repeat every morning for the rest of our existence.

CHAPTER XXIV

I HAD FORESEEN THAT Heph would be unhappy once I told him the entire conversation Hera and I had in her office. He wanted to go with me, and I really couldn't find a reason for him not to go. While he accepted that it wasn't going to be too dangerous a task, maybe, he wanted to be with me.

Walking into Hera's office, she looked past me at Heph who trailed behind me with the cane he used very rarely anymore. She looked surprised that he had chosen to accompany me.

"He insisted on joining us," I explained as I stopped in front of her desk.

"I figured."

"Hello to you, too, mother." Heph didn't look happy to be there, but I knew that he was ready for the trials to be over. He didn't want that lingering threat to exist anymore. All he wanted was for us to be able to live our life in peace.

"Hello, dear Hephaestus. I am always pleased to see you, but not with that look on your face." She knew as well as I did that him being there meant it'd likely go how every other time did. He'd petition for her to stop the trials somehow, to have mercy on me. I loved him for that, that he just wanted to make my life easier. But things couldn't be changed. They would have needed to be fixed centuries earlier. It was my fault things were like that, but I was trying to quickly fix it, to complete the trials so we could live our new life together.

I didn't want to interrupt, but I figured I could at least find out what the trial was before Heph started trying to get Hera to find a way to release me from my oath. "What do I need to do?"

"Straight to it then," Hera said with a sigh. "You must acquire a pure heart." The confusion was clear on my face. Did she want me to purify my heart? Or did I need to find someone with one. "Not your own. Bring a pure heart back with you."

"A mortal? It is against the peace treaty between the pantheons to slaughter mortals indiscriminately." Not to mention the wrath of the more fearsome beings that ran the afterlife hub. While I worked with them from time to time when they needed me in the therapy realm, I did my best to keep them happy. Well placed gifts and never breaking the treaty did wonders when trying to stay on their good sides.

"I didn't say mortal. I don't particularly want *those* people coming after me for causing untimely deaths." It wasn't that Hera was afraid of them, it was more that they could make all our lives incredibly miserable balancing the scales. "What is the epitome of goodness, innocence, and purity?" They were synonyms, but I wasn't about to correct her. She could say it however she liked. But I was dreading what the answer was.

It took a few moments to figure it out but then the answer appeared in my mind. I couldn't stifle my gasp as I stared at her. "You are truly sick and depraved."

My words didn't phase her. Hera merely shrugged, an expression I couldn't decipher on her face. "When you're finished, deliver it to Hekate. Tell her my debt is paid."

"They were hunted to extinction by the mortals thousands of years ago. How could I possibly find one?" Did a sorcerer have one? Had one of the gods of another pantheon kept one as a pet? Or maybe someone knew...something.

"There is an island that no mortal can find or reach. It's protected by...another pantheon. I heard they are actually thriving there, without humans to taint their existence."

Of course, Hera would know where to find one. That was our queen. "How do I find it?"

"That, I don't know. Like I said, it isn't our pantheon that has put the barrier around the island. Before you ask, no, I don't know which one it is. I didn't think to ask when she gave me the task." Hera obviously never had any intention of going to get one herself. Had she thought of foisting the task off on me once she heard what Hekate wanted? And what had Hekate done for her that she had a debt? There were too many questions and not an answer in sight. Hopefully Hekate knew where to find the island.

Could I do it? Could I kill such a pure creature? As much as I missed them, I never thought I would see one again. And now that I could, I would have to kill it? Heph wrapped his arms around me, obviously sensing the turmoil in me. I savored that comfort he gave me, but I knew that I couldn't turn back. The trial was set and there was no way I could refuse it. I just wasn't sure I would be the same after it.

From the look on Heph's face as I tilted my head back for a kiss, I knew that he and his mother would be having words. "Send me to Hekate," I requested, pulling back from the tender kiss that warmed me to my toes.

Heph didn't even have a chance to let me go before I was sent from the office by Hera's power. I was dropped in the woods, and I was ever grateful that I had opted for boots and jeans again.

My gaze was drawn up, a relic of some kind hanging from the tree above me. As I looked behind me, there were more figures and symbols hanging from various branches. Whatever they were, they didn't work on our kind. I could feel the power coming from them, but my guess was that it was to keep mortals away. And perhaps it might work like an alarm that something immortal had arrived in her lands. There was a small cottage up ahead that I could barely make out between the trees. I could hear the howl of her wolves as I walked closer.

I knew there would be various animals that she kept close to her, it was her way. It'd been many, many years since I'd last seen Hekate. I wondered how she was faring in the modern world. Though, I supposed she was avoiding it, given that she still preferred to hole up in the woods.

Then again, I realized how wrong I could be once she stepped out on the porch. Her hair was dyed a pale lavender, her brows dark and thinly drawn on. She'd fallen into a goth aesthetic since I last saw her. It was a good look for her. There were some that just looked even more beautiful when darkly made up. It enhanced those gorgeous looks she'd always had.

"You lost?" she asked, crossing her thin arms over her chest. Hekate wore a large, loose, thin, black sweater that hit her at mid-thigh and hung off one slender shoulder. I couldn't tell if she was wearing bottoms, but her legs were wrapped up in black fishnet tights. Her lips had been colored the same black as the heavy makeup accentuating her large bright eyes. Even the silver hoops she had put through her lip, nose, and brow didn't look out of place. She'd been stunning the first time I saw her, but she always looked uncomfortable somehow. Not anymore. It was like she was finally busting out of her shell. "Hello?"

I realized I was staring again. Perhaps my powers were making a comeback in a way. I thought that I had merely stared at and admired Heph because he was mine. But I had done it a bit with Hera, and even more with Hekate. I was mesmerized by beauty again. It'd been a long time since that had happened.

"My apologies. No, I meant to come here. Hera sent me."

"Ah. So, she won't get her hands dirty." Hekate scratched the back of her leg with her other fishnet clad foot. That explained why she was still on the porch; she had no shoes on. I wouldn't want twigs and leaves stuck in my tights either. "You're late."

That was a curious thing to say. "What do you mean?"

"Someone already brought me one." She looked irritated by that. "I've spent decades alone and now I can't get a moment's peace. When one of you needs me, you all do."

"I have to bring you one."

"I don't need a second one. And I also don't want the cost of a unicorn life to be on my head twice."

The realization that I couldn't finish the trial set in as ichor began filling my chest and throat once more. I doubled over, coughing as I struggled to breathe past it. My body was trembling, and I couldn't hold myself up, even pressing my hands to my legs. I fell to my knees, my hands stinging as the twigs dug into them. There was a thunderous pounding in my ears, and I couldn't make out Hekate's frantic words. But I felt her power flow over me before everything went dark. It was warm, comforting, and all I could think of was how much I would miss Heph's embrace.

"What the fuck was that?" Hekate asked as I opened my eyes. The metallic sweet taste of ichor was still there on my tongue. It was real.

Turning my head, I sighed. I was curled up on a worn maroon loveseat. My gaze went to the full couch, and I understood. There was an unconscious and wounded mortal on it. First Nyx and Eros, now Hekate. Why was everyone taking in mortals? Oh, I did that, too. "I swore on the ichor to complete the trials set forth by Hera."

"Idiot."

"I did it for Heph."

"I heard about that. Did you get my present?" While she hadn't made it to the ceremony, she did send a gift to us. It was an amulet that I hadn't really thought about much. But I was beginning to wonder what it was, what it would do.

"Yes. It was lovely."

That made her snort as she sat cross-legged on the coffee table with a deck of tarot cards. There was a steaming mug of tea beside her that was unlike anything I'd smelled before. "It wasn't meant to be lovely. But I'm glad you liked it."

My gaze went to the ground and my previous intention of putting my feet down was gone. As I twisted in the loveseat, I drew my knees up. There were various breeds of snakes slithering around the floor of her den. I didn't want to risk angering any of them. I spotted some dogs sleeping behind the couch, a few Dobermans that were beautiful and sleek. Between them and the wolves, I wondered if those were all the animals she had there. They probably weren't. She likely had more in other parts of the house. She'd always loved animals.

"So, you saved me?"

"Temporarily."

"Thank you. Truly." I was going to owe her a big favor for that. Not that I minded. I was sure that Heph would send her a gift as well when he found out.

"Why did it happen?" She knew about the oath, but apparently, she wanted specifics.

"I cannot complete the trial. You refuse to take a second pure heart and I need to make good on the debt that Hera owes you."

Hekate sat in thought for a few moments, shuffling the deck of tarot cards in her hands. "What if I just transfer the debt to you?"

"Will that work?" Not that I minded owing her a favor, it meant I'd get to continue living.

"I can remove the spell keeping you safe for now and see if it does once I transfer the debt to you." She sighed as she got up from the coffee table, setting the cards beside her mug. The snakes on the ground moved, clearing spots for her feet like they knew which way she was going. It was intriguing. They repeated the strange dance as she returned, sitting in front of me with a rolled piece of parchment I could feel more than one person's energy coming from.

Without instruction, I wiped up some of the ichor that was still coating my face and pressed my gold-stained finger to the parchment. The sensation isn't one that could ever truly be described. There were too many things that happened at once to ever explain how it felt to form a contract like that with another deity. It's something that one would have to try for themselves to understand.

As soon as the contract of debt was transferred to me, my energy replacing the one I assumed was Hera's, Hekate waved her hand between us. I felt the power she'd wrapped protectively around me before pull away, draining back into her. We both waited, tense for whatever might come. But nothing happened. I was grateful that I would survive after all, that I wouldn't have to hurt Heph like that. Perhaps it was wrong, but I was even more glad that I wouldn't have to slaughter a unicorn. There was something I was still curious about.

"Thank you. I know that I owe you a favor, but I feel like I owe you two now. But there is something that I have been wondering."

"You're welcome. And maybe I'll have an answer," she muttered, the parchment disappearing from her hand as she picked up her still steaming mug. I wondered if she used her powers to keep it at the perfect temperature, whatever kind of tea it was she was drinking.

"What pantheon saved them? I heard that one was protecting them."

"One that we wouldn't want to anger or battle ever again." That narrowed it down to two or three that I could think of. Though one was still a power to be feared. The others had dwindled down a bit after centuries of neglect.

I didn't need to know. None would take kindly to trespassing. It was better to let it remain a secret known by few. "I will accept that as an answer. Could you return me to Hera? Please?" My gaze went to the wounded mortal, but she obviously had no intention of explaining who it was. It wasn't my business to pry into her affairs. If she needed assistance, she could always call for me. I owed her after all. I wondered if Heph would feel the same, if he would feel indebted to her. Hekate did find a simple way to clean up the mess made because of whatever deal Hera had with her.

Nodding, Hekate reached out and took my hand. Warmth spread through me, and I was back at Hera's office. I chuckled as I appeared sitting on top of her desk. Hekate did seem to have a fondness for sitting on things that weren't seats and she decided that she should share that joy. I was amused, but I doubted the queen goddess would be.

CHAPTER XXV

I thought it strange that Hera wasn't immediately upset that when I appeared sitting on top of her desk, that she didn't have some witty or scathing comment about it. That was because she had her head in her hands and no way to see that I had appeared. While I knew that she could feel my energy or power as easily as I could feel theirs, I suppose she was distracted. By what? My giant muscled wall of a husband standing over her and shouting about how I had done enough, and she should call the last trials done already. For the first time in as long as I could remember, I felt bad for her. It wasn't something that I had felt in centuries towards Hera, and I wasn't sure how to recover from it.

While I could've remained silent and let the show go on for a little longer, let him vent out whatever frustrations he still had left, I wanted to step in. Besides, I had plans for those pent-up feelings he was taking out on his mother.

"This is a very loud welcome," I teased in a raised tone so I could hopefully be heard over Heph's booming voice as I climbed off Hera's desk.

It did the trick, thankfully. Heph turned to look at me, stopping midsentence. The ire on his face melted away and he moved around her desk to gather me into his arms. "You were much quicker than I expected you to be."

"Someone beat me to it. But Hekate has relieved you of your debt. And I was not asked to needlessly slaughter a pure and beautiful creature," I explained as Heph looked me over. It would've been wise to wipe away the ichor that had coated my face and shirt after the little incident that Hekate had saved me from. But in my haste to get back to my beloved, I didn't think to do it. Not until he was inspecting my skin and trying to see what had caused the ichor in the first place. Obviously, it wasn't from a kill that I already admitted I didn't have to do.

"Dite." His tone told me he was expecting answers.

Hera avoided my gaze, visibly relieved that his attention was off her. "When Hekate told me that someone had already brought her a heart, she told me that she would not accept another." I realized that he hadn't observed the battle with Ares and that something similar had happened then. "The oath took it as my inability to do as instructed and that I was going to have to break it. Hekate fixed everything so it really should be fine now."

The expression on his face told me that it was not fine. He was upset. That anger was directed away from me back to his mother. "Did you contact Hekate to see if she had already gotten what *you* were supposed to give her?"

When Hera winced, I took pity on her and wrapped myself around him. "Rather than doing this, which you could always come back another day to do, we could go home." My tone was one he was very familiar with. Just as he could give me a single look to tell me that we were in for a good time, I could use the barest bit of inflection to tell him the same. It was one that he always reacted to, and this situation made no difference. With one last glare at his mother, Heph threw me over his shoulder and took us home.

I was grateful that he wasn't going to stand there and argue with her. There were better ways to deal with those feelings after all. More constructive outlets. At least, in my opinion.

As he set me down, Heph turned and walked away. It was a jarring change that left me anxious as I looked after him. Was he in need of space? Did he just want to go work on something to get the frustration out? I could respect that, but I didn't want him to bottle up whatever it was he was feeling. It wasn't healthy.

A few moments later, Heph returned with a damp cloth in hand. He grabbed my chin with his other hand and began wiping the ichor off my face. The gentle touch didn't match the frustration in his eyes and the hard line of his mouth. I wanted desperately to reach up and smooth out his creased brow, to caress his face until he had calmed. But I couldn't. I wouldn't. From the expression on his face, I knew it was better to let him show me what he needed first. Either that, or we were in for a long, heated discussion. The latter didn't appeal to me nearly as much, though I knew we'd have a discussion about things either way. I rather it be after we worked out our stronger feelings and had that open and honest conversation in bed, wrapped up in one another.

Heph tossed the gold-stained towel in the general direction of the laundry room, his gaze firmly fixed on my face. It was a struggle not to squirm, but I managed to meet his eye. "What am I going to do with you?" he murmured, pulling me against his chest and wrapping his arms around my body.

"I have a few ideas, my sparrow. Perhaps using me as an outlet for your frustrations?"

At my suggestion, he nudged me back and gazed down at my face, trying to gauge whether I was serious or not. "Beyond our usual play?" It was something we'd discussed before but never actually tried.

I couldn't really blame him for his hesitation. What I was suggesting went beyond him using pleasure and other tools at his disposal to 'punish' me. But what better time was there to try it? It was something I had been curious about since my revelation regarding our dynamic. "I think this is the time to try it. Unless you find that all your ire has dissipated."

He didn't answer me. His actions told me that he was going to trust me to know my limits and he would take me at my word. Without discussing what he wanted, he pushed me down, guiding me to my knees. Heph let all his irritation and worry out, clear on his face and practically coming off his body in waves. If experimenting with some things that I had been wanting to try would help him, I was more than happy to get past my anxious feelings and be his relief.

Heph stripped off his well-worn duster and grey shirt with smooth and methodical movements. There was a menace to them, like the promise of violence from a predator preparing to strike. It sent a shiver through me, my body reacting nearly painfully. I craved everything he was silently promising. For him, I would play the good girl and stay on my knees, do only what he wanted me to do. I knew that everything I needed and wanted would be taken care of one way or another, but I wanted to make it all about him first. Or entirely. I wouldn't mind either way. His hands went to the top of his pants, unfastening them as I stared up at him. He hesitated for a moment before pushing them down and taking his length in hand. I couldn't help licking my lips as I watched him pump his hand over it a few times. It was hard and ready and the sight of him like that just increased the throbbing between my thighs.

His other hand reached down, wrapped my hair around his fist and guided my head forward. I could've been extra good and just parted my lips, but I looked up at him with an expectant expression. Heph arched a brow as he tapped the head of his cock against my lips, silently telling me what I better do.

The urge to brat was there, but it wasn't what we were doing. It wasn't what I was meant to be. Obediently, I opened my mouth. He didn't wait for me to move my mouth over his length. Instead, he used that tight grip on my hair to position me as he thrusted into my waiting mouth. Through countless nights of playing together, he knew what I could take, but he was going to push me to my limits. Heph moved his hips forward until my nose was buried against the trimmed red curls that sat at the base of his cock.

I'd shown him early on my lack of gag reflex. But even I needed to breathe. The strain on my lungs turned my skin a deep red, my eyes watering as I tried to fight that pain. Heph watched me closely, and when my hands went to his hips, he moved back enough to let me draw in a breath through my nose. It took in as much air as I could, and gently squeezed his skin. As soon as I did, Heph began a brutal pace. He vigorously thrust into my throat and pulled back, using my mouth as he would use any other part of me. And while I might dislike how his thrusts left me with tears streaming down, my nose running, and drool trickling down my chin, I knew that it was the state he wanted me in. The heat in his eyes as he looked down at me told me just how much he loved making me into a mess that he could use any and every way he wanted.

All I could do was try to time my breaths to when he pulled back, my mouth opening a little wider, so he didn't catch himself on my teeth. I wanted to suck him, to pleasure him, but I knew that he was enjoying himself. Letting him use my mouth as he was, that was what he needed. And it was a wonderful preview of everything else I knew would come. He'd likely been holding a lot of those feelings in since the first trial, if not also those that he had during our estranged marriage. One bout of face fucking wasn't likely to solve everything. But it could be a marvelous start.

One thing that always proved true, at least for me, was that during oral sex the larger an appendage was, the more difficult it was to go on for longer periods of time. I had gone hours with endowed male presenting partners before and I suffered for it after. It was the one kind of pain and soreness that I didn't want. Except with Heph. With him, I was eager to have the sore jaw, the aching in my throat, all of it. For him, I would endure whatever pain he gave me, and enjoy it.

When his hips began to lose their rhythm, I was surprised. While he wasn't a quick draw, it was still not as long as he usually lasted.

I loved how he used my hair as his handle, tightening his grip and tugging, pulling muffled moans that had my throat vibrating against his length. But when he yanked my head back and pulled his length free of my mouth, I was confused. Was he ready to try something else? My eyes widened for a moment as his other hand pumped quickly over his shaft. As soon as he cursed and groaned out my name, I let my eyes flutter closed, the heat of his seed spattering across my skin. It was a first for me and I didn't have many of those left. Never had I let someone do that before.

Always before, I thought it would feel humiliating, like I was being degraded. It didn't though. It felt like Heph was claiming me. And truthfully, I enjoyed a little degradation at his hands.

Heph released my hair and before I could reach up to wipe my eyes, a cold damp cloth was wiping everything away. From the scent of metal on it, I knew it was the one that he'd used to clean me before. Blinking a few times, I smiled up at him, noting his expression. He was concerned, but I wasn't sure if it was for my well-being or if he thought I'd be upset by what he'd done in the end. There was no reason for his concern. I'd enjoyed every moment so far and was eager to see what else he had in store for me. As he watched me, he kicked off his boots and finished removing his pants. It was the sign I yearned for, to know that he had even more planned.

He regarded me for a few more moments before he grabbed my hair in his fist once more and used it to pull me to my feet, guiding me by it to the couch. I was surprised when he shoved me against the back of it, but I just held onto the back of it and waited for instruction. None came. Instead, he reached beneath me and ripped the top of my pants, drawing a groan from me. I loved it when he showed off the incredible strength he had. The way he ripped apart my top was just as thrilling, the tattered material falling around us and baring my skin. He shoved my pants down to my knees and when he stood up again, I whimpered at the sensation of his length tapping against my bare ass.

There would never be a day when I wasn't grateful for how quickly he recovered, that he was seemingly always ready for me.

It seemed like he was out of patience, shoving my bra down to expose my chest before pushing me over the couch once more. One hand roughly fondled my breast as the other slid down my stomach to delve between my thighs. I cried out as he shoved two fingers into me, thrusting them roughly as his length slid between my cheeks. There was so much stimulation happening and I didn't know if I needed to breathe and have a small break or beg for even more.

"Got a question for you, little dove." His tone was guarded, like he was afraid of how I might react.

"Yes?" I gasped, my hips rocking as I sought more...more. The answer was that I needed more.

"Do you want me to hold back?" I shook my head 'no' in reply. "What if I make you bleed? Hurt you in ways I haven't before." It was dawning on me what he was asking and why he was so concerned. But I didn't want him to be hesitant, I didn't want him to hold back.

It took me a moment to find my words, just wanting to savor the way he drove those digits into me longer. "I meant it. Anything." We both knew that if something he wanted to do pushed me past my limits, I'd use the safe word. And we had a signal if I couldn't speak. Bound and gagged, all I had to do was release a bit of energy, something even I could manage, and he'd stop if I needed him to. So when I told him to do anything, not to hold back, I meant it. "Please," I whimpered, pushing my hips back against him.

"You're sure?" Heph asked, pressing kisses to my cheek before licking along the shell of my ear. "You'll be bloody and sore in ways that you haven't been before." I nodded, whining for him as I grabbed at his arms. It was clear to me what he wanted, and I wanted it. Perhaps he was unlocking a masochistic side to me that I didn't know I had. And while it wasn't something I'd want to do often, there were times like this when I knew that I would enjoy every ounce of agony he'd inflict.

Some might say I was crazy for wanting him to do what he intended, but it was just one more thing I was curious if I'd enjoy. I knew that it would be just absolutely painful to begin with, but I wanted it. And he was helping with how he was getting me close to the edge of bliss with his hand skillfully and roughly moving against my core.

The hand he'd been abusing my breast with disappeared as he drew his hips back. My breath hitched as I felt my excitement rise, the anticipation almost too much to bear. His length poked between my cheeks as he lined himself up with my entrance, one that we had enjoyed rounds with before, but never like this. There was no oil, no lubricant, no attempt to ease the sting as he pushed the head of his cock forward. I breathed out, willing my body to relax as I leaned forward as much as I could. Heph took it as the invitation it was and thrusted into me. I screamed out, my hands flailing before grabbing onto the couch and clawing at it. The hand between my thighs tipped the pain into an edge of pleasure. It was enough to keep me from crying out the safe word or trying to get away. Perhaps that was why Heph paused halfway into me, waiting to see if I would beg for things to end. It was only a moment, but when I didn't give him any indication that I wanted to stop, despite the tears streaming down my face once more as I struggled to catch my breath, he started a brutal pace. The way he slammed into me, driving me over the back of the couch showed me that the vigorous way he'd fucked my face was practically gentle.

His free hand gripped my hip with a tight grip that promised to revive the bruises already healing on my skin. I loved how often I had bruises of his fingers left after our fun, which was most days on some part of my body.

I couldn't catch my breath. Between the tearing and searing pain of him driving his endowment into my ass, the fingers he was slamming into me and practically shoving me over the edge into my orgasm with, there was no time. One moment I was chasing that peaceful abyss, and the next I was being burned and shredded from the inside with pleasure that I couldn't handle. All I wanted was a moment of unconsciousness, a reset, but it was something that the agony he was inflicting on me wouldn't allow. But when I reached for his arm pinned between me and the couch and tugged at it, he was merciful. Heph pulled his fingers free and shoved them in my face, forcing them into my mouth to make me suck them clean.

Obediently, I licked and sucked them clean, the feel of his thrusts becoming more pleasurable as my body adjusted. When he was content that I had cleaned his hand well enough, it lowered to my throat, wrapping around with the perfect pressure that cut off nearly all my air and left me moaning even louder. I wasn't sure if my throat was more sore from the way he'd used it or how he'd been making me scream, but his taking away my ability to continue crying out for him was a kindness I don't think he intended.

The slap of our skin sounded through the room, mingling with his grunts and my stifled groans and gasps. Even Heph didn't have words, no dirty comments. I was surprised that even while he fucked my face, his usual stream of lewd and derogatory statements was missing. Perhaps the next time we did something like this, letting him take out all his aggression as he used me for his pleasure, he might.

As his hips stuttered, jerking and breaking his rhythm, the hand around my throat squeezed, cutting off that last bit of air. It was alright though; he knew it was. He moved his other hand from my hip to abuse the breast that had been neglected before. Between the way he was moving the couch fucking me hard against it, the grip he had on my throat, and the way he dug his fingers into and squeezed my breast, I was thrown headlong into another orgasm. Besides aftercare, he was gifted as a pleasure dom, driving me into that pleasure as many times as he wanted. Though that was probably just a secondary effect of his current goal. I knew that my pleasure wasn't what mattered, that I was his toy to use as much as he wanted. All that knowledge did was increase my arousal.

Finally, I was granted a slight reprieve, darkness dragging me under for a few moments as I was lost to my release. The next thing I knew, he was shuddering and pressed to my back as the heat of his release filled me. His hands had moved, his arms instead wrapped around me, holding me close to him.

We stayed like that for a few moments, but it was only his grip that kept me standing. As the endorphins faded, the first stinging pain return. Heph pulled out as gently as he could. I looked over my shoulder, watching him wince as he saw the ichor coating his length. He was quick to go grab another wash cloth, hurrying back to use the warmth of it to clean me up.

"What do you need?" he asked as he gently moved me, lifting me into his arms once he cleaned himself off.

"Honestly, I think I am still in that headspace. For once, I really could not tell you what I need." There was an unreadable look that flashed across his face before he schooled his features. He laid me on the sofa on my stomach and kissed my head. For a moment, I thought he was going to leave me there to grab supplies, but he thought better of it.

Usually when he used his power, it was only things that he could forge, fire, or for transporting us. He never really summoned other things from other parts of the house. He liked to try and live as humanly as possible. But leaving me alone when I was in such a strange and vulnerable headspace was unwise. Heph knew things that had surprised me. While he'd never put them to use before me, he knew them. Since he wasn't sure what I needed, he decided to try something basic. I watched as one of my favorite soft blankets appeared on the couch by my head, along with some of my favorite plushies.

Heph knelt by the couch, pressing a kiss to my shoulder before turning his focus to the part of my body that was still leaking ichor. I knew neither of us really cared if the couch was messed up, but I still felt bad because of the look on his face as he inspected it. As much as I wanted to reassure him, I knew that nothing I said would fix whatever he was working through in his mind right then. He held a little pot that looked like something Hekate might have laying around, his fingers of his other hand dipping in and then spreading the salve over my aching skin. The effect was pretty immediately soothing, and I was able to breathe more easily. When he did the same to my throat, I was confused until I realized that he'd gripped me hard enough to bruise towards the end when I lost consciousness.

"Now you should be able to sit up with me without hurting as much. Clothes, yes or no?" he asked as he put the salve on the coffee table.

"No, if you will be naked under the blanket with me." I was grateful that he was easing the pain, but I was happier that he looked less upset. It wasn't that he was angry all the time, but there was always a weight in his eyes, his shoulders, and I never knew how to fix it. There was still some there, but it was a lot better. And since we were coming up on the last trial, I was hoping that it would be gone entirely soon.

"Deal," he said as he cleaned up the ichor and helped me sit up. Heph sat beside me, drawing me into his lap and helping me shift until I could lean against him without causing more throbbing or burning pain. He draped the blanket over us and drew the plushies closer for me to grab should I want them. I rested my head against his neck, happily cradled in his embrace.

It surprised me how he used his powers again to get me water, juice, and snacks. We both needed those things, but normally he'd just get up to retrieve them. I was glad though, I wanted to remain as we were then. When Heph handed me the remote to the television, I contemplated putting on sci-fi, but I realized that I wanted to watch anime with him. Normally, I would just agree to it once he decided he wanted to watch something or show me one. But for the first time, I wanted to start one. Well, continue the one that he had introduced me to recently that had been quite enjoyable. The stunned look on his face made me smile. I loved that I could still shock him at times.

"Wise Man's Grandchild?" he asked with a chuckle. I nodded. "I didn't realize you'd been enjoying it that much."

"I was just as surprised as you are." Which was the truth, but at least he'd find a genre or two of anime that we could enjoy together. I loved that we could share something that made us happy, something mundane. It made me feel warm inside, happy and content in ways that I hadn't thought possible.

For the first time in a while, there was no fear, even in the back of my mind, about the trials. I was completely in the moment with him, and enjoying the preview of the comfortable and calm life that we had ahead of us once everything was over. It was something that I had never let myself think possible before, and I was glad that I had been gifted the chance to have it.

CHAPTER XXVI

"She's gotten lucky with the last two trials, but I am sure she told you that I had already warned her that this will be the most difficult trial of all." Hera leaned on the edge of the desk as Hephaestus limped back and forth across her office with his cane.

"I was hoping you were just trying to scare her," he grumbled. When we'd gotten to her office, he'd been ranting and raving and trying to get her to set the trial to something that I had already done or that would be simple to complete. While he didn't know what the last trial was either, he was still livid that I was going through with it. His frustration flitted back and forth between Hera and me, but we'd also taken turns calming him down until he decided to just pace back and forth.

"If you're quite finished, I would be more than happy to tell you what the last trial is." At Hera's words, I moved into Heph's path and wrapped my arms around him. He stopped and stood stiff against me, but slowly began to relax.

I looked over at the queen goddess and nodded. "We are ready," I told her. Somehow, I was able to keep my nervous energy under control. Perhaps it was because I was focused on keeping Heph calm.

Hera shifted, one could almost call it fidgeting, though the queen didn't fidget. Something about the last trial made her uncomfortable it seemed. "You have given me a great number of grandchildren in the past. The final trial is to give me the same number again. With your husband."

While Heph looked stunned, I was gaping like a fish. I wasn't quite sure I heard her correctly. She wanted grandchildren. Again. "I had nine by...before." Hera nodded. "You want nine grandchildren? That will...that is not a quick thing to pull off. And we have yet to discuss whether-"

Heph cut me off, placing his hand over my mouth as he gazed down at me. "Do you want them?"

Guilt churned my stomach. He thought I might not want to bear him children. Pulling his hand from my mouth, I smiled up at him. "If you are prepared to chase after those powerful little beings, I will happily bear your children. I just was unsure if that was something you wanted. And that many."

"There's no time limit on this. You could take centuries if you need to. But you must eventually have all nine." That was fair and it meant that we didn't have to start immediately if we weren't ready.

"Thank you for the consideration." My gaze went back to Heph as I reached up to cradle his face. "Do you want this?"

"I do. I always have." And in that moment, I understood why it was the final trial. There were so many things that I had refused Heph, that he'd gone thousands of years without. But I never knew if watching me be a mother to his nieces and nephews was just as painful. I never knew if he wanted children. Hera did. I knew that they'd talked things out, worked through things that had bothered him. But until then, I hadn't realized that his desire to have children with me was part of it. Everything was clicking into place, and I felt incredibly slow.

My smile widened and I leaned up to give him a tender kiss. "Then I gladly accept this final trial. I think the number was a little intense, but I would gladly give you a dozen children if you asked, my sparrow."

His cane disappeared as he scooped me up into his arms, laughing joyously. "Then we should get started."

Hera cleared her throat, but Heph didn't care. He wrapped his powers around us, taking us home as Hera started to say something. If it was important, she could always call later or text. But nothing was more important to Heph right then. I could tell.

He wasted little time in carrying me to bed. And the smile didn't leave his face as he tenderly made love to me until we could no longer move.

"I hope they have your hair, and your heart," I murmured, resting my chin on his chest as I laid atop him. My body was completely spent for the moment, perfectly sated by his skill once more. "Maybe your eyes, too."

"You think those rounds took?" he asked as he ran his fingers along my spine, his other arm was folded back behind his head.

There was no way for me to be certain it had, it wasn't exactly something that I turned on and off. And unless I went to Hekate for a ritual, there was no guarantee. Though we might not have to go as far as a ritual. Understanding finally dawned on me. I knew what the gift was. Her foresight was amazing, I only wished that she could use it for herself. It was one drawback to her abilities, sadly.

"While I hope they did, I just realized that we received something that would make this much easier." He gave me a questioning look and I decided to try something I had been afraid to for so long. I wasn't sure it'd work but I decided to try and test my powers. My eyes widened as

I had no difficulty using them. Later, I'd try other things, but I wouldn't assume that they were entirely back to what they once were. Instead, I reached my hand out and grabbed the antique gold amulet floating through the air, the red stone glinting in the light. "Hekate's wedding present to us. I never asked her what it did, but I understand now. I can hear it," I explained.

It also made sense that when Lola had been helping sort the presents, she'd lingered on the box sent by Hekate. Everything was clicking in my mind. I'd have to send her a proper thanks later. Just as I thought that, my phone chimed on the bedside table. Heph reached over to grab it and handed it to me.

> if u still think u owe me a
> 2nd favor, got a weird
> gross 1 u can do 4 me

It came from an unknown number, but I had a feeling I knew exactly who it was. Rolling over, I rested my back against the headboard as I curled against Heph's side so he could read the text conversation as it unfolded.

> How did you get my number?

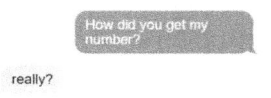

really?

That was really a dumb question on my part, but I was still curious if someone else had given it to her. Since I hadn't been as close to others in the pantheon for decades, I hadn't really given out my number to many people outside those who needed it. Just those that I needed to stay in contact with or the few that I wanted to. More entities from the afterlife hub had my number than others from my own pantheon. Which, with the trials mostly done, I was excited to start up my work with them again.

> You are right. That is not important.
>
> Thank you for the gift. I understand now.

i kno

so we got a deal? a gross favor u can pay back next yr?

> yes, we do.

cool. enjoy ur dick down time

Heph laughed as he took my phone and set it aside. I could save Hekate's number later. The look on his face told me we hadn't even begun trying for real yet. He grabbed the amulet I had set on the blanket in my lap and put it on me, instructing me to lift my hair so he could.

"Now that you're getting an extra boost, we can actually try. Remind me to make and send her some gifts later. For saving you and for thinking ahead," he murmured as he rolled over and hovered above me.

"Yes, my beloved," I managed to reply before he stole my ability to speak once more.

EPILOGUE

As I collapsed onto my stomach, Hera rubbed at my back, murmuring praise. Heph kissed my hand before he let me go, moving to check on the wailing child Eileithyia was tending to. Lola wanted to be there for the birth, to bring my first child with Heph into the world, but something had come up. And it was something that I wished that I could go and help her with. But she promised that she wasn't alone and told me that she wanted me to focus on a healthy and successful labor.

Hephaestus helped keep me from running off to help her. He knew how important Lola was to me, but he also agreed that I needed to rest and prepare for our little one.

I never knew preparing the house for a child could be so enjoyable. When Heph was picking out anime characters to paint on the nursery walls, I reminded him that we would have nine in total. My intention was for him to pick nine and just paint each of their rooms with a different anime. He took that as me telling him to paint the Hashira from a certain popular anime and do the nursery in their patterns. It was an amusing decision and I loved how happy he was as the murals were painted.

Our children would be raised in the mortal world, taught human happiness and the enjoyment of mundane things. It was something that we didn't discuss for more than a minute because we knew the type of life we wanted to give them. It was just unfortunate for them that their parents were nerds.

Hera helped me roll onto my back, wiping at my face as she brushed my hair back. It was strange for her to be so attentive and loving towards me. At least at first. As soon as I had told her we had conceived, she was incredibly supportive and helpful. And once Lola couldn't be as involved anymore, Hera had stepped up even more. Perhaps she just wanted to watch Heph's happiness up close as much as I did. Watching him read the parenting books, baby proof the house, and prepare the nursery like a child at Christmas were things that I treasured and hoped he felt through every pregnancy.

"Thank you," I murmured. "Mama," I added when she shot me a curt look. She'd taken on more of a mother role with me, something I appreciated since it was something I had never had. And it'd been a pleasant surprise when she asked me to use such a term for her.

"Look," Heph cooed as he came back over to the bed. He laid the wriggling newborn in his arms on my chest and sat beside me. Even though she was still grey and had a slight gold tint, I was glad to see that his red curls had won out. Though I wasn't sure if my current appearance would sway the way our children would look or not. It wasn't something that had been experimented with as far as I knew. Still, I was just glad that I got to share those tender moments with Heph.

"She looks like you already. Look at that hair, and that nose," I teased, cradling her to me. It'd been a long time since I held a baby, and I couldn't help the tears that welled up in my eyes.

"But she has your lips," Hera pointed out from my other side.

I shifted so Hera could touch the little darling in my arms if she wanted to. "Grandma has to take on babysitting now. Aunt Lola will be gone for a while." But she'd get plenty of pictures sent to her. It was something she'd demanded the last time I had seen her.

"I will always be happy to watch this little angel." When a knock sounded on the door, Heph got up to go check on it and Hera leaned in close to whisper in my ear. "Thank you for giving him all the happiness he deserves. And for proving your love, through everything."

"I promise to keep making him happy. Forever," I whispered back as Heph let my older children into the room to meet our little Sakura blossom.

And I did let him pick anime names for all our children, it was a joy that I could never deny him. The way his face lit up as he wrote out his favorite names was too wonderful, and I was never bothered by the idea. After all, it was just one more way that I could continue to make him happy forever. Like I had sworn and would swear a thousand times over. Just as he did every day.

    I had finally found what I needed most, and my powers were finally back to normal. Everything was in balance and while it wasn't how everyone might find their happily ever after, we had found ours. And we'd fight through every death season to keep it.

HEPHAESTUS' ANIME LIST

**Note: these anime series are ones that he enjoys, but it is not a comprehensive list. He has also read all the manga available for each of these as well as others that haven't been made into series yet. These are just some fun tidbits that I thought I would share about our mutual love of anime. This is also in no particular order. And I thought it'd be a nice little extra for y'all to enjoy.

Bleach – He's made all his favorite zanpakutou and hung them in his homes. Also, it's an all-time favorite of mine I've been watching for forever.

Black Clover – Yami is his favorite character, but he has a soft spot for Noelle since she sometimes reminds him of Dite. This is also top tier for me.

My Hero Academia – A quirkless wonder becoming all-powerful? What's not to love? I didn't want to watch this at first, but we both love it so very much now.

Naruto – The author has not watched it for reasons, but he thoroughly enjoys it.

One Piece – Same as above though the author is considering watching this one.

Demon Slayer – I binged it for Heph and read the manga. We loved it and hated the ending. He wants his Mitsuri to love him, scars and all.

That Time I Got Reincarnated as A Slime – he went in afraid it was all just fan service but was pleased to see that it was a great series. With fan service. We love this.

Sword Art Online – we disagree on this one. I can't bear to watch any more if more comes out, but he thoroughly enjoys the battle sequences. We both enjoyed the spinoff though!

InuYasha – Yes, he has made Tetsuaiga, Tenseiga, and So'unga for himself.

Blue Exorcist – It's just a fun time to be had. For the most part.

The Ancient Magus' Bride – I don't think I need to explain this one.

The Sacrificial Princess and The King of Beasts – we both thought this was better than the one above, also needs no explanation.

Overlord – Do I really have to explain this one?

Future Diary – When he just needs some mindless violence.

Fate/Stay Night (and all other Fate series) – I don't know. I watched them, he liked them. They made the list. I have no strong feelings either way.

I tried to get him into **Jujutsu Kaisen** but it just didn't work out. Gojo's beautiful eyes weren't enough. And he was incredibly unhappy when I suggested **Is It Wrong To Pick up Girls in A Dungeon**. So, he doesn't enjoy anime that tie in Greek gods. But he does seem to like isekai, which are what he uses to lure Dite in.

Victoria Moxley is a dark romance author, who also edits novels, designs covers, and does some beta reading for good measure. Because being a Domme and nerdy gaming goth girl wasn't fulfilling enough for her. Oh, and we can't forget her contributions over at InThePantheon.com as the scribe for Aphrodite and as an assistant editor. She can be found on tiktok and twitter as @daleksndemons.

She is a former prison sergeant that's been writing for the voices in her head since 2000. Most of her writing can be found on various platforms and blogs. If she's not writing, she's gaming, making graphics/gifs, or building mods to bring the worlds of books and gods to Skyrim.

Fun Fact: She can wrangle mice, rats, snakes, and scorpions. The only thing she's deathly afraid of is geckos. Yes, those creepy little pink guys. They send her screaming and crying. (Flying is also terrifying, but she can easily avoid that. Geckos are far too common in Texas)

Printed in the USA
CPSIA information can be obtained
at www.ICGtesting.com
LVHW021322180224
772034LV00011B/272

9 781957 893518